Sonja Winternoller

It's all about L.O.V.E.

Brigitte Bloemen
Marina Dobler
Miriam Lohr
Sonja Winterholler

It's all about L.O.V.E.

*Michael Jackson stories
you were never meant to read*

Books on Demand GmbH

This book contains true stories.

Die Deutsche Nationalbibliothek verzeichnet diese Publikation in der Deutschen Nationalbibliografie; detaillierte bibliografische Daten sind im Internet über dnb.d-nb.de abrufbar.

Original edition

Published by
Copyright © 2010
Brigitte Bloemen
Marina Dobler
Miriam Lohr
Sonja Winterholler (ed.)

Publisher/Print (Herstellung/Verlag)
Books on Demand GmbH,
Norderstedt

ISBN
978 3 8391 4941 6

Edition
first edition

Index

                                  Page

<u>Opening address</u> *Anton & Franziska Schleiter*	18 – 22
<u>His message was: Love!</u> *Alex Gernandt*	23 – 24
<u>Happy birthday, Michael</u> *Andrés Salinas*	25 – 31
<u>If only we could turn back time</u> *Hoda Karamzadeh*	32 – 33
<u>You ain't seen nothing yet</u> *Kerstin Reinke*	35 – 42
<u>Gentle soul</u> *Bonnie Lamrock*	43
<u>„...nothing falls like London rain.....nothing heals me like you do....''</u> *Katharina Roggendorf*	44 – 50
<u>You</u> *Michaela Huber*	51

The sheets *Christina Sanchez*	52
Pinch me! *Marina Dobler*	53 – 78
Neverland Feelings *Miriam Lohr*	79 – 80
Michael in Oman *Samira Harib Mohd Al Maskry*	81 – 84
From Munich to Duisburg, a true miracle *Zimmy*	85 – 90
Cologne Calling 3rd July 1988 *Shaun Redfern*	91 – 95
My short trip to London *Vanessa Pereira*	96 – 99
August, 28th, 1958 *Dagmar Herrmann*	100
Running into Michael *Diane Hotchkiss*	101 – 102
The letter *Alice Oderinde*	103 – 104
Thank you for the memories *Jannik Per Jørgensen*	105

A story of a very special friendship *The Appleheads*	106 – 203
London *Charlotte Svee Hestnes*	204
All the magic in your eyes *Sabine Fritah-Lenze*	205 – 206
My little gift's journey *Dawn Trethewey*	207 – 208
The "Omni"-experience or "Oh, he's already coming!" *Sonja Winterholler*	231 – 248
Blue Skies, August 29, 2004 *Sandra Mojas*	249
My meeting with Michael *Dagmar Herrmann*	250 – 260
Make that change *Hoda Karamzadeh*	261 – 263
American Bandstand 50th Anniversary *Marjorie De-Faria*	264 – 275
Munich 1998 or Let US entertain YOU *Brigitte Bloemen*	276 – 293
Ain't no sunshine: Goodbye gloved one *Pranav Dixit*	294 – 297

Crazy Times Heidi Laurito	298 – 308
March 17th 1996 Paris, FRANCE... Kader	309 – 317
I love you Dagmar Herrmann	318
Seeing him live Gabriela Bejan	319
HIStory Tour Bremen 1997 Michael's arrival Kerstin Reinke	320 – 322
The soundtrack of my life Glenda Furia	323 – 324
The Dangerous "balcony" Show in Tel Aviv (1993) Julia Orendi Birgit Hoffmann Dagmar Wendel & Monika Reimann	325 – 330
Basic needs simply didn't matter Laura Czerska	331 – 336
A fan's life Eva Lassmann	337 – 340
Escape! Dagmar Herrmann	341 – 342

My inspiration *Mark Makowski*	343 – 344
Prague 1996 - MYStory *Olaf Haensch*	345 – 349
In the eyes of those who love him *Sandra Mojas*	350 – 352
„I give you more than a hug" *Sybille Wittmann*	353 – 355
The purest smile I have ever seen *Goncerenco Sherin*	356
Dear Michael *Brigitte Bloemen*	357 – 358
A cold winter's day in Berlin *Agnes Spett*	359 – 361
My life as MJ „fan" *Harald Hehmann*	362 – 374
Argentina 1993 *Anonymous*	375
My meeting with Michael Jackson *Gina Banic*	376 – 381
The Elephant Man's left hand *Sandra Mojas*	382

„Wetten, dass..?" *Petra Fischer*	383 – 390
A poet's notion *Carina Zieroth*	391
Like a big brother... *Michael La Perruque*	392 – 396
Home-to-him sickness *Marina Dobler &* *Katharina Roggendorf*	397 – 408
Dream come true *Marjorie De Faria*	409 – 414
Meeting Michael – How one single day has changed my life *Silke Milpauer*	415 – 429
„Thanks Michael, it means the- world to me, I love you" *Kader*	430 – 432
WE are Michael Jackson *Franziska Neurieder*	433 – 435
Quotes *Michael Jackson*	436 – 440

> Love you so much, please Love Me Too
>
> Love Michael Jackson

Preface

by Brigitte Bloemen, Marina Dobler, Lisa Hochmuth, Miriam Lohr & Sonja Winterholler

Michael Jackson

This name alone initiates some kind of emotion or opinion in almost every person on our planet. For nearly four decades, Michael Jackson has been in a worldwide spotlight. His talent as a singer and dancer stays unequalled in pop history; his music, his performances, short films and tours revolutionized our entire pop culture. Countless articles, reports, books and essays have been published about him, all trying to offer insight into every aspect of his professional career as an entertainer and, apparently even more interesting to some, into his private life and lifestyle. Fact is Michael Jackson's life is highly documented – truthfully or not. So what can still be said about Michael Jackson that the world doesn't already know?

Well, there is another side of the man, the myth, the legend. It's his fans. Michael Jackson's career would have never been the same without the millions of fans all over the world who stood by him for over 40 years. They were very important not only for Michael Jackson, the artist, but also for Michael, the human being. His fans stayed by his side in good times as well as in bad times and kept him grounded when the media tried to condemn him. Even when the whole world turned against him, in his trials and his tribulations, on his fans' support Michael could always count. But what is the reason for their unbroken loyalty?

This book contains stories and poems that no journalist, no biographer and no editor could ever write about Michael Jackson! These texts were written by Michael's fans and friends and tell you about the unique relationship, the very special bond that existed between them and Michael. By reading these stories you will discover a facet of Michael Jackson that the general public is not even aware of and you will get an insight into why Michael's fans have the reputation of being the most loyal of all.

The idea to compile this book was in our minds long before June 25th, 2009. Originally we had planned it as a present for Michael. When he announced his London concerts, we thought it would be the right time to make our concept a reality. So at the beginning of June 2009, we began to contact fan clubs, communities and individual fans around the world to collect contributions. Surprisingly a personal friend of Michael told us that he had heard about our idea and loved it - and he promised to tell Michael about it when meeting him the next day. That day was June 23rd, 2009.

Then the unbelievable happened on June 25th, 2009…

It took several weeks before we could think about the planned project again. Now, however, it made no sense to continue with it because it was designed for Michael. We had intended to show him the joy he brought into his fans' lives, how he has inspired them, how he has changed lives and how even little courtesies on his side meant the world to us. We were not sure if he ever fully understood all of that. He probably did not know how much fun it all was for us! On top of that we were certain that the Michael we all got to know would have loved reading about his fans' experiences and their encounters with him (or at least their efforts) from their perspective. We believe he would have laughed a lot!

Suddenly this goal was all shattered. It made no sense anymore to continue the project and so we intended to let it die with him.

But for some reason it did not disappear from our minds and questions began to form in our heads. We realized that the next generation(s) of Michael Jackson fans would never be able to experience him the way we have. How would they know what it was like being a Michael Jackson fan in the "MJ-era"? How would they ever learn about what Michael was really like, how he cared for his fans, how he never missed a chance to show us his love? Would they ever hear about "window games" and "lightshows" and would they ever know that Michael was, in contrast to what the press says, one of the most accessible stars for his fans? We knew they would not find anything about that in the media!

We realized that only we, his fans, who have experienced all that, only we can tell these stories and our love and admiration for him serves as a mirror of Michael's personality.

So gradually we realized how wrong it would be to let it all go. We soon felt the need to bring this project back to life, to do the best we can to portray and thereby preserve the Michael we have got to know over the years. Suddenly we had become contemporary witnesses of one of the most talented artists and of, no doubt, the greatest entertainer that ever lived. But, maybe much more importantly, of one of the sincerest human beings we have met and a true example in sharing his values.

So that's how we started all over again.

Admittedly, it was a difficult timing for a lot of fans found it painful to remember their personal memories in a time of mourning. Others, however, saw it as a way to keep Michael alive by remembering him in their stories. We all shared the feeling that this book should be put into practice and that it was important to do so – maybe now more than ever!

Michael influenced millions around the world! He touched hearts and opened up his own to generously invite his fans in. And we have learned some important things from him – to love, to care and to give! Therefore we decided that all proceeds from this book will go to charity in Michael's name.

Being a Michael Jackson fan, for us, always meant a lot of joy, believing in the impossible, going for your dreams, never giving up hope, friendship, escaping everyday life and having incredible fun! It truly was a walk on the wild side – and we loved every second of it!

May this book help to keep his memory alive for many generations of fans that will follow. Not of Michael Jackson the mega star, the Moonwalker or the King of Pop – just of Michael, the man who so self-sacrificingly tried to show the world that it is all about L.O.V.E!

Opening Address by Anton & Franziska Schleiter

The Schleiter family were close friends of Michael and his family for many years.

When we were asked if we would like to contribute some lines to this book, we gladly said „yes" because we got to experience very closely the special bond between Michael and his fans over many years and we feel happy to be able to share this with you.

„Fan" is, in our opinion, too simple of a word to describe the relationship between Michael and all of you because the affection and love that each one of you has for Michael, and that he has for you, would be better described with words like friends and family. Michael has touched so many lives and we came to understand, now more than ever, what important role he plays in each one of your lives, like he does for our family.

For millions he is an inspiration, a role model, a light. For him, all of you play just as an important of a role. He loves you with all his heart and we remember many occasions that show how much he cares about you.

Whenever we would stand next to Michael at the hotel window we got goosebumps from all the emotions that were created by the singing and shouting fans. There was literally so much love in the air. Michael was always aware of every noise you made, even if he wasn't at the window.

by Anton & Franziska Schleiter

A view from MIchael's window

Michael looking at banners in his hotel room

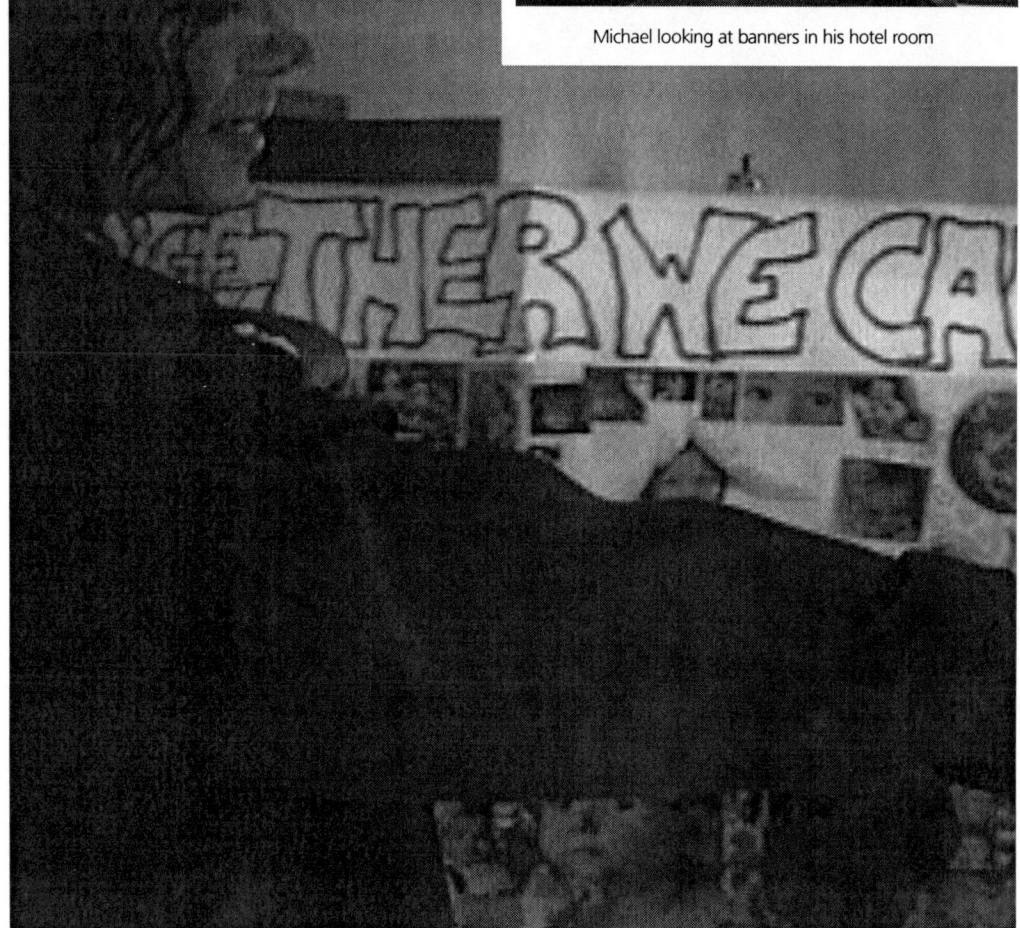

We would hang out in his room and he would start to sing along to the songs you sang or tell us how sweet the sentences were that you shouted. When you were dancing his moves on the street, he would laugh out loud and enjoy watching you. He loved that.
He would point out pictures and posters that caught his eye, so we could go and pick them up for him. Then he would look at them in his room and his eyes would shine bright with excitement. We have a video where he unrolls a big poster with children pictures and he says with so much joy: "YES! It's my favorite. Oooh, I looove it! This is going back with me in my arms."

Michael and we were always so amazed at all the wonderful artwork that you created. It showed how much love and effort you put into them. We always spent so much time just looking at everything. Michael truly valued the things you gave him and would store every single thing at his house.

He told us so many times how much you mean to him and we understand very well why, because everything you do comes out of love.
Often, when some of you came to meet him, he would tell us to hug you so that we also could feel the love you give. He was always so right.

Your personal stories and experiences with Michael are truly magical and will never be forgotten - it is something that stays in your heart where nobody can take it away from you. And what makes us so unbelievably happy is knowing that all of you will continue to live his love and his messages and pass it on to the coming generations.
And this way, through all of us, Michael will forever live.

Love,
Anton & Franziska

by Anton & Franziska Schleiter

Franziska and Anton with Michael in Munich 1999
Picture by Elisabeth Apfel (ElisabethApfel@gmx.de)

His Message was: Love!

by Alex Gernandt, Germany

Alex Gernandt is assistant chief-editor of the biggest European teen magazine, "BRAVO". During his career, he has done many exclusives on Michael and has met him several times. He was one of the few reporters Michael trusted!

There is no star in the world that has as loyal fans as Michael Jackson! Even in this aspect the King of Pop manages to achieve a superlative. The incredible enthusiasm, the infinite love, yes, the almost god-like worship of millions of fans that Michael evoked over the decades is beyond comparison!

Not only with his brilliant songs, videos and stunning breakthrough performances Michael won the hearts of the people, but also by his exemplary humanitarian efforts and an unwavering commitment to make this world a better place... Michael was a dreamer and a visionary. His message was love!
He gave us meaningful songs like "We are the world", "Man in the mirror", "Heal the world", and the "Earth Song". He personally took care of sick and vulnerable children around the world, had hospitals built in conflict areas, and donated to cancer research. While doing all of this, he never put himself into the spotlight. And that makes him so special!

Many admitted their admiration for MJ after his tragic death. But his true fans always stood by him - even in difficult times! They saw through the game of the tabloids that tried to increase their circulation with alleged scandals. The real fans always saw the real Michael - the Michael, we will forever remember...

by Alex Gernandt

Alex with Michael in Budapest
during a break of the shoot of his HIStory trailer

Happy Birthday, Michael!

by Andrés Salinas, Spain

Ever since I missed Michael's 45th Birthday Party in Los Angeles, I made a promise to myself to be with Michael for this 50th Birthday. And I always imagined it in a very different way from how it really happened. Who wasn't expecting a huge 50th birthday bash organized by some celebrity 'friend'?

So at the beginning of 2008 the first thing I did at work was to ask for holidays at the end of August. Months were going by and there was no word of any birthday parties being put together. Michael was living in Las Vegas during that time, moving from a house to different hotels to another house…We decided to book our flights in May and take the risk of going to Las Vegas and try to find him. That of course if he didn't decide to move to another country!

August came and Michael was still living in Las Vegas. A few months before one of the Las Vegas bloggers mentioned the street of the place where he was reportedly living, Palomino Lane. With this address and the one of the Palms Studio where he was recording we felt we had a chance of finding him.

We flew to Los Angeles and spent a few days there: Universal Studios, Disneyland, Warner Studios… During these first days some rumours were saying Michael was in New York! And then in Canada! And then in Santa Monica with Pamela Anderson! We decided not to pay attention to any of these gossips, some supported by what clearly were pictures of lookalikes, and continue our plan. Actually we went to check the Santa Monica rumour! One of my friends in the group had never been to Neverland so

by Andrés Salinas

we decided to take a different route and stop at the ranch before going to Las Vegas. The idea was just to buy some food at the Los Olivos Grocery and have some kind of picnic in front of the gates. It is so calm and peaceful there! I recognised one of the security guys at the gates from the time during the trial in 2005 and I asked him how everything was at the ranch. "It's OK" he said. Just a few minutes later we saw a couple of trailers leaving the property…We were aware of the critical situation at the ranch but never expected to see that! Some of the rides were passing by in front of us, the Ferris Wheel, the Zipper…I couldn't believe my eyes! They were taking away the rides that some of my friends were able to enjoy one day…Ironically my nickname in forums is Zipper, because I always thought that would be my favorite ride… Tears and sad faces in all of us. We cancelled the picnic and continued our road trip to Las Vegas ... hoping that Michael wasn't doing some shopping in NY!

So we arrived in Las Vegas days before his birthday. We got there by 3 pm, desert city of Las Vegas, month of August...40 C!! A quick check in at the Palms Hotel and straight away to have a look at that Palomino Lane... It was not a very long street, just a few blocks, so we decided to leave the car on one end and walk to the other trying to figure out which one was Michael's house. I will mention again the 40 C and that there were no shadows in that street! And that of course we didn't know for sure if he was living there. It was months ago when I found the name of that street. After walking all along the street we agreed on 4-5 possible houses, even though neither of them seemed like a place where he would live. Walking back to the car to have a second look we noticed a black suited guy with one of those things on his ear, standing on the front yard of a house that we didn't consider a possible one! But that guy was clearly working as security so we stood nearby for a few minutes. Another security guy came out to the front yard. Both looked at us standing on the other side of the street. Moments later they came to us...What we heard from them was like magic to our ears! "He knows you are here and wants you to know that he loves you and appreciates you being here. You are more than welcome to stay

by Andrés Salinas

here." They told us we could give them any letters or gifts and they would hand them to Michael. Neither of us had an MJ t-shirt and nobody mentioned his name in the conversation but we all knew we were talking about Michael. I guess standing there with 40 C we could only be fans! We had just arrived to Las Vegas and had found him within an hour!!! And he knew there were fans outside and didn't mind having us there!!

It was just me and my friends in front of his house. Around half an hour later the gates opened and an SUV left. It was the first car we saw, we had no idea of what to do, we didn't know if that would be his, so we basically did nothing! When the car was a few meters away the back window rolled down and there he was!! He had half his body outside the window, he was laughing and waving back at us!! We finally reacted and started running after the car, what made him laugh even more!! He was wearing a white t-shirt. The car disappeared turning right at the end of the street. We felt extremely lucky. I myself had experienced some other unsuccessful MJ trips in the past, but this one was becoming the best one! He came back at night time and stopped the car for us. Prince, Paris and Blanket were inside with him. We all shook his hand, even several times! He had his face covered with a veil but we could see him quite well through it. He told us they went out to have some ice cream and had a good time. We told him we were coming from Spain and that we would have lots of presents in the coming days. He kept saying 'thank you' all the time. That night, like many others, we went to have a dinner celebration!

Back in the hotel we found out that he had been to the show KA at the MGM. The next day we went to buy some presents for Michael and the kids before going to his house. We bought some baseball caps, some merchandising from the show KA, and a magic game for the children. In the early afternoon the car left again. It seemed like it was just going to leave without stopping but it slowed down, the window rolled down and he had something for us! Inside an empty CD case there was a note. He had written us a message... „Just know that I truly love and appreciate all of you, from the bot-

by Andrés Salinas

Andrés holding Michael's message

tom of my heart. I will do the best for you musically and creatively, visually. "I love you". Michael Jackson -08."
That message made us feel the most special people in the world. Telling us one more time how much he loved us and promising that he would do the best for us. Always thinking of giving the best to the fans. When he came back they didn't stop the car. But he left the house again a couple of hours later to have dinner at Planet Hollywood. That was the moment we showered him with all of our presents. The kids were very polite and thanked us for the presents. Michael and Blanket seemed to really like a DVD collection of the 3 Stooges. In the coming days he was rumored to appear at two events, the MTV VMA and the BMI which were honoring the Jackson 5, so I asked him directly if he was going to attend. "I can't, I have to work" he said. I asked him if he enjoyed the show KA the other night and if he would recommend it. "Oh yes, totally! I loved it!"
A few other fans arrived as his birthday got closer, but we were never more than 15 fans. But as fans started to show up, the paparazzi did too, guarding his house all day long.

The big day arrived, our King was turning 50! We bought lots of things from a Disney Store, we got balloons and of course a birthday cake! Because of the cake that was melting with the sun we gave it to his security together with all the presents and the balloons. The security thanked us and took everything inside the house. They told us Michael would go out in the evening, in case we didn't want to stay there all day in the sun. We went to do some shopping for a few hours and then came back to the house. Later we got some bad news. The security came to us to tell us that Michael had to cancel his plans of going out because of the paparazzi, he didn't want to be followed on a day like his birthday and have his day ruined by the paparazzi, and preferred to stay at home with his children instead. We understood his decision but couldn't help feeling sad for not seeing him on his birthday. But somehow we felt we celebrated his birthday together. We spent the evening outside his house. We all got some pizza delivered by his bodyguards! And later on the day Michael made a very touching gesture. They were probably cele-

by Andrés Salinas

Andrés with his friends in front of Michael's house with their birthday presents for him

30

Pizza Michael ordered for the fans

brating his birthday in the back yard and at some point he released the balloons we gave him. We stared at them as they went higher and higher in the sky until we lost sight of them. I took it as his way of saying that he got our presents and that he was thankful. A bit before midnight we all gathered outside in front of his gates and sang 'Happy Birthday' for him before going to bed.

We didn't see him for a few days, maybe because of the paparazzi or maybe he just felt like staying at home. But almost every day we could see the children from the outside riding their bicycles around the house. And we got more pizza in two other occasions!

Since we were staying at the Palms we wanted to get as close as possible to the recording studio that he was using at the time. The studio was in a different tower of the hotel, but being guests we had not much trouble getting there. Being right outside the door of the studio, on the other side where Michael was creating magic for us, was a wonderful feeling.

We had the chance to see him once again. He stopped the car when leaving the house. He was with the children this time, too. We asked him if he liked the birthday presents. "I loved them. I loved the Peter Pan statue". "Did you really like it?" we asked. "Are you kidding? I loved it!" he said with a huge smile. The 'are you kidding moment' was my favorite moment of the trip. I can still hear him say that while giggling at the same time.

Our last day came, we just had a few hours left before going back to Los Angeles to take our flight back home. The security guy told us we could give them things and they would get Michael to sign them for us. I had never asked him for an autograph as I always preferred to talk to him while I had him in front of me so I thought this was a good occasion to get my first autograph. We gave them some photos we bought during our trip, and I gave them my Bad vinyl. They gave us all back signed in two hours. "God bless. Michael Jackson'08" is what he wrote on my vinyl!

And that is how our trip came to an end. He made us sooo happy during those days. I just wish we made him half as happy. Thank you, Michael. I love you.

by Andrés Salinas

If only we could turn back time

by Hoda Karamzadeh, Sweden

If only we could turn back time
We wouldn't be too blind to see that
in a world of lust, violence and fear
he spoke of love, peace, hope and valor.
If only we could turn back time
And there he would be again, this young
boy, telling our whole life with his words.

If only we could turn back time
We could see him moonwalk across
the stage again as his smile lights
up the skies.

If only we could turn back time
We just needed to stop for a moment
to hear him one last time. Now we
see him from a distance, never up-close
and real.

If only we could turn back time
We wouldn't imagine him singing,
dancing and moonwalking among
the clouds.

If only we could turn back time
And God could give us one more chance.

If only God could give us one more chance
To light him up when his path was dark.

If only God could give us one more chance.

If only we could turn back time
So we could say "in your sorrow, we'll comfort you".
It's all too late now, it's all too late.

Freedom is a precious asset. Michael Joseph Jackson,
you are free now like the soft breeze in the dawn.
Fly Michael, fly up in the skies. We are always looking
up at the sky just hoping we could get a sign. Especially
at night when in the magnificent universe above, the
brightest star of all shines, we know it's him.

If only we could turn back time
Maybe we would realize he had already given
us all his life.

If only we could turn back time…

by Hoda Karamzadeh

You ain't seen nothing yet

by Kerstin Reinke, Germany

Like so many of our "Michael-journeys", our trip to Monte Carlo/ Monaco also started at Munich's central station. Coming from different parts of the city and its surroundings, we always met up there. It was May 9th 2000 and Michael was said to get a special award at this year's World Music Awards taking place the next day, May 10th, in Monaco.
This time, we were only 4 friends of our group travelling together, the others had already arrived in Monaco a day earlier which we couldn't make due to work or final exams taking place at that time.

After everybody had arrived, the usual excited chatter set as we boarded our train. And off we went. At around 5 pm we arrived in Verona/Italy where we had a few hours stopover before our "connecting" train would depart at 1.30 am at night. During these hours we explored Verona, which is such a beautiful city. Our Verona memories: marvellous ice-cream, even better pizza, stunning Arena dI Verona, lots of bats, Romeo and Juliet's tiny balcony (at least we thought so), then quickly brushing our teeth at the train station's platform and off we went again. Back on the train we at least got a little bit of rest in our sleeping car cabin.
The moment the sun rose we could already see the amazing Mediterranean Sea, lemon trees, gorgeous little houses and finally Monte Carlo. It was a dizzy day so we saw the high buildings of the city suddenly appear out of the blue.
After some "mountaineering" through the city that is entirely built on the side of a mountain, we ultimately reached our hotel.

Refreshing shortly, we headed to the Hotel de Paris where Michael was staying to meet our friends.
The day before, Michael showed himself at the main entrance of his hotel to greet the fans but after a few minutes or mere seconds he quickly went back inside. At least that's what we heard. We were actually relieved that we had not missed too much. And this day was still very young, nobody had seen a sign of Michael yet.

Soon we met some other familiar faces we now knew for some time. In front of Michael's hotel, it always was kind of like a family reunion celebration. Everybody was meeting friends and exchanging stories, talking, laughing and of course speculating how the day will go on and what Michael might do. Today, however, it was clear that Michael had to go to the Award Show in the evening, after all, that was what he was here for. It seemed Michael was preparing himself for that appearance all day, because he wasn't seen anywhere till the evening.
But my friends and I had lots of other things to see at the "Hotel de Paris" that rainy afternoon. We saw Mariah Carey, Ricky Martin and Jean Claude van Damme, all leaving in time for the show. Michael, however, took his time.

Meanwhile the clock already showed 8 pm and we were sure the Award Show at the "Sporting Club" must have already begun. We started wondering if Michael was still in his hotel or if he had secretly took off through the back entrance. So some fans headed towards the "Sporting Club" others to the beach in front of the club where the show was broadcasted on a huge screen. We decided to stay and wait at the hotel.

Two hours later – we actually thought that the show must soon be over – Michael's driver came out and told us that Michael needed a bit more time to get ready. We couldn't believe it but our hope to finally see Michael rose again. Indeed a few minutes later the vans were parked in front of the hotel's side entrance. We ran from the main entrance around the corner only to see someone with black hair rushing into the van.

by Kerstin Reinke

Obviously Michael was in a hurry now to make it to the "Sporting Club" in time for his appearance which was scheduled towards the end of the show. So all we got was the sight of the vans back lights and a few honks.

Our initial reaction was to run to the beach to at least see Michael there on the screen accepting his award. However after running a few minutes, we decided to rather go back to the hotel to be in the first row when Michael would come back.

We waited on the same side-entrance from where Michael had just left. And this time our decision was right. We managed to get a "first row spot" at the barriers and only seconds later the convoy of cars came around the corner. One of the vans parked directly in front of us. Now we were looking at blacked out windows. Its a weird moment, seeing yourself mirror in the windows of his car and not knowing how to look or what to do - simply looking stupid.
Soon some fans began to take pictures of basically black windows however through these camera flashes we could now clearly see Michael's face behind the windows. He sat in the car and looked directly at us. I was honestly scared a few seconds and then again, I didn't know what to do, now even more, knowing Michael is directly watching us.

Miraculously we felt the nervousness increase even further as nothing actually happened over the next 2 minutes. The screams of the other fans became louder and louder until finally the van door opened and Michael exited. Now the car was between Michael and us, so we couldn't see him. Hectically we searched for a solution to get higher up to see over the van. But the flower boxes next to us were already occupied by other fans and all other poles and barriers were overcrowded as well. Suddenly some fans lost their balance and slipped back to the ground. This was our chance and our feet finally found a little spot on the flower boxes to step up. Finally we could SEE Michael!
He simply looked amazing. He smiled and was dressed all in

by Kerstin Reinke

Michael at the Hotel de Paris in Monaco

black with two silver dragons decorating his jacket. Energetically we had to defend our place on the flower boxes for we constantly were pulled down again. The sunroof of Michael's van was still slightly open, so we managed to get a hold there and finally rescued ourselves onto the roof of the van. But even up there we felt other fans ripping and tearing at our clothes and feet. Thus I lost hold after a while and dropped back to the ground. Laying right at the rear end of the van I tried to get up again now. But then I saw Michael moving a few steps closer to the barriers directly next to me. Suddenly, there were no more barriers between him and me. I kept sitting down on the street and just watched him writing autographs and shaking hands for a few moments. I felt paralyzed and somehow couldn't get up. Police had their hands full getting the masses under control again as Michael moved back between the two vans and headed towards the entrance door. Again he disappeared out of my sight. Many fans jumped down from the barriers or vans to get a glimpse of Michael. Only after Michael was inside the hotel, the situation slowly relaxed.

We lay in each others arms for a while now, crying out of joy! Those moments, as short as they might have been, were so intense that I will never forget them…
But Michael's words from the Award acceptance speech that night turned out to become very true for us the following day: "You ain't seen nothing yet!"

BIG Surprise at Hotel de Paris, May 11th, 2000

In the early afternoon we sat at the ocean side of Michael's hotel, enjoying the nice view (not the ocean of course but Michael's hotel windows) and a late brunch. Suddenly a girl we knew came running towards us. She told us that it looked like something at the side-entrance might happen soon and that we should better go there now. Immediately we threw our baguettes and balloons away with which we had just waved to a "Michael-to-be" shadow at one of the windows and ran to the mentioned side entrance on the other side of the hotel.

by Kerstin Reinke

Apparently Michael wanted to go on a shopping tour so we wisely secured a good spot at the barriers. The vans were already parked in front of the exit door and indeed a while later Michael's kids were carried to the vans, followed shortly by their dad. The fans were holding up banners and pictures and once again hysteria broke loose. For a quick moment Michael looked at us, waved and then sat down in a little black SMART, inconspicuously parked between the two big vans.

This time he wore a red mask. After some honking his little car moved a few metres before being surrounded and completely trapped by a mass of fans. Everyone jumped around ecstatically, knocking at the windows of the little car and blocking the street. Michael was clearly visible for us all the time, sitting in this tiny car with only two seats, literally no trunk and of course no blacked out windows. He was waving at us but also seemed a little nervous seeing the masses surrounding him.

The police were busy making some room for the car to move forward. Finally, with a little help by the big vans, the Smart managed to speed off. Caught in the excitement, most fans ran after the cars but gave up after the first corner. Little cars can go fast, too.

My friends and I immediately went back to the side-entrance. We adjusted the run over barriers back into place and occupied the best spots behind them, at the left side of the wall next to the entrance door. Moments later the barriers were completely occupied by fans again, all waiting for Michael to come back.

And indeed only minutes later the convoy returned. The Smart stopped only three metres away from us and we could see Michael sit in there. He pointed at some pictures that he wanted to sign. Meanwhile his children were brought back into the hotel. This time Michael took a lot of time and even signed some pictures twice, like the one of my friend which he signed on the front and the back side, probably because each side showed a different picture.

by Kerstin Reinke

Michael at the Hotel de Paris

The bodyguards collected gifts and banners for Michael, too. I held my self-painted "Blood on the Dancefloor" flag and a Peter Pan postcard in my hand. As Michael exited the car and went past the fans towards the entrance door, he personally went over to me and took my presents. My heart literally sank into my boots when he paused in front of me, only about 30 centimetres away from me and looked at all the banners his fans were holding up. While looking at some collected banners and signing some more pictures, he turned around so his back faced me. At that moment I simply needed to touch him. Gently I reached out with one hand and softly stroke over his blade bone a few times. His silky shirt felt awesome and I had the feeling that he even enjoyed it. Despite the excitement I also tried to take some pictures. I managed to take a very special snapshot of Michael in a moment when the light that fell on his hair reflected in the shape of a heart.

I tried to memorize everything. The moments he stood so close to me, they actually seemed so long, almost like eternity. Still he was holding my flag in his hand while giving more autographs. I passed on a few pictures from fans behind me to him so he could sign them and then I passed them back to their owners. It was such a unique situation, so special.

Suddenly he turned around, looked me directly in the eyes and took my hand. Then he took one step to the side and unfolded my flag. Two corners of the 90cmx90cm square, silky flag he passed on to one of his bodyguards but kept holding on tight to the other two corners. Then he opened a black marker, literally painted a huge autograph onto it and then gave the flag back to me. I was totally surprised. I didn't anticipate something like that for actually it was a gift for him. He lovingly looked at me and told me: "It's wonderful". I was lost for words.
Twice I told him "Thank you, thank you, but it was for YOU!"
But he said "It's so wonderful, but it's for YOU! This is for you."
For a little moment he held my hand again and pressed it real tight. Then he disappeared into the hotel. I couldn't believe my luck and tears of joy ran down my face.

by Kerstin Reinke

Soon after, my heart had just gone back to normal rhythm, the vans were parked at the entrance again. Again his kids were first brought to the cars then Michael followed. Now he just waved very shortly blew some kisses before he took off to go shopping.

We defended our spots at the barriers and waited for about 90 minutes until Michael returned. His now sleeping children were quickly carried inside. All fans tried their best to stay quiet to not disturb them until they were inside the hotel. All you could hear were shushes coming from all sides.

Wisely Michael stayed inside the van a few minutes longer and spent this time telling his bodyguards which banners to collect for him. I had a second painted flag brought with me which I now decided to hold up as high as I could. On this one I had painted Michael sitting on a swing, surrounded by children. I couldn't believe my luck as soon one of the bodyguards stood right in front of me and smilingly took my flag. Grinning from one ear to the other, he positioned himself in front of the van to show Michael my painted flag. I held my breath, when Michael all of a sudden pointed both his thumbs up and enthusiastically jumped up on his seat. He was so sweet.

Shortly after, he left the car to sign more autographs and then he stood right next to me again. He held a marker in his hand and was searching the crowd with his eyes to find the owner of the pen. Then he lightly shrugged his shoulders, nodded friendly towards me and before I could protest I had the marker in my hand. Thereafter Michael waved one last time and vanished inside the hotel.

Overjoyed I sat down on the ground. A whole day of standing squeezed behind barriers leaves its marks. Every single bone was aching, some bruises too but those wonderful moments with Michael were simply worth it all.
Forever I will think back to that day, for I will never be this close to Michael, for so long ever again…

by Kerstin Reinke

Gentle soul

by Bonnie Lamrock, USA

I remember looking up at him as he gave his speech at Webster Hall 2002, during a Fan Celebration in New York. Luckily they allowed me in the "press booth" so I was right at his feet, at the bottom of the stage. I felt like I was dreaming.
He was so beautiful, not only his outer beauty but his spirit as well. I can tell by the way he addressed his fans that they were so important to him. He would smile and giggle when the fans would scream to him as he continued to speak. He knew we really loved him - I know that in my heart.
I've been very fortunate to have seen Michael Jackson live three times as well as having worked at his 45th Birthday party in L.A. I will never forget those memories.
He was a very gentle human being - innocent and gentle.

„...nothing falls like London rain.....nothing heals me like you do...."

by Katharina Roggendorf, Germany

The first memories that come to my mind when I try to remember „London 2000" are my soaking wet clothes and terribly aching feet, almost no sleep, yet at the same time absolute blissfulness.
The summary of the most important moments of four nights in London: It was Friday. It was raining cats and dogs. We were waiting in front of Michael's hotel „The Dorchester". One of his vans had been parked only minutes ago directly in front of the entrance, what created the impression, that he would come out very soon, and made us leave our rain refugee and position ourselves behind the crowd barriers on the right side. Very soon? After one hour our jacket was wet, after two hours all of our clothes and our banners („dare to get the thrill in Munich", „thanx you know what you did") were soaking wet, after three hours we were wet as if having taken a shower. Still no sign of Michael. We were „trapped". For "beaming" ourselves wasn't an option, we had to make up our minds: go or stay. Having already been at the Royal Albert Hall in the morning (like Michael's bodyguard Wayne Nagin, maybe even accompanied by Michael; it took us 3 hours by feet to get there from the Tower of London) to check out the arrangement of the crowd barriers and the possible entrance, we knew we would be able, if we arrived early enough, to stand nearby the entrance and would therefore be very close to him when he would enter

the hall walking over the red carpet and most importantly, we would be protected by a roof. Encouraged by our imagination we started to make our way to the Royal Albert Hall, yet still praying for our decision to be the right one. You never know with Michael. When we arrived there at about 3.30 pm with our snacks that we had bought on the way, we hardly believed our luck, there was still enough space for us and so we joined the other fans behind the crowd barriers directly nearby the entrance and slowly started to relax. It turned out that we had done everything right. We were going to see him and he was going to see us and our banners and everything would just be perfect. We were so happy! It was cold, the wind was icy and there was no end of the rain in sight. Having still a lot of time left till the show would begin, I seized the opportunity to jump over to Hyde Park that was just on the other side of the street. I couldn't resist looking for a toilet and with it even found a possibility to dry my hair at least a bit to make myself presentable to the human eye again. Light-heartedly I returned to my friends but our luck should not last too long. At almost 5 pm the security and police showed us the real entrance Michael and Liz would take, the place where the press was supposed to wait (very near and under a roof) and the place where we, the fans, were supposed to „die", miles away in the pouring rain. We couldn't believe it, we didn't want to believe it, that must have been a bad joke, our eyes instantly filled with sadness and disappointment, a pitiable sight even too much to take for the security, that after a while rearranged the crowd barriers so that we were at least a little closer. The positioning of us, grateful and released, and our banners began again and at about 5.15 pm we were ready for Michael. Only that he probably wouldn't come in the next three hours. Again it got uncomfortably wet (is there still a superlative?), I could have easily wrung out all (!) of my clothes. I only wanted to get away, but how could one, needless to say that there was no place in the world where one would have rather been, because we were going to see him. At about 7 pm the audience started to arrive, the number of police men in yellow rain coats increased, and some time around 7.30 Wayne came and our excitement rose to the top. He checked the situation and began wai-

by Katharina Roggendorf

ting in front of the entrance of the Royal Albert Hall. He was as cool as always, watching us and reading our banners. We tried hard to force Wayne to a smile, shouting „Wayne, Wayne stop the rain", but he showed no emotion. Suddenly we got the impression that the rain let up, in comparison one could even say that it stopped. Wasn't it always like this? Whenever Michael showed up, the rain stopped, even if only for a few minutes. At 8.10 pm his car, a normal Mercedes with normal windows, arrived from the back, it drove by us (we saw him sitting on the left side, on our side, Liz was sitting next to him on the right side) only to stop right in front of us. He instantly started waving at us. It was like a dream, in that moment there was only him and me. The world around me didn't exist anymore. Nothing was important anymore. Happiness and joy filled my heart and left no room for trouble and pain. It felt as if I had lived only for that moment, never before had I felt such strong emotions for someone. Suddenly his door was open and we were able to see him completely. We waved back at him and shouted, he only stopped to help Liz out of the car pushing her elbows, then he slid over on the right side of the seat to get out himself what enabled us to see his penguin tailed suit. Man, he was so cuuuute :-) They proceeded some meters towards the stairs, turning every now and then to wave at us, climbed the stairs, still waving at us and smiling at the cameras and then got swallowed by the hall. I had tears in my eyes, all the tension of the last hours unloaded itself (one never knows for sure if one is able to see him), but I regrets no second, it is all worth it, these few seconds waving at him and him waving back are all worth it. After a roller coaster ride of feelings there's only absolute blissfulness left.

Full of joy yet with an empty stomach we took our banners and started to move as fast as we could (my feet were aching terribly, I still don't know why I left Munich with uncomfortably tough boots), without any goal but with the urgent need to eat something and rest somewhere. Thank God there's Mc Donald's. We ate a bite, but most importantly, we tried to dry our clothes at the toilet, holding all possible parts of our bodies under the warm air, even our butts. Most certainly we would get the worst cold we ever had. But there was no time at all to worry about that. We

by Katharina Roggendorf

were on the road again returning to the Royal Albert Hall just in time to see the first fans rushing out, smiling and laughing, all enthusiastic about the „show". When we started to prepare ourselves again for Michael to come out, a security guy told us, he had already left the building with Liz 5 minutes ago, using the exit at the back of the building.
We trotted to his hotel through the pouring rain. Where there had once been my feet there was only pain then.
The cold and strong wind made it rather easy to decide where to spend the rest of the evening/night. His suite was located at the side of the hotel so we found ourselves in a narrow street that fortunately provided some shelter from the unfriendly weather, of which we really had enough, but at the same time enabled us to stand right under his windows and his balcony. A magic night was about to start. We sang, we shouted, it was so wonderful to finally be able to let the feelings we carry inside our hearts out, expressing our love and gratitude. The joy we felt was infinite, every once in a while my whole body shivered from the cold, the atmosphere was incredible and could not even be destroyed by the fat bald guy who threatened to call the police. The whole hotel was awake, there was light in every room, every window was open, nobody could sleep. We did an amazing job! Then suddenly (about two hours later when we were singing „Earth Song", howling like wolves at full moon) a man appeared on Michael's balcony, with him Wayne and with Wayne Michael, who was waving down at us. Everybody screamed, shouted and sang, it seemed like eternity (didn't last longer than a minute). They disappeared again. Happiness filled the air and nothing was impossible. Nobody could stop us from expressing our love to him and since words and songs in a moment like that were the only possibility, we continued, not knowing that it only had started. At 2 am we decided to go on till 4 am. Shortly after he returned on the balcony, alone, he raised his arm and threw down a „package" that flew directly towards us and turned out to be a Harrod's plastic bag containing 2 „banners" and - to give the package some weight to improve its ability to fly - a red apple. There are no words that can describe what it feels like touching the banners (or pillows) with his messages, it is like

by Katharina Roggendorf

"wow", the girl who did get it must have been in heaven. But there would have been still enough time to admire them and who knew, maybe he was still on that balcony, so I walked away from the others to get a better look up and indeed there he was again, the situation repeated itself, maybe one can compare it with playing football, there was this thing „sailing down" from the sky towards me, my eyes were following it, not letting go of it, it was coming nearer and nearer and then it was in my arms and I was diving to the ground. I couldn't believe it. I had the package! Something that seconds ago was in his hands now was in mine. It was something too big to grasp, so unreal, it was totally crazy, it was simply magic. I would take it home. It read: „DeSTRoy TABLOIDS - BURN THEM- I LOVE YOU- gOOD NigHT". At about 4 am the last banner found its way down to us: „I will LoVE YOU FOREVER - I PROM-SE - I must SLEEp NOW". We all were more than happy, photos of his messages were taken and everyone went „home". We were looking for a place to crash, not too far away, we were shivering, our teeth were chattering, our whole body was shaking, yet at the same time our cheeks were hot and were glowing in the dark. Fortunately we found a public parking garage only around the corner with a very friendly security guard, that at first couldn't believe his eyes and the expression on his face made us only guess what we must have looked like, but then he seemed to understand and showed us a „warm" place in the staircase of the garage. Scared about what we would find we took a look in our bags, even the money in the purse was dripping wet, „mashed sandwich" was everywhere. Our thoughts were light-years away from normal, we were laughing („the other part of my map is swimming through London"), we were talking nonsense, we weren't able to form full sentences, we found out that blowing on our knees warmed up the whole thighs and finally we fell asleep. Not for very long. At 5 to 6 am we „woke up" filled with panic that it might have been to late. In a hurry we left the parking garage not without thanking the security guard who even asked us if we were warm then. With our teeth chattering again we answered and then quickly headed to the Dorchester again, the others were already behind the crowd barriers opposite of the garage, we only had seconds to get our banners out before the gate opened and

by Katharina Roggendorf

two vans came shooting out like two rockets and he was gone. We couldn't help running down the street, but only to see him leave. Tears were rolling down our cheeks, again he took a piece of us with him, again it hurt so much and again we felt completely lost. One never got used to it. After a moment of total confusion we got a grip on ourselves again. It was Saturday morning, our flight back to Munich would be Monday morning, two days in London. We decided to have breakfast first, then bought a newspaper, spent some time at Harrod's, spent the whole day walking around in the city. The adventure wasn't over yet, since I had no place to sleep at night. I cuddled up in my sleeping bag in a corner of the staircase of the house my friends stayed at, not really closing an eye, but again happy inside, happy about the things we experienced during the last two days, every once in a while touching the banner and looking at his message to make sure it wasn't a dream. Sunday we all felt better, but without Sonja I couldn't have moved one tiny bit. Her pair of Sneakers saved me. I would have loved to take a shower, but it had to wait. After breakfast we decided to discover Covent Garden, returned to our parking garage (where I had thrown away the rest of my apple) because I suddenly felt the urge to collect the apple stalk (I carried it in my purse as a lucky charm for quite some time until one day I realised I had lost it) and we seized the opportunity to ask for a „prespotz", „prospect", „prospectus", „paper with pictures" at the Dorchester - it took quite a while till they knew what we wanted and they got us a very nice brochure of the hotel.

Sparing me another night alone in the staircase the three of us decided to go to Stansted Airport already Sunday evening, it was like heaven there, warm, dry, safe and it didn't take long before we fell asleep snuggling down in our sleeping bags on the cosy seats in the waiting area, but certainly not before having allowed us something delicious to eat, finally!! The events of the last days were running through each of our minds, we couldn't help laughing every once in a while, no, we laughed nearly all the time, but when thinking of him, longing filled our hearts and it hurt.

Monday we returned into our all-day lives in Munich, I even had to work in the afternoon, but could have never gotten there without having taken a hot shower before, finally :-)

by Katharina Roggendorf

The last message from Michael on that day

Michael on the balcony of The Dorchester

Spending the night at Stansted Airport

Katharina eating Michael's apple with his message on her knees

You

by Michaela Huber, Germany

You are the rainbow on a rainy day,
you colored my life, scaring darkness away.
You are the compass in my life when I'm lost,
you gave me hope when I needed it most.
You've changed my life in every single way,
and I miss you more with every passing day.
You are not like anybody I ever knew,
you are something special, just simply YOU!
I miss you Michael, my sparkling star,
now shining so bright but also so far.
On earth you were an angel in disguise,
and now may you rest in paradise.

The Lord took you to a better place,
a place with no name, a place filled with grace.
Now, you're free from anguish and pain;
no more despair and sorrow again.
Now, the world knows your invaluable worth;
you were such a precious human being on this earth.

I thank you deeply for all you have given;
for all your strength and for all you have striven.
I thank you deeply for your lovely reverie,
your inspiration and your encourage for dignity.

I love you Michael, I really do;
you're always on my mind and I'll pray for you.

You will forever rock my world!

by Michaela Huber

The sheets

by Christina Sanchez, Spain

I have seen Michael four times in concert in the years 1988 and 1992 here in Spain.
I remember thinking that he looked exactly like on DVD or pictures.
I also remember him standing close to the edge of the stage, looking down to us and me not going crazy at all. I stayed calm and repeated "My God, it's him!"

In 1992, I went to the Oviedo concert and I was staying at the hotel's garage exit as his car came out. He waved and smiled to us fans through the two front seats of the car.
Two days later I did the same thing in Madrid. This time I waited for him at the hotel garage entrance and as his car arrived he got off and again quickly waved towards us before disappearing. I won't forget the feelings and thoughts that ran through our heads when we saw his amazing smile and his beautiful shining black hair.

Once a couple of girls and me got into his hotel after he had departed and made it to the floor in which he had stay. The hotel staff was already cleaning his rooms. I peeked inside his suite and saw a white piano and nearby a kind of portrait he had obviously drawn on some sheets with a black pencil. I still wonder today why I was not brave enough and took those sheets with me. So stupid!

Pinch me!

by Marina Dobler, Germany

Finally!
The jumbo jet took off! And with every second it ascended higher into the air our excitement synchronistically rose to new yet unknown heights. Yes, we did it again! We were on our way to Michael and this time we were flying around half of our planet to see him. We felt that with each mile the plane covered the distance, it not only brought us closer to him but also further and further away from our everyday life. It was a wonderful, magical and adventurous feeling. So many weeks of preparation lay behind Sonja and me, so much excitement inside us and who knew how many adventures before us.

Even though we had travelled quite a lot to see Michael in the past few years, the fact that this time we were travelling to California, his home, was very new for us and more thrilling than all other trips before. Alone the chance to get to see all these places we had only read of in books and magazines with our own eyes was already a dream coming true and yet it was supposed to be topped. We had managed to buy tickets for the "Michael Jackson 45th birthday party" in Los Angeles's Orpheum theatre and if everything went well, we would even get to see Michael there. We were so excited and yet beyond all, we also felt a bit sad and unusual for our other friends had not joined us this time. The distance was simply too overwhelming. But we promised to tell them everything once we got back and therefore took a travel diary with us.

The 14 hour flight gave Sonja and me enough time to reflect our past experiences as Michael Jackson fans. It somehow felt as if it was all meant to be. I had found Michael in a time of my life when I felt lonely and misunderstood, a difficult time called adolescence. Reading about him and his life back then showed me that I was not alone with my problems. Even someone as amazing as Michael Jackson had to experience these kinds of feelings and that knowledge alone already helped me a lot. Yet his powerful music and lyrics gave me the strength I needed to go on and find my own way. He was my anchor in the sea of my uncertainty, my guide through the jungle of my confusion and my guidepost in the search for values in my life.

But it got even better a few years later, when I found many people who were a lot like me and who were also fans of Michael. They thought the same, they felt the same and we soon had the feeling to know each other for years already. From that moment on, the world was not big enough, the goals not high enough and the dreams not unbelievable enough. No matter where in the world we were or in which circumstances, be it in front of Michael's hotel in the middle of a freezing night or in the middle of all the commotion of 9/11 in New York City. Whenever we were together we felt safe because we felt at home and whole. I guess that's what people call kindred spirits and I am so thankful that I found those through Michael.

"Ladies and gentlemen we are now approaching Los Angeles International Airport". The captain's announcement ripped us out of our dreams and ruggedly catapulted us back into reality. But was this reality? It seemed more like a dream, a dream coming true!

THE DIARY

Thursday, August 28th, 2003
What a day! First thing in the morning we had to pick up our rental car and manage to drive through this huge city to Santa Ynez Valley. We were quite nervous. These 7-lane highways and all these traffic snarls and jams made our nerves go blank. Thanks to Sonja's amazing ability of "map reading" we bravely managed to get through this mess. Yet once were out of L.A. we were

by Marina Dobler

truly rewarded with a stunning view over the endless blue Pacific Ocean next to us and a cloudless deep blue sky above us. Elated and yet excited we cruised up the highway 101 with Michael's music blasting from our speakers. "You rock my world, you know you did…" Luckily no one could hear us singing along. We felt so free, so excited, so happy and blissful! How much better can life get?

With "Let me show you, let me show you the way to go…." we got closer to Santa Barbara. It was difficult to not get distracted too much by our high-spirited mood and the catchy song, after all we still had to find the right exit from the highway to get to Neverland which was quite a bit off the highway. Once we had left the highway, we drove over hills and through valleys, over bridges and past the deep blue Cachuma Lake before we got to see a sign which read "Figueroa Mountain Road". Once we had turned into this winding, bumpy, little road, we almost couldn't contain ourselves. "We are almost there!" I screamed. Our excitement rose with every second we got closer to Michael's home, so presumably it was to blame for that we missed the entrance gate to Neverland at first try.

'Stop!', Sonja screamed, 'there it is! There are even some fans!' How embarrassing! We actually had driven past the gate about fifty meters already! Being keen to not attract too much attention of the few fans that already waited at the simple, totally inconspicuous wooden gate, we skilfully turned our car and parked. Excited as hell inwardly yet as nonchalantly as possible on the outside we strolled towards the other fans and greeted them. We recognized a few of the faces from other Michael trips we had made and immediately began to relax.

"So this is Neverland?" I asked still a bit disbelieving while looking towards the wooden lane with grazing cows on soft, almost dried out hills between huge old oak trees and a tiny little guard-house next to the wooden gate. It was so not what I had imagined it to be. "Yes" said one of the waiting fans "but this is just the outer

55

by Marina Dobler

Marina and Sonja in front of Neverland

gate". Though, before we could ask more, an uncertain excitement rose among the fans. A woman in uniform came up and spoke to us "Ok everybody, clear the driveway!" Just then we saw a black Rolls-Royce approaching the gate from inside. Sonja and I held our breath. Slowly the gate opened and all 20 or so fans stepped aside obedient yet perplexed. So many thoughts crossed our mind in just one single moment. Was this Michael coming out in his car? No, this couldn't be! We had just arrived a few minutes before, how could we already be THAT lucky? But if! No way. Then a second guard came out and ordered a few fans to step back a little more yet at the same time informed us "Guys, it's not him! So don't follow, ok!"

With that said, the black shimmering car slowly rolled through the gate, closely followed by a black Jeep. Once it came closer towards us we actually felt that Michael was in there. His aura was immense. We had experienced it several times before, during other trips. You could feel him before you saw him. And indeed just as the car was about to pass the first fans in line, the blacked-out back window opened and then we saw him. With a huge happy grin on his face he waved towards all of us. "Oh my God", Sonja managed to say, "it's really Michael!" I just stood there shorttaken and tried to smile and wave back. But once Michael's car was on the street, it sped up and left us all standing there with open mouths. Sonja and I were speechless. We had just arrived and already we had seen him!

Of course all fans were now wondering where he was heading to and some even tried to follow his car although the guards had strictly forbidden that. For us it was more than enough to have seen him smile and wave towards us. It couldn't get much better, could it? We had not expected anything like that. But after a while as we had recollected ourselves, we remembered that we still had to look for a place to sleep that night and to buy some food. And so, although it was hard, we finally managed to leave Neverland and check out the cute little town of Solvang, only a couple of miles away from Michael's ranch. There we quickly found a cosy

by Marina Dobler

Bed & Breakfast and the required supermarket. We surely would have enjoyed this lovely town with its timbered houses a lot more if our minds were not already back at Neverland. What had we missed since leaving?
Once back there we heard that Michael had returned a while ago. There were rumours that he had been to the dentist with one of his children and other rumours that some of the waiting fans were allowed inside Neverland yet nobody seemed to know if it was true. Before long, dusk set in and a beautiful starry sky appeared above our heads. The air smelled of dried grass and was so clear that we could even see the Milky Way with its millions of stars up there. It was a truly magical evening, as suddenly a strange sizzling sound interrupted this calm atmosphere. Looking up we saw an amazingly huge shooting star flying in a little curve above us before disappearing right behind some Neverland hills. We were all taken aback. Never had we seen something like this! And even the gate guard came running out towards us and asked "Have you guys seen it!?" "It was remarkably huge!" Indeed this was not an ordinary shooting star, it actually was more like a comet with a blazing tail! Just like in a fairy tale. It appeared this environment was magical, as magical as Michael was for us. Of course Sonja and I – as probably most of the other fans - had quickly made a wish and now it no longer lay in our hands what would happen while we were here. As overwhelmed as we now were, we almost did not notice that it had gotten real chilly. Only as some fog came up and coyotes and wolves began to howl in the surrounding hills, it actually felt a bit like in the "Thriller" video and we found it was a good time to call it a day.

Once in the car we recognized that we had not really eaten anything since breakfast and were very hungry. Before our journey we had read a little story about Michael and a Taco Bell restaurant in Buellton, a town only a few miles away from Solvang. The story tells that Michael sometimes drove to this unspectacular little fast-food restaurant late in the evening to get himself something real greasy to eat after his kids went to bed. It says that his favourite dish was menu "number 7". So Sonja and I thought why

by Marina Dobler

not give it a try and drove to Buellton. Curiously I ordered this infamous menu. But what a big mistake! After a few bites I had to realize that "number 7" indeed seemed to consist of grease only and so my stomach and I had a terrible night ahead of us.
Quote of the day: "Number 7 is not as hip as I thought!"
Friday, August 29th, 2003
"Happy Birthday, Michael!"
After a night with not too much sleep (due to number 7) we woke up - no, actually it was more like carefully blinking with one of your eyes and in the next moment being catapulted right onto cloud number 7 (oh no not number 7 again!) by your anticipation. Today was HIS birthday and we were here to join the other fans in front of the gate, to celebrate him and to hopefully be able to yield our presents to his guards. So right after breakfast we got ready, put on our self designed "Munich Birthday Delegation" shirts, got our Bavarian birthday banner and presents together and drove off to Neverland. Once in our car it hit us again, for driving through this beautiful landscape that Michael called home in connection with his music was an experience of its own. It somehow felt as if here in this surrounding it was easier to understand who he really was and what moved him. I know it sounds strange – but that's just how it felt.

As we arrived at around 10.30 am, a few other fans were already there. It was a beautiful sunny day and so we joined them sitting in the grass in front of the lane, chatting and imagining how Michael would spend the day. Actually it was quite busy at the gate that day. Many delivery cars drove in and out as well as a blacked-out limousine (congratulators?), a locksmith (has he locked himself out or in?) and to top it all, a ready-mixed concrete lorry (what the hell is he doing on his birthday?). More and more fans arrived and with them the atmosphere got crazier and funnier by the minute. Balloons, garlands and other decorations where put on the trees and lanes and Michael's music boomed from some car speakers. Now it really looked like a birthday party.
In some scarce moments when it was a bit more quiet, we could hear the telephone ring in the little guard house. It was already

by Marina Dobler

late afternoon as shortly after one of these calls a guard came out towards us waiting fans and asked if we wanted to give anything to Michael. "Of course!" we almost all replied at the same time. And so with a huge smile on our faces, Sonja and I ran towards our car and got out our white and blue Bavarian gift bag for Michael. The kind guard patiently collected all the stuff from us fans and put it on the deck of his pick-up car before driving towards the main house. "Wow! Now he will get to see our presents!", I thoughtfully told more to myself than anyone else. "Yes! And I am sure he will laugh a lot" replied Sonja, grinning back at me. We had brought all kinds of funny and strange stuff from our hometown Munich – last but not least a CD with Bavarian brass music.

Now everyone was in high spirits. Some fans began to dance scenes or more a parody of Michael's videos and we all sang and clapped our hands while watching. It was a lot of fun and our loud laughing and singing echoed through the valley. After a while I coincidently looked away from the fan crowd, towards Neverland. There, in still quite a distance, I recognized a little white golf cart with a person dressed in black on it, slowly driving in our direction. "Sonja, look!" I told my friend and we both immediately knew it was Michael on that cart – as again we could feel him somehow. Now the other fans also got notice of this strange little cart and without further ado all the fans began to wave to him. In that moment the golf cart made an abrupt u-turn (it almost tipped over) and quickly disappeared behind the next corner, leaving a cloud of dust behind.

We were all puzzled, amazed and amused at the same time. It was really Michael and he must have gotten scared as he had to realize that we all had recognized him although he was still far away from us. "He definitely is underestimating his aura!" Sonja exclaimed. After a while of pondering we came to the conclusion that Michael probably wanted to check out where all the music and laughter came from and/or how many fans were at the gate. It was exciting to know he was so close and obviously interested

by Marina Dobler

in us fans on his birthday. Hyped up we continued with our little party yet not without having a look towards the direction he left, every once in a while.

But it wasn't before long that our gaily celebration was disturbed. A police car drove up and stopped right at the gate. The strict looking officer went directly to the guard house from where we could hear him talk to security. Shocked we turned down the music and tried to find out what this was all about. We had a bad feeling that we were about to be sent away, probably because we were too noisy or blocked the street. But a few minutes later the officer simply drove off again without further ado. We were perplexed. Yet, before we could find some explanations, one of the guards came towards us. "Can I have your attention!" she said determined. Then she continued: "You guys need to get away from the street. So please everybody go back to your cars and…" Oh no, I knew it! They are sending us away, I thought to myself. But before I could even finish my train of thought the guard continued "…and drive in!"

What?!!! Everybody looked around puzzled. "Did she say IN?" asked Sonja wide-eyed while I looked back at her just as shocked and slowly nodded: "Ehm, I think so." It took a moment to sink in but as all the other fans already ran towards their cars and began to queue in front of the gate, we knew it was true. "I can't believe it!", I screamed once in our car. "Me neither!" retorted Sonja just as hyped up while hectically searching for some compact powder in our bags. The same scenes seemed to happen in most of the other cars as well. Girls checking on their make-up in the rear mirror and refreshing their lipstick while driving. What a sight! Once at the gate, we were admonished to leave all cameras inside our cars before being escorted by a guard in a pick-up truck inside Neverland.

I was so nervous I almost forgot how to drive! A few moments later we arrived at a big parking space next to the most beautiful entrance gate I have ever seen. Meanwhile it had gotten all dark

by Marina Dobler

but the millions of lights that shone from inside of Neverland produced an enchanting glow. We were told to queue because we needed to sign a document stating that we agreed not to take pictures etc. This gave me a little time to realize where I actually was. Me, here in Neverland! It was so unbelievable that tears immediately began to roll out of my eyes. One of my biggest dreams was coming true in this very moment! Never had I thought that one day I would indeed be able to visit this beautiful place – but here I was. It all happened so fast and was so unbelievable, the atmosphere so magical, that I had to pinch myself several times to check that I was not dreaming. Looking over to Sonja, I saw that she was dealing with the same emotions and seemed to be in a similar state as myself.

After the signing, we were told to go through the golden entrance gate with the inscription "Dieu et mon droit" (God and my will). "Ah, so that is the motto here!" Sonja giggled and I had to grin back for some images were popping up in my head which I quickly tried to block out. Awestruck we went through the gate towards the little red train which awaited us there. Once everyone had taken a seat, it set in motion with a loud tooting. The journey of our lifetime began. I did not know where to look first. I felt like a sponge trying to soak up as many impressions as I could. The cool air stream touched my face, classical music coming through invisible speakers hidden everywhere in the flower beds touched my ears and millions of little lights illuminating dozens of gnarly old oak trees touched my eyes. Their light bathed everything in an enchanting golden glow, making it even harder to believe that all this was real. Again the loud hooting of the train echoed through the dark and Sonja and I repeatedly pinched ourselves as we rumbled past the lake with its huge lighted fountains and the romantic stone bridge leading towards his beautiful house before eventually arriving at the amusement park.

All the rides were also lighted and in full swing. The sight alone simply overwhelmed us. AdMiring it all, Sonja and I did not dare to move away from the train at first but as a guard saw us rooted

by Marina Dobler

to the spot he kindly came up and encouraged us to just enjoy ourselves and move around freely, like all other fans. Still awestruck we slowly moved towards the chairoplane. We could not believe our eyes as we saw that this ride had been made in Bavaria, our home, so naturally it was that ride that finally broke our reluctance. Music by R. Kelly blasted from the speakers. "This is heaven!" I screamed to Sonja and we couldn't stop laughing the whole ride long. Afterwards we joined some other fans entering a huge swingboat called "Sea Dragon". "Move your body like a snake" it sounded off the speakers just as the swingboat set in motion. A little taken aback at first (for we weren't sure who had said that) we quickly realized that it was only R. Kelly's voice. Again, we laughed the whole ride long, tears of joy pouring out of our eyes. None of us wanted to get off this ride after the first round and so we were allowed to stay on for a second round. This time the song "Ignition" echoed through the night and since we all had seen "The private home movies" we knew it was one of Michael's favourite songs. "Aaaah, I can't believe it!" Sonja screamed and I felt just the same.

Afterwards we really needed to visit the restrooms. The friendly guards showed us the way to Michael's cinema where we could use the facilities. Oh my God! His cinema! The same one we had seen on TV years ago during the interview with Oprah Winfrey. And now we were here – using his restrooms! Believe me, this was an experience of its own.

Once back at the amusement park we decided to ride auto scooter. It was a lot of fun, especially since we had a little problem with our steering wheel at first and so repeatedly collided with the fog machine to the rhythm of Lumidee's song "Never leave you". Deep fog surrounded us all due to the animated machine and made more colliding with other fans inevitable. We laughed so hard. Afterwards we strolled with glowing cheeks towards the nostalgically merry-go-round. Just the sight of it catapulted us back to our childhood days and immediately we calmed down. But as I got on a horse one very embarrassing thought crossed my

by Marina Dobler

mind "Did he ride this horse too?" Afterwards Sonja confessed to have had the same thought so we decided that we urgently needed something to cool down.

A nearby ice-cream cart was very convenient for that cause. That day I ate the best strawberry ice cream of my life. One look on a big clock shocked me a bit for it was almost 11 pm! Time flies when you are having fun – that much is true. Slowly most other fans also came strolling towards the little square to get themselves some refreshments after all the excitement and fun. And then for the first time since we had entered Neverland, a song by Michael was played. "You rock my world" blasted through Neverland. What a sound! Many fans started dancing and singing along but since Sonja and I were not good at both and did not want to embarrass ourselves more we strolled away from the crowd a bit.

Actually our intention was to look for a trash can for the sticks of our ice cream. But then an idea stroke our minds "We should at least collect some stones for our friends at home as a souvenir" suggested Sonja. What a great idea! And since we were a little away from the crowd and the guards, we took our chance to quickly rummage around in a nearby flower bed. We felt totally unobserved in this dark corner while looking for some stones. "Damn, no stones in here!" I called out to Sonja, puzzled. "Neither over here!" she retorted a bit distressed. "Shall I take some leaves instead?" I asked now also getting nervous for we did not want to be seen by a guard.

Still kneeling on the ground bend over the flower bed, Sonja and I suddenly had a strange feeling of being looked at. Slowly we both lifted our heads a little and to our great shock saw a darkly dressed person with a hooted sweater and a cap on his head sitting on an unlighted golf cart only a few meters away from us. The moment he recognized that we saw him, he quickly sped off into the dark, obviously amused and grooving to the music with his hands in the air. Sonja and I looked at each other with open mouths. "That was Michael?!" I finally stammered and Sonja

by Marina Dobler

only nodded "I think so…" Obviously he had watched us fans enjoying his park and he probably thought that the dark corner from where he looked would be perfect to watch. The scales fell from our eyes now. Of course, that was so typically Michael. He loved to be the fly on the wall and probably had watched all of us since we had entered Neverland. Sonja and I now quickly tried to rethink if there were any more embarrassing moments he might have witnessed us in. Unfortunately we counted many…
With highly red cheeks, Sonja and I returned to the crowd, not without having finally collected some stones from the train tracks. We were wondering if anybody else had noticed Michael. A little later we found out that a few fans had also seen him but luckily kept calm as well. We decided to stroll around a little more but before long the guards told us that it was time to say Good-bye to Neverland. Of course that moment came way too early for us. There would have been so much more to see and experience but it was close to midnight now and even the most wonderful dream eventually has to end. The kind guards brought us to the waiting train again and one of them told us that we could sing something for Michael if we wanted. Some confused fans asked if Michael would be able to hear it since the house was quite a bit away from the amusement park. But the guard replied that he certainly thinks so while smiling whimsically. Sonja and I had to smile too, for we also knew that Michael was surely somewhere very near and watching us in that very moment. Convinced by the guards' reply all one hundred fans, now already sitting on the little train, began to sing "Happy Birthday to you, Michael!" from the top of their lungs – more or less simultaneously. The song was repeated in more than four languages until we reached the parking space. What a sight this must have been! But more so, what a sound that echoed through the usually so peaceful landscape that night.

At the parking space everybody stopped singing and instantly a sad melancholy feeling spread among all of us. Now it was all over, way too quick. Although we had been in the park for several hours it felt as if we had just arrived. Looking back towards the golden entrance gate, we had only walked through a moment

by Marina Dobler

ago, let my emotions break through. Tears began to roll down my cheeks "Thank you Michael! Thank you so very much!" I gratefully mumbled, closing my eyes and deeply inhaling the cool grass scented air one last time before we had to enter our car.
The way back to our Bed & Breakfast was a very silent one. We both needed a while to comprehend, to let it all sink in. But soon we began to talk and almost couldn't stop. We talked almost the whole night through, repeating over and over again what we had just experienced in order to remember everything and to finally believe it.
Quote of the day: "Dreams really do come true, if you let them!"

Saturday, August 30th 2003
What a morning!
Waking up was pure torture. Red eyes and hoarse voices were unfortunately not the only symptoms we were suffering from too little sleep. But once our brains managed to fully wake up, they recalled what had happened the night before and even more importantly reminded us what today would have in store for us. Soon enough adrenaline pumped through our veins and made us jump out of our beds. Of course, we were sure that yesterday night could never be topped but we were quite curious how the fan club had organized Michael's Birthday party and if he would really show up.

Before long we found ourselves on the Highway 101 again, this time heading towards Los Angeles. Once we had arrived in our hotel we decided to rest and refresh ourselves a bit from the long drive. But soon excitement began to rise within us, knowing that only in a few hours we probably were about to see Michael again. But we had a problem. Should we really dare to wear our Bavarian dresses (Dirndl) at the party? We would most likely attract some attention which had been our plan in the first place (especially Michael's attention, of course), yet now we felt a bit too shy for it, visualizing all the gazes.
But after some discussion we decided to just do it. It took some courage to get out of our car in downtown Los Angeles in these

by Marina Dobler

dresses while being watched by some extra cool rapper guys hanging out there at the parking lot. However they seemed to be quite perplexed at first, but of course their mood quickly changed to being amused. "Hey Ladies, where are you from?" one of them called over, while the rest of them grinned and giggled. But Sonja and I tried to play cool and completely ignored them while walking as unimpressed as possible towards the Orpheum theatre's entrance.
In the entrance hall we took part in a raffle to win a Meet & Greet with Michael or a trip to Neverland but unfortunately we were both unlucky. A hot wave of excitement rolled over us as we finally entered the auditorium. Yet once we had found our seats it got even worse. Now we could see the balcony where Michael would be seated and this balcony was only a few meters away from us – beeline. We were so curious and excited and tried to imagine such important things as what he would wear and if he would look down to us. The auditorium was soon fully seated and after a while the light was dimmed. Excited chattering from fans that seemed to see more than we from their angle, signalized us that something was up.

Of course the reason was Michael! He appeared on that balcony with his entourage, looking amazing yet cool as a cat while smiling and waving down to us fans. Everybody started to cheer and wave back to him immediately. "Michael! Michael! Michael!" hundreds of fans screamed and he seemed to enjoy it a lot seeing us buzzing with excitement. "Damn, he looks really hot in those glittering tight jeans and the white shirt!" I shouted to Sonja with glowing cheeks. "Yeah, he really does!" she agreed dazed and added, absolutely absorbed by his look "But how on earth shall we concentrate on a show now?" Only he finally sitting down released us a bit from our state and so we managed to sit down as well in the end. Gladly the vibe in the whole auditorium calmed down a bit once the room went all dark, so the artists who had to take the stage were not disrupted too much during their performances. A big-band dressed up as roman soldiers started the show. It was amazing and crazy at the same time. But Sonja and

67

by Marina Dobler

Michael on the balcony in the Orpheum Theatre

I were in a difficult conflict. We wanted to watch the show yet at the same time see Michael without staring at him all the time. So, as inconspicuously as we could, we checked back to the balcony every now and then and saw that Michael excitedly followed the show, clapping and cheering after each performance, giving thumbs up to all the brilliant and courageous performers.
Yet, after a while, Sonja and I had the feeling to be intensely looked at – a familiar feeling by now yet not a very pleasant one. The look we felt came from the direction of that balcony. So of course we looked up to check and were a bit shocked (to say the least) to see Michael looking down at us. Though once we looked, he quickly looked away, ducking behind a kid sitting beside him and nonchalantly followed the show again. This happened two or three times and thrilled, yet confused us a lot. "What is it?!", I still wondered while Sonja already seemed to have found the actual quite obvious reason: "I think our "attention" plan worked but probably the Dirndl dresses were too strange a sight for him!" Well, who can blame him?

Later on, Brian McKnight entered the stage and performed "Lady in my Life". It was very beautiful and touching but once he began to play "Happy Birthday" for Michael, all the fans quickly joined in singing from the top of their lungs. Unlike the night before in Neverland, we were now able to see Michael looking down to us, smiling and folding his hands to thank us all. He looked so cute. Towards the end of the show Michael suddenly left his balcony. Again the room filled with high tension. Everybody was wondering if he would enter the stage or if he had already left? Steve Harvey, the host of the evening, began to talk but it was difficult for him to keep us fans calm, for we guessed what might be about to happen. And indeed, only a few moments later Michael himself entered the stage, followed by a bunch of bodyguards. Now the auditorium was shaking. Everybody sprang up from their chairs to cheer and applaud for him. It was unbelievable!
Sonja and I could not contain ourselves either and so abandoned to the impulse and ran towards the stage like many others fans. A bit handicapped by our Dirndl dresses we did not manage to

by Marina Dobler

get in the first row. But Sonja had the bright idea to step on the backrest of one of the folding chairs to get a better look. Without thinking I followed her example, but quickly found out that it was quite a shaky affair up there. My only rescue from falling down and making a big mess was a big, bald-headed man next to me who looked a bit like one of Michael's bodyguards. But there was no time for me to think how embarrassing it would be and so I plucked up my courage and simply put my hand on the man's bald to stabilize myself. Luckily Michael's presence was so overwhelming that this guy obviously did not mind me holding on to his bald. Probably he did not even notice it. Now I could see Michael really close and safely follow his speech. Luckily, he could not see us in that awkward situation from his angle.

He was so cute and seemed a bit embarrassed by the frenetic, not ending applause. Some of the things, he said, were: "I look into the future with great optimism.", "...I will make you all proud to be a Michael Jackson fan..." and "...I want to make Neverland more accessible for the fans!" "My children are your children and all the children of the world are our responsibility..." and then announced that he is about to launch a new philanthropic organization called "Go for your dreams!" in which we fans could become "ambassadors" in our home country. He continued, "I urge all young people to go for their dreams, cause when they do, many problems will be solved in the world...", and said "...it would make me extremely proud, if you, the fans, would become ambassadors for `Go for your dreams´ all over the world..." Then he closed with the words "...life is beautiful, I love you, you are the best, thank you so much!" We cheered and were so happy and blissful about the things he had said and planned. It felt so good to see that he obviously was buzzing with ideas and dreams and intended to involve us fans in these beautiful projects. Everything was so exciting and we were in heaven that evening!

This was yet another dream coming true because for years we had dreamed of supporting Michael with his charity work and now everything seemed to become possible. The future ahead

by Marina Dobler

was full of happy anticipation, bright and as colourful as a rainbow. No limits and no boundaries could hold us up with Michael on our side. We would change the world together with him.

After his speech, a girl who stood close to the stairs leading up to the stage was allowed to meet Michael. She was excited as hell and so Michael hugged her real tight. But there was a problem. On the way to the stage she had lost one of her flip-flop shoes and now stood before Michael with only one shoe on. He quickly understood the problem and as the Gentleman that he was, he tried to pick up the shoe for her without being caught by the many hands of the fans. Once he had managed, he kneeled down before her – just like in the Cinderella tale – and put the flip-flop back on her foot.

The girl was pink in the face out of excitement and embarrassment. But Michael seemed to enjoy the scene. He grinned like a Cheshire cat (we did too) and hugged the girl again. Meanwhile a choir had positioned onstage together with all the performers of the evening and they started to sing "We are the world". Michael almost took the microphone to sing a solo but suddenly decided against it. However he sang along without a microphone like we all did. Afterwards a huge birthday cake was rolled onto the stage and everybody sang "Happy Birthday dear Michael!" again. Together with a guy from the organisation team Michael cut the first piece of cake, took a little bite and handed the rest of his piece towards some fans in the audience. On his way out he paused in front of some artworks fans had made for him to look at them more closely and then he was gone.

Sonja and I beamed at each other "He is so amazing!" she called out. But I had other problems now. Quickly I stepped down from my shaky chair before the bald-headed guy came to his senses and then Sonja and I directly went outside to see Michael leave in his huge white limousine. What an evening!
Quote of the day: "Not only tight glittering jeans do irritate people – Dirndl dresses do too!"

by Marina Dobler

Sunday, August 31st, 2003
As our alarm clock woke us up, we simply could not move at first. Again, we had slept way too little due to all the excitement of last evening. But this time we were prepared! A single word: Red Bull! Thanks to this energy drink we managed to get off the ground and actualized our plan to be at Neverland before midday. We just arrived as the last two buses of raffle winners drove into Neverland to spend the day there. Sonja and I felt a bit downcast, although we had no right since luck had been on our side the last few days and more than one dream had come true for us. Nevertheless it was hard to watch and not be allowed in that day, knowing what a magical place they were about to discover.

Some other fans who also waited outside told us that Michael had not arrived back from L.A. yet. So hope rose inside us again. We realized that we had another chance of seeing Michael if he was to come back sometime that day. And so we relaxed and sat down on the grass beside the lane, exchanging all those exciting experiences of the last few days with the other fans. In the afternoon more fans arrived, but still no sign of Michael's big white limousine.

At around 3 pm a girl, we had not seen before, tried to mobilize us all to stand up and queue in front of the gate. We thought it was a joke and did not take her seriously. But she asked us again and promised that she would get us all in. We looked at her bewildered, but she kept being persistent. Hesitantly a queue of fans formed and eventually all 30 or 40 people stood there in line, still with big question marks on their faces. But that girl indeed went to talk to the security at the entrance gate and to our greatest astonishment the gate opened! Now we all stood there with open mouths. "I don't believe this!" I stammered to Sonja who also disbelievingly shook her head. We felt like dreaming again. Some guards came towards us with papers we had to sign (again an agreement to not take pictures etc at the ranch) and afterwards the same procedure as Friday night began. Escorted by security we drove in with our cars, parked at the parking space next to all

by Marina Dobler

the buses and went through the golden gate again to where the little train already awaited us.

The only huge difference to Friday night was that it was daytime and we could see everything! We saw the whole beauty of Neverland and how big it actually was. On our way to the amusement park we passed wonderful statues of playing children, an Indian village, a place for waterballon fights, the lake with fountains, flamingos, swans and ducks, all those huge old oak trees, all the wonderfully colourful flowerbeds and also his beautiful house. As we arrived at the amusement park, fans and children with their parents were everywhere enjoying a beautiful day. All the rides were in full swing and laughter filled the air. And, unlike Friday night, people were allowed to stroll around Neverland as they pleased. "Can you please pinch me?" I asked Sonja for I could not believe it. But pinching did not help. It was too surreal that we were here yet again! "Nobody at home will believe us!" she said, and looking at each other we started to laugh out loud. Once calmed down again, we headed for Michael's cinema because it was too hot outside without the shadow of the trees.

Carefully we entered the auditorium which was all dark. On the screen we saw the final scene from the "Thriller" video. Irritated as we were it took us a while to find a free seat in the dark, but once we sat down our senses were conquered with yet another sensation. The seats were velvety, soft and very cosy and on top moveable into every direction, with plenty of legroom. Wow! So that's how Michael watches movies! But quickly our attention was drawn back on the big screen because the "Ghosts" video just started. However it was not the normal video we knew, it was a different version with scenes we had never seen before. The uncut version! "We are watching his videos in his cinema!" stated Sonja, suddenly shocked. Seeing him on the screen saying "...it's too late, you're my guests!" did not make it easier for us. We were absolutely overstrained with impressions and emotions. After "Ghosts", we saw an unreleased trailer, similar to "Brace Yourself", probably once intended for a DVD or a concert. We screamed a

by Marina Dobler

lot cause to watch all these scenes at his home was sometimes just too much for us! Yet, as the "Superbowl" performance was about to start, Sonja and I decided to leave the cinema for we wanted to see more of Neverland by day. But we did not leave without depositing our Bavarian flag which had Michael's picture sewn onto it (instead of King Ludwig II) at the counter. We hoped he would get it somehow.
Outside again, we decided to walk down the little street on which Michael had disappeared into the night on Friday. Following the path, we soon saw his house, slowly approaching it over the grass. It looked so beautiful and cosy and the entire house environment radiated an atmosphere of special calmness and peacefulness. It was a place to feel at home. There were other people strolling around so we dared to come even closer and finally stood on a little sandy playground with some toys and a swing, directly in front of the house. We went on the swing for a moment inhaling the atmosphere and trying desperately to comprehend the sea of impressions and emotions. Across from us stood a little wooden playhouse and engraved to its small door were three words: "Daddy loves you!" As we read these three little yet so meaningful words we almost started to cry. We knew Michael was a wonderful dad who loves his children dearly, but to see and experience it in this environment was even more moving.

A little later we walked further around the house and arrived at the swimming pool. The water was very warm from the sun. "What a shame that I did not bring my bathing suit!" Sonja joked, and I agreed "Yeah, what a pity" before we both burst out in laughter by the sheer imagination. "Well, it's a law to get wet in Neverland!" I added, citing Michael's word. We strolled around some more, yet did not dare to watch through a window of the house. This would have felt wrong for he already opened up so much, we did not want to intrude his privacy. We walked by a punching bag - on which Sonja almost broke some of her fingers - and a trampoline before we heard the guards calling that it was time to go back to the amusement park. We sensed the atmosphere of departure and indeed once we arrived there, the first train with

fans had already departed. A look on the clock revealed that it was already 6.30 pm! Again, time was flying! As we finally drove out and came past his house, we saw a cook arranging something through one of the windows. "Ah, well it`s time for dinner" Sonja remarked, "probably he will be home soon!" And in fact, just a few minutes after we had driven out, Michael arrived in this huge white limousine, followed by some fan cars. We waved and screamed "Thank you, Michael!" towards his car but unfortunately he did not open a window that evening. We guessed that he probably was a bit annoyed by the stalking fans and just wanted to get home to have dinner with his kids. We were so thankful and happy, it is hard to express in words.
Quote of the day: "…and we went on his swing!"
September 1st, 2003
Today we had our first sleep in since being in California. We also managed to finally buy some more groceries at the supermarket; after all we could not count on Michael's popcorn, ice cream and candies to keep us alive every day. Around lunch time we had run all our errands and so of course we drove to Neverland again. Again a few other fans were also there. They told us that they had not seen nor heard anything from Michael yet. "Probably he and the kids have a sleep in today as well" Sonja remarked, which made me grin a little while imagining. It was a really hot day and soon we had to escape under one of the big oak trees. There we had some chill out time and fun with the other fans. It actually felt a bit like normal holiday after all the excitement of the last days. We watched the cows grazing the hills, eagles circling in the sky and squirrels playing around their burrow. We even tried to lure some squirrels with our cookies but to no success. Since we had a lot of time we noticed that Neverland was in the possession of conspicuously many birdhouses, located not only in the trees but for example also next to the gate etc. Since we had nothing else to do, we pondered what the reason for this incident might be. Our theory was that the birdhouses must have little cameras inside so Michael can see everything happening inside and in front of Neverland without having to leave his house. Later in the afternoon a black limousine arrived. About an hour later we

by Marina Dobler

heard the steam train tooting and sometimes the wind carried a bit of classical music out to us. Once we even saw the little white golf cart again. But he, or whoever drove it, was too far away to notice us few fans. Most likely it was Michael showing some guests around. Shortly after 8 pm a guard came out to us fans and told us that we needed to leave now for it was dangerous out there at night. And since nothing too exciting had happened in the last few hours, we, somehow elated, followed the order. Back in our Bed & Breakfast we had enough time to reflect the last few days which were the most exciting days in our life so far. The first signs of wistfulness came up and after completing our diary, we each wrote a letter to Michael in which we thanked him for everything. We hoped to be able to hand the letter over to him or his security the next day, our last day. Covered in a blanket of happiness and thankfulness we finally feel asleep.

September 2nd, 2003
Our last morning in Santa Ynez Valley had broken and actually this was the first morning here without feeling jet lagged. How unfair. After breakfast we decided to quickly make a little detour on our way to Neverland and check out the sea first. It was a warm and sunny day in Santa Ynez Valley, but once we got closer to Gaviota Beach, deep fog enveloped us. What a pity! We could not see anything except from a tame seagull named Goo-Goo and a sign warning us from rattlesnakes. So before long we were on our way back, not without making another stop at Lake Cachuma, from where we had wonderful clear views. But then we had enough of sightseeing and straight-line drove up Figueroa Mountain Road, "Break of Dawn" blaring out of our speakers. Again driving through this beautiful landscape that Michael called home, with his music on, was an experience of its own. We had the feeling to finally fully understand the songs and its lyrics. In the case of "Break of Dawn" this was really something, as you might imagine.
It was a quiet day again with no sign of Michael. One last time we enjoyed the peaceful atmosphere in front of the lane, one last time we watched the cars with workers driving in and out of the

by Marina Dobler

ranch and one last time we enjoyed the beautiful flora and partly thrilling fauna (tarantulas and snakes) out there. But as much as we wished that we could stay, time did not stand still for us. Luckily we were able to give our letters to one of the guards who promised us to pass them on to Michael. Yet that did not make it any easier for us to say goodbye. In just a few days we had begun to feel at home. Michael had made us feel welcome and at home. Due to his generosity, kindness and love some of our biggest dreams came true.

Late in the afternoon we eventually pulled ourselves together and said Goodbye to Neverland and the few remaining fans. It was very hard. Heading back to Los Angeles we cried many tears but then we remembered one of the signs on the way out of Neverland. On this sign were three little children angels looking down from a cloud and under them the words "Good-bye for now!" We liked that idea of "for now"! It actually deeply comforted us in that moment. Though we needed to leave now, we could come back any time to see Neverland and be close to Michael again. That day Sonja and I made a vow to be back as soon as our bank accounts would allow us to. Though little did we know then what incident would bring us back much sooner than we imagined. But that's another story – yet not a happy one for it was the beginning of the end.

Now, only a few years later those three little words "GOODBYE FOR NOW" that I once was so lucky to read in this magical, beautiful and peaceful land once called Neverland, a place where dreams did once come true for thousands of people – children and grown-ups alike - have become the most significant words for me. Once these words comforted my friend and me when we had to travel home from a fantastic journey we did not want to end. Yet now these words have become so much more important for they are all that is left and in them lays the hope of the world. The hope to meet again somewhere some day with all the loved ones we have lost - and to be together again.
Michael, I want to thank you so much for all you have done!

by Marina Dobler

I will never be able to thank you enough for changing my life and giving me the best years of my life, great friends and wonderful incredible memories as well as values for life that are so important in times like now.
You were too good for this world. You were ahead of your time.
In the promise of another tomorrow, Good-bye for now dear Michael!
I love you forever!

by Marina Dobler

Neverland Feelings

by Miriam Lohr, Germany

Wind caresses me softly
Playfully chasing the leaves around my feet
The sun wraps her wings around me
Smilingly embracing me with her warmth
The feeling of complete peace
Gets a new definition
In the presence
Of your love
When I close my eyes
And take a deep breath
I can smell the sweet odour of your aura

Joyful laughter floats through the air
And disappears between the mountains
Smiling eyes wave at me
„I don't know you
But I know what you feel"
My soul stretches
And breaks the chains
Of pretending and hiding
It rejoices in „myself"
This is home!

by Miriam Lohr

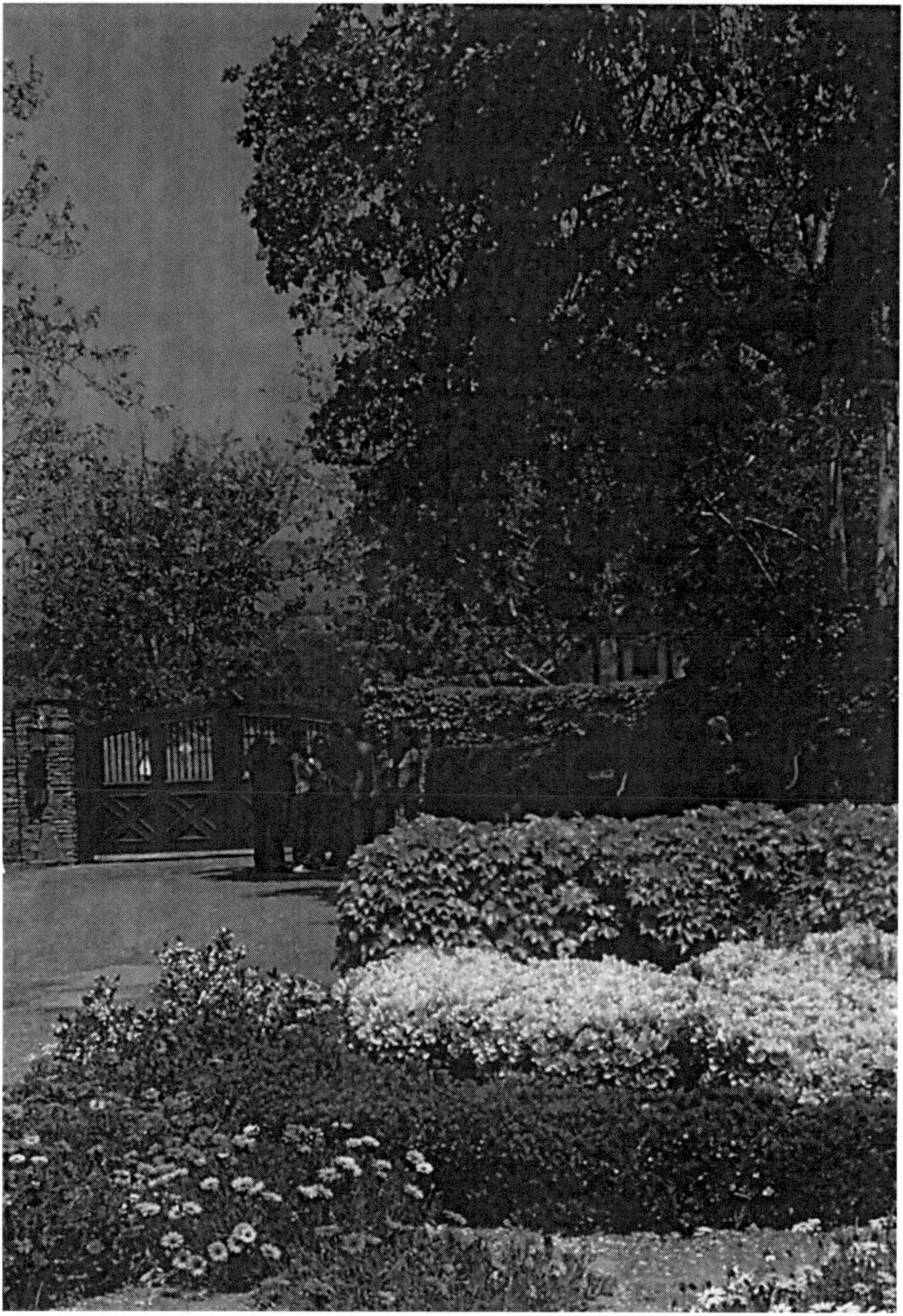

Michael in Oman

by Samira Harib Mohd Al Maskry, Oman

My name is Samira from Muscat and I'm 31 years old.
I am a huge fan of Michael Jackson since I was four years old. When I was little I was a fan of "Shakin' Stevens" also but somehow, I think it was in 1980, I fell in love with Michael's voice. The songs which I recall from back then are "One day in your life" and "I can't help it". But then "Thriller" came out and got me started. God, I loved Michael Jackson from there onwards. I never get bored watching this clip but nowadays it's hard to get "The Making of Thriller" on DVD! Back in those years everything was on video tapes and yes, it was easy to get.

"Thriller" also became my favourite album. I still have so many cassettes at home for it's hard to get this stuff on CDs here! I also started collecting his pictures from newspapers, magazines, posters etc and still do until this very day. I'm always looking forward to something new from Michael. His music is amazing. You can dance to the tune yet his music relaxes your mind. And I simply love his dance moves! This man was so gifted and talented.

I never saw Michael live in concert but I did watch all the concerts on DVD - and wow they are magic. I never get bored watching the Bad and Dangerous tours on DVD. Here in my office I have even set up a screen saver with Michael Jackson on it, too.

During all those years of being a fan I always said to myself that one day I will meet Michael Jackson in person. And believe it or not but my dream really did come true when Michael visited Oman in 2005.
At first it was just a rumour that he was in town but I didn't believe it! But as the rumours kept on I got suspicious. I knew that tracking Michael down, would be like mission impossible,

but I thought if he indeed is here I just have to meet him!
So, my friend Fahad and I went to the Grand Hyatt Hotel. There we waited for hours and hours and it soon became clear that Michael indeed was in the hotel. It was the 16th of November, 2005, and my birthday was on the following day. But sadly, we didn't get the chance to meet him that day. Though I didn't give up that easily, I really wanted to meet my idol in person!

The following day (my birthday) I called the hotel and asked if it was possible to speak to Michael Jackson. Of course, the receptionist refused, and added that Michael didn't want to be disturbed.

So another day passed without any sight of Michael and I was growing desperate yet at the same time very determined so I called the hotel again. This time I asked the receptionist about Michael Jackson's whereabouts and luckily found out that Michael was going to be at the "Al Bustan Palace Hotel" tomorrow!

Next day I was at my station in NSC, anxiously waiting by the clock, counting down the minutes, so that I could pursue my mission. Finally it was time and I went to the "Al Bustan Palace Hotel" together with Fahad. We waited for so long but nothing happened. Though exhausted and tired I nevertheless decided to return the next day.

It was a Sunday when I returned to wait in the lobby of the "Al Bustan" hotel. I prepared for a long wait but suddenly a security guard approached me. It was the same one that I saw at the Hyatt a few days ago. He said ,You haven't seen him yet?' ,Come with me and I'll introduce you!' I froze and couldn't believe what he had just said to me.

But indeed, a few moments later, there he was, wearing a red shirt and black trousers, his hair open loose and staring at me through his black sunglasses. My first reaction was to run to Michael and give him a hug. I said ,HI I'm Samira, and I'm a big fan!'
It really was a pity that I didn't have a camera with me, but it

by Samira Harib Mohd Al Maskry

all happened so fast. However I managed to get his autograph. ‚Love always, Michael Jackson.' he wrote on the inside cover of his book. He was simply amazing and so kind. I will never forget that day of meeting my idol.
Finally my "Mission Impossible" was complete!
I MET MICHAEL JACKSON!

by Samira Harib Mohd Al Maskry

Samira in traditional clothing

Samira's autograph

From Munich to Duisburg, a true miracle

by Zimmy, Germany

When it became more and more certain that Michael indeed would come to Europe's most famous TV show called "Wetten, dass..?", all fans went totally crazy and everybody wanted to go to Duisburg. Well, everybody wanted to go but not everybody was able to go... That was the case with me. I really wanted to go and see Michael but I just couldn't make it because exactly on that date I needed to attend a dress rehearsal and had a theatre performance at 10 o'clock in the morning the other day. I was very sad but strange enough I still somehow believed that I would make it there.

In the coming weeks all fans tried to get tickets for the show. So did I, but unfortunately I was unable to get one, for the show was already sold out 6 months before and that although nobody knew at that time that Michael Jackson would be performing. The only chance to get in was to pay an awful lot of money for tickets on the "black market"! Prices around 1.000 Euros were nothing but extraordinary. But that was too expensive for me and on top of that nothing had changed in my theatre schedule. So bad luck, I thought, but deep inside me I still believed that somehow I would get in.

A few weeks before the "Wetten, dass..?" show I attended a fan meeting in Munich (Michael's second hometown at that time). We were so excited to hear that Sony had arranged 40 extra

show tickets just for the fan club. They decided to make an auction so all fan club members could bid for the tickets. Afterwards the collected money was donated to the "Heal the world" foundation.
I was not bidding because I knew I would have no time to go to Duisburg and I still felt very sad about it. All tickets, but one, were auctioned off, so the leader of the fan club decided to make a game. We had to answer questions about Michael and the one who knew most of them would get the left ticket. Well, it came like it obviously had to come, the way you usually read about in fairytales: I won that ticket.

I was happy yet sad at the same time because now that I even had a ticket I knew that I still couldn't go. There was no chance for me to skip or reschedule the rehearsal for there were around 20 people in that theatre play and on top of that it was the last rehearsal before the premiere. I was not happy at all. I began to think that now that I have a ticket and can't go I take the chance away from another fan that might have been able to see Michael. But in my heart I somehow still believed that I would be there.

The thing with those won tickets was that we did not get a real ticket to hold in our hand but only a voucher. We needed to collect the real ticket in Cologne, a few days before the show. Although this again was impossible for me, I still began to look for flights. But there weren't many affordable ones left.

However I checked again to see if there was a small chance and indeed this time I found one flight which left Munich at 5.50 pm and would arrive at 7.15 pm in Düsseldorf. Suddenly I was so excited again. From there I only needed to catch the suburban train to Duisburg and indeed I found a possible one leaving at 7.18 pm and arriving in Duisburg's central station at 7.55 pm. From there another train would go to the hall where "Wetten, dass..?" was broadcasted, arriving at 8.40 pm.
The only "little" problem was that the show was scheduled to start at 8.15 pm and to get into the hall after the show had already

by Zimmy

begun was simply impossible. My mood changed from excited to depressed again. It was impossible. But damn, I had this ticket and I wanted to go! And somehow I still believed that I could make it. So I made a plan.
First I had to change the time of the rehearsal so that I could take that flight in the evening to Düsseldorf. Hey, did anyone of you guys ever tried to convince 20 actors to stand up early in the morning to do a rehearsal at 9 am instead of in the afternoon? But still I thought it was a very good plan.

Then I would run from the gate to the suburban train and then.... STOP. What kind of plan is that? From the aeroplane to the train in only 3 minutes? Well, all of you guys have experienced the pleasure of flying, so I am certain you know how much time one needs to just get out of a plane, right? Never mind. Okay…so then I will take the suburban train to Duisburg's central station, change to the other train which will take me to the broadcasting hall. Sounds good, doesn't it? The "only" problem might be that I have never been there and so I would surely need some time to find the right terminal. But well, if I wouldn't make it in time I still could take the next train and arrive at 8.40 pm at the hall. But then the show would have already begun…oh no, I am running in circles.

And then something terrible came to my mind. I had forgotten about picking up my ticket in Cologne the day before the show. I needed a reliable person not only to pick up my ticket but also to wait for me in front of the broadcasting hall even though the show might have started already, with my ticket.

Oh my God! This "plan" was no plan. It was simply impossible, I knew it. Or let's say my head knew it and I really should have accepted that: IT'S NOT POSSIBLE. But my heart believed in it, much more than before.

And so I went through with my plan. First step was to ask the director if we could change the time of the rehearsal. He said:

87

by Zimmy

"Well, if no one has a problem with that then we can do it". So I asked and explained the situation to all 20 people of the production team and believe it or not, they all agreed. It was so amazing that they supported me to get a chance to see Michael.
Then I booked that flight. And afterwards asked a friend to pick up my ticket a day before the show in Cologne and wait for me at the hall until 8 pm.

Until today, I don't know what made me say this to her. I did not do it on purpose; it just came out of my mouth in that very moment. I guess I was not really thinking. She also was lucky enough to have gotten a ticket for the show so she couldn't wait a minute longer than 8 pm. But I did not consider that. I just said I would be there in time and now that I write all this down, I still can't believe it that I was so certain about it.
"Be there at 8 pm", I knew it was not possible, simply not possible for me to make it in time.
But I kept on believing...

So finally the big day came and we indeed had that rehearsal at 9 am. Then I quickly went to the airport, entered the plane and waited for the take off. But outside it had begun to snow, it was November, and suddenly an announcement of the captain told us that the wings needed to be de-iced, so we would arrive 15 minutes late in Düsseldorf.

Can you imagine how I felt at that moment? But I was so stubborn. I did still believe. I know someone has to be really crazy to still believe in this plan – but well, I did.

Once we arrived in Düsseldorf at about 7.30 pm, I ran to the suburban train terminal. I ran and ran and tried to follow the right signs. Someone had told me earlier that the train station was only 2 minutes away from the gate but I soon had to find out that that was not true. I ran and my lungs almost burst through my chest. The moment I arrived at the platform, I literally screamed: "Which train goes to Duisburg? Which one!?"

by Zimmy

In the very last second I jumped inside the right train, almost not able to breathe anymore. But hey, I had made it. In that train I met two girls, obviously fans as well, and asked them, when we would arrive in Duisburg. They told me that this was an express train which would go directly to the main station Duisburg. This was good news for me – very good news indeed! I was getting more excited for my goal came closer. I told them that I had a ticket for the "Wetten, dass..?" show but since I could not show it to them, they didn't believe me. So I told them everything, and asked if they knew to which terminal I needed to run, in order to get the right connecting train. They began to understand that I had told them the complete truth and so one of them said that her sister is waiting at the main station to pick them up with her car and that I could go with them. I was so happy. People support you for Michael - that felt really good.

And so we arrived at the hall at exactly 8 pm. But where was my friend with the ticket? Oh no, I thought, she is not there anymore. I felt so downcast within a second. After all I had gone through now nobody was there with my ticket. I was so unbelievably sad. So I told one of the securities about my disaster and pleaded that they let me in. I knew how ridiculous this must have sounded for someone else. No one would believe me that story.

But then the unbelievable happened. I coincidentally met one security guy that I knew and he made the impossible possible and let me go through. And so, just four minutes before the show was about to begin, I stood in the 4th row at "Wetten, dass..?" right in front of Michael's stage.

Watching Michael's performance on "Youtube" you can see me standing there in an orange shirt, in the moment when Michael stands on the cherry picker. It felt so unreal and it was so unbelievable.
I am fan of Michael since 1988, visited 23 concerts, two of them in New York City on September 7th and 10th, 2001, so I was also in New York City on September 11th, 2001. Michael personally

by Zimmy

gave me an autograph in Monaco, I talked to him during his stays in Munich...etc. There are so many stories to tell.
But why did I choose this story?
We all know that Michael is magic but for me this trip to "Wetten, dass..?" was really a true miracle. I wanted to show you that things can happen even though they seem impossible. Just believe in them and then just do it. It doesn't matter what you are doing but keep on running for your goal.

by Zimmy

Cologne Calling
3rd July 1988

by Shaun Redfern, UK

My name is Shaun Redfern and I have been a fan of Michael Jackson for over 28 years.
And I am proud of it!

Born on June 16th 1968, I have four sisters Janet, Sheila, Eileen & Joan who are all older than me. My family always loved music.
Joan, my youngest Sister was the same age as Michael Jackson, so she used to watch the Jackson 5 cartoon series, when it was on TV, I do remember watching it with her some mornings. Joan always used to say to me 'Ben' was always her favorite song by Michael Jackson as she had the 7"single. I know this is where I began to listen to Michael's music and my sisters have left an imprint on my taste in music which was never to go away.

While at school, my very first Michael Jackson record I bought was the 7"Single 'Rock with you'.
My first Album, though, came to me by chance, literally, as it was about to be incinerated at a local depot when I said, I wanted the album, and that LP was 'Destiny'. I always used to play 'Blame it on the Boogie' over and over again.
It wasn't until the 'Thriller' video came out, that I began to follow Michael Jackson properly. My sister came to visit me one day and we rented the video from a local shop, I initially couldn't think what the fuss was about, my sister kept telling me that Michael was about to hit big time. As soon as the film started I remember being blown away by it and I just loved it. Vincent Price will always stick in my mind when I watched 'Thriller' for the first time. After watching this film, I bought the 'Thriller' album.

by Shaun Redfern

I then began to spend years buying Michael Jackson's back catalogue. Collecting Jackson 5 7"singles, Jackson 5 albums and all other Jacksons material by reading Record Collector Magazines so I could buy the older Motown records. This was to be my main source for the old material which I was chasing for the next two years and successfully collected.

So, when the 'BAD' album was released and they made the announcement that this was to be Michael Jackson's first World Tour, I knew I had to get tickets. I had some tickets for Wembley Stadium, also Leeds (Roundhay Park) but I wanted to see Michael before he reached the UK so when I saw an advert one day in a Sunday Newspaper to see 'Michael Jackson in Cologne' it was a chance I had to take.

On the morning of July 2nd, I made my way to London Victoria by train from Stoke on Trent as there was no pick up in the north of the country. This was my first time abroad on my own which in itself was scary. I went with a fairly new travel company, so I wondered if I lost my money as I remember at the time my mother saying to me, answering an advert in a Sunday newspaper could well be a con, but I wasn't to be ripped off and at 11 pm they picked me up at London Victoria Coach Station and we made our way towards Dover to pick up our Ferry to Calais and go overland to Cologne via France and Belgium.

After 10 hours on the road, we arrived at the city of Cologne and as we made our way towards our hotel we could see all the Michael Jackson fans dressed like Michael making their way to the stadium. At this point as you can understand I was beginning to get very excited.
After spending some time in the city to have something to eat and do a bit of sightseeing, we boarded our coach outside the hotel and made our way to the 'Müngersdorfer Stadium'.
On arrival at the stadium, as with all other coach trips, I was given my ticket, it was then I knew my dream was to come true and I would see my hero!

by Shaun Redfern

As I reached the ticket gate some other Michael Jackson fans asked me to join them so I wasn't on my own which I accepted. We then handed our tickets to the ticket collector who kept them, which I found very disappointing. The ticket was a photo of Michael Jackson shaped in his 'BAD' pose. I wished I could have kept that as a souvenir.

Once in the stadium I was directed to the pitch with my new friends and we waited for the opening act, Kim Wilde, to come on stage. The atmosphere took me by surprise as I always thought the Germans would be laid back, how wrong could I be! As soon as Kim Wilde came on stage a German guy said to me: "Come on, let's party!" and we all started to jump up and down, and this was just the support act!

After Kim Wilde had finished her set, I started to feel my adrenalin go mad and began to feel sick. The thought of seeing Michael Jackson was beginning to make me ill, so, in the end, I had to leave my new friends to get some air on the outside of the pitch as my nerves were terrible and I felt I was going to faint! It's a feeling that I just cannot describe because people think it's funny that I got so excited and got myself into this state. I was in a frenzy and just could not wait for Michael to come on stage any longer.

As soon as the electronic board on the back of the stage came on, I started to forget my sickness and I could see Michael Jackson's trademark white socks and shoes go across the screen which announced Michael was about to come on stage. At this point I moved back nearer the front again, next to the screen where I had a fantastic view.

There he stood with his arm in front of him and hysteria was everywhere. Michael Jackson was finally here! I just could not believe he was there!
When the opening beats of 'Wanna be startin somethin' started I just felt like crying as I was about to see my hero perform for

by Shaun Redfern

the very first time. It was a night I will never forget! I got to see Michael perform 'Billie Jean', 'Beat it' and 'Thriller'. The show was everything I had wished for. Michael's dancing got me spellbound, especially the 'Moonwalk', and his voice was great. It was what I had saved up for a long time since I never got to see Michael with his brothers on the Victory Tour. This was also the first time I got to see Sheryl Crow and the brilliant musician Jennifer Batten who was also to be in Michael's band for the Dangerous and HIStory Tours. Michael Jackson ended the show with 'BAD' and it was brilliant!

When the concert had finished and I made my way to the coach, I was really deflated as after being on such a high it was time to come back down to earth. A feeling of disappointment followed as I knew it was all over for this trip but it definitely wasn't to be my last.

On my return to the UK, my local newspaper asked me if they could take my picture and do an article on me with regards to all concerts that I was going to watch all over Europe. What made me really surprised was that it was in full color and also on the front page of the 'Evening Sentinel' (see picture). They also requested I had my skin darkened even though at the time everybody was going mad about Michael's skin going lighter. I enjoyed doing it as I hoped Michael Jackson would see it!

I would eventually get to 17 Michael Jackson concerts in my life and even though I spent a lot of money going to them, I wouldn't change a thing!

Now Michael has gone it's very sad, but I will always think of seeing Michael back in 1988, I smile as I was lucky to see him. He will always be in my heart and soul! I have my DVD's to watch and all my records to listen to. I have also made loads of friends on the way through Michael Jackson. One thing is for sure, Michael Jackson changed my Life!

God bless Michael Jackson and long live the 'King of POP'!

by Shaun Redfern

Shaun on the cover of the 'Evening Sentinel' newspaper

My short trip to London

by Vanessa Pereira, Germany

On Saturday, 8th of October 2005, it started.
Jaqueline, Michelle and Tina told me they want to travel to London to see Michael Jackson and they asked me if I want to travel with them. I took the chance to see Michael Jackson for once in my life.
I was 16 years old, so I've never really had the chance to see him. So that was my opportunity to finally do so!
Furthermore I had a little money in my piggy bank and I had holidays at school. All in all, best premises to travel to London to see Michael. Also, my parents were happy that I started my trip to him.

We arrived at London Luton airport. We flew with EasyJet, but London wasn't that easy. It was a bit difficult to get into the city from the airport, but with some effort, we soon sat in a bus for one hour that took us to Baker Street. I was so happy when I heard the song „ABC" from the Jackson5 in the bus; I thought that might be a good omen!
From Baker Street we went on to Oxford Street to where it crossed with Park Lane. Next to the Hyde Park there it was: the luxury hotel „The Dorchester", where Michael and his children were staying.

When we arrived in front of the hotel, we heard a girl speaking on her phone saying: „I saw Michael Jackson, I saw him!" So we asked her what happened. We got to know that we had missed Michael about 30 minutes. He had left the hotel to see the musical „Billy Elliot" with his children. We had been too late! Whate-

ver! We spend the whole day waiting for Michael. After hours and hours, more fans gathered till there were about 300 fans in front of the hotel.
When Michael came back from the musical, the chaos started. There were cars everywhere! Finally, there were just three options how Michael could get into the hotel: first, through the main entrance, second, the garage to the right, or third, a shabby backdoor at the left. Suddenly all fans and the press ran towards the street, then back to the main entrance. Some barriers stood next to the main entrance, but they weren't very useful anyway.

Finally it was clear: Michael got out of his car at the backdoor on the left side of the hotel. Everyone waited just for this moment. We, the fans, and the press with big TV cameras started to move to see Michael Jackson. We ran. It was such a huge crowd that suddenly started to run, you could be happy if you outran at least a few people. As the car stopped and Michael got out, there was a wall of people that neither Jacqueline, Michelle, Tina nor I could see him. I stood about three meters away from Michael, but these three meters were full of people. I tried hard, I jumped, I held my digital camera up in the air to film, but nothing. A sudden, hard push from the back carried me to the front in an instant. I thought 'OK, that's my chance to see him', but Michael was already in the hotel and I didn't even get a glimpse of him.

There we were, standing in front of „The Dorchester" with our big banners. Jacqueline had made a big red-golden heart with the inscription "I love you Michael". I also had a litter board banner with "We love you Michael" written on it while the other side said "HI to Michael from GERMANY".
The crowd in front of the main entrance started singing songs like "Michael Jackson is the King of Pop" and chanted "We love you" which created a good atmosphere. We all hoped that he showed himself at the windows somewhere. Jacqueline and I held our banner in the hope that Michael would notice us.
I don't know how long this MJ-fan-party lasted, but it was great to be with so many fans there. The music played until the middle

by Vanessa Pereira

Vanessa and her friend finding their way through London

of the night. At about 3 am it started to rain, we were tired as well, so we started our search for an accommodation. We really tried to find something at Piccadilly Circus, but there was nothing. We sacrificed our last pounds for an Underground ticket to Bayswater. There we immediately found a hostel. Everything was alright ...

The next morning, October 9th, began quite well. After having a typical English breakfast with tea and toast, we, once again, made our way to Hyde Park and of course to Michael.

The morning we spent at his hotel. Around 1 pm the forecourt was already full of people again. The press bustled about, so you couldn't count how many photographers there were. Everyone waited and waited. This waiting took hours and hours. Meanwhile the photographers got bored, so they started taking pictures of us. Yes, of Jacqueline and me. They wanted to take pictures of us, because of our nice banners and because we came all the way from Germany just to see Michael Jackson.

After that, Tina and I lay down on the hayfield in front of the hotel. From that position we could see all windows of the hotel. Suddenly it seemed that one of those windows was opened. And sure enough, a male shape looked out. Everybody screamed „Michael" - but it was just the window cleaner of the hotel whom we probably confused a lot. So funny, everyone, including us, was screaming after a hotel cleaner. He finished his job at this room and went away.

In the evening, Jacqueline, Tina and I had to start our trip back to the airport. As we arrived there, we got a SMS from Michelle who stayed a few days longer, visiting a friend of hers. She wrote that Michael had donated pizza for the fans with the message "Thank you for your love".

Naturally we were a bit sad having missed this, but all in all it was a nice trip, even though we haven't seen Michael.

It was great to spend time with other Michael Jackson fans, and we were having a terrific time together.
Sharing that feeling with fans is the best thing you can do!

by Vanessa Pereira

August, 29th, 1958

by Dagmar Herrmann, Germany

Is the rejoicing of the lark
even brighter on that day
and the ringing of the bell sounds
stunning like a beat of drum?

Greets the rosy dawn happier
the sleepy world than other days
And the bread chars in the stove
because the baker pauses work?

Neither shawms, nor fanfares
Telling of this mirthful hour
And the world hasn't learned
What is this time on every lip.

Sweet child with golden throat
Still motionless, so seems the world -
But with arrival of your soul
the spark already has been placed.

The hearts already beat more mildly
Lighter seems the shine of stars
and in the vale of tears of pains
the tone of love is getting through.

It's messenger of grief and joy
Language which a child can speak
Child and man, today I still see you
in this unchanged light.

Running into Michael

by Diane Hotchkiss, USA

Even though I have never seen Michael live during a show or concert, my daughter and I once were lucky to accidentally run into him.

It was about the time when Michael had held his son Blanket over the railing in Berlin. My daughter and I were at the Hilton in Orlando because she took part in a pageant there. We were just coming out of the hotel building as at the same time Michael walked out of "Bennihan's" Japanese restaurant.

At the moment I saw him I was in total shock and said to my daughter: "Oh my God, do you realize who this is?" But she said "No mommy." I have to add that at that time my daughter was only 11 years old. Curiously she looked at me. I told her "It's Michael Jackson! Oh my God, I used to be so in love with this guy!" So she said: "Mom, you have to say hi to him!"
So we nervously went up to him and my daughter bravely said: "Excuse me, Mr. Jackson, but my mom would like to say hi to you."

Just at that moment my cell phone had rung and my husband was on the line. I quickly told him who was in front of me, actually all I kept saying was: "Yes, Brian, it's really Michael Jackson!" Meanwhile my daughter introduced herself to Michael and he kindly asked her some questions and just talked to her. Quickly a crowd of people had surrounded us and so Michael finally took my phone and started talking to my husband, telling him "Your family is very pretty and your daughter is sooo sweet." Actually he had about a 5 minute's conversation with my husband. After he had hung up, Michael kindly took the time for a picture with my daughter and me.

Then he walked back to his limo. Just in that moment I realized that he still had my phone.
Luckily one of his bodyguard realized as well and came back to give it to me.

My husband later told me about the conversation he had with Michael and that he had told him that if it wasn't for the song "Man in mirror" he would not be here today. He told him that after hearing that song on the radio it helped him to stop doing drugs (that was before we got married) and that it is a shame that the media wants people to believe that he (Michael) is a bad father and that he knew he wouldn't harm his own child (referring to the baby dangling incident in Berlin).

Michael thanked Brian for saying that and he told my husband that he simply got so caught up in that moment (in Berlin) and added, "... you're right, I love my children and would never harm them in any way."

Of course my daughter finally wanted to know more about Michael and so I told her that he is a very nice man with a big heart and the biggest superstar that you could ever come across.

by Diane Hotchkiss

The letter

by Alice Oderinde, Germany

It was November 21st in 2002 and Michael attended the Bambi Awards in Berlin to receive the "Pop Artist of the Millennium" award. After the show Michael celebrated with his fans, standing on the hotel room balcony waving and smiling. It was a great experience, the atmosphere was fantastic - hundreds of fans in front of the Adlon hotel, singing and screaming.

Later in the evening Michael left the hotel for a late trip. My friend and I noticed it by chance and decided to wait in the basement garage until Michael returned to the hotel. Only very few fans were there. So we thought we'd have a really good chance to be able to say hello to Michael at his arrival and give him our banner and our letters and also a picture of him that I had drawn. The banner said "Tommy Mottola is a cold man" – my friend had originally made it a few months earlier to take it to the Anti-Sony Demonstration in London. But we added some other little texts and pictures, also some funny stuff.

A few weeks earlier, three short snippets of previously unreleased songs had appeared on the internet: "If you don't love me", "For all time" and "Monkey Business". We wrote on the banner that we really liked the snippets and would love to hear more. We also wrote that the fans are always totally excited about new material and suggested to release the three songs in whole.

In the meantime it was getting later and later and still no sign of Michael. We were getting really tired and frustrated and put a time limit. If he wouldn't arrive within the next hour we would leave, heading for our warm hostel beds. Unfortunately when the time was up Michael still had not returned. We decided to at least leave him a message since we had to leave Berlin the next morning and wouldn't have another chance to give him our presents. We took the banner and put it on the front window of one of the cars of Michael's crew. We also wanted to leave our letters and my picture and so we clipped it all under the car's wiper.

The next day we were already on our way home, still excited about having a wonderful time in Berlin but also a bit sad because we didn't get the chance to say hello to Michael the night before.

A few weeks later we were given two wonderful surprises. First, I got a letter from one of Michael's bodyguards. I opened it and the first thing I saw was the picture of Michael that I had drawn and left in the garage! I was getting nervous – what was that supposed to mean? I took it from the envelope and gasped: Michael had signed it! I read the letter attached – it said that Michael had received our banner and letters and was really happy about it. The bodyguard also wrote how excited he was to work for Michael Jackson and that they had decided to send me the signed picture instead of Michael keeping it. How nice!

Another week later the next surprise followed. Guess which three songs were suddenly available on the internet in full length?

by Alice Oderinde

Thank you for the memories

by Jannik Per Jørgensen, Denmark

The first time I heard about Michael Jackson was in 1993 when I was 6 years old.
As curious as it may sound, he has been a part of my life ever since - understood in the sense that I always took solace in his music and joy. Through Michael, I collected the best memories of my life, friends and also some amazing trips around the world.

I remember the day when my biggest dream became true. It was 1997 and I was going to Michael's concert on his birthday, August 29th. My heart was beating really fast and it did not stop pounding until the day after the concert. Back then I could not grasp that I really had been to a Michael Jackson concert.

My dream came true again in 2006 at the World Music Awards in London. I remember my absence from school during those days and my brother honestly defending me, telling that I was really „sick". I had "Jackson fever", he said and he actually was right.

Michael, you have really touched me deeply and thinking that you're gone now makes tears come up every time. I want to thank you for all the beautiful music you've given us and thanks for all the wonderful and fantastic memories you have given us. Thanks for all the wonderful friends you brought along for me. Thank you for healing the world. Thanks for everything. We love you. You will always live on in my heart.

A story of a very special friendship

by The Appleheads (Lisa Hochmuth, Heike Arbter, Carina Zieroth, Jessica Loose & Miriam Lohr), Germany

There's that legend that says that once in your lifetime, something BIG happens and changes your whole life forever. After this turning point, your life will never be the same. We know that this legend can become reality!

We are Jessi, Carina, Heike, Miri and Lisa. We all became Michael Jackson fans in the early 1990's and we became friends through Michael's music in the mid 90's. A little later we decided to call ourselves "The Appleheads" - that was long before we knew that Michael called himself and everybody else "Applehead". We just thought that name would fit our craziness.

Getting to know each other really changed our lives. It soon grew into something more than just sharing the passion and commitment for Michael Jackson. We realized how similar we were to each other, how we had the same outlook on life, the same interests, the same goals. Although we were coming from different parts of Germany, we became as close as friends can be. A special bond developed between us and led us to many adventures in different places in the world.

Our story is about fun, joy and laughter, but also sadness and tears – sometimes one directly after the other. And although we have experienced so many every day situations together, which were made special just by the fact that we experienced them together, it were of course the once-in-a-lifetime experiences that will always hold us together like glue.

We were driven by our big dream –
meeting Michael Jackson in person!
Let us invite you to read about our life-changing moments.

09/07/1996 – HIStory Tour Prague/Czech Republic
Finally! Finally he was back! Finally we were old enough! Finally we had the chance to see him live!

It was surreal when we reached the boarder to the Czech Republic and the custom official's first question was "Are you going to see the Michael Jackson concert?" and we all screamed "YES!" It was surreal when shortly after crossing the boarder we saw lights in the air and joked that they probably came from Michael rehearsing – and in the end that turned out to be true. It was surreal when we arrived in Prague and "Earth Song" could be heard throughout the city. We just couldn't wait until the next day!

At 9 am we arrived at Letna Park to queue. There were already quite a lot of people and the security already couldn't handle them. It was torture! But it didn't get better when we were let in, because there were no sections and all 140,000 people pushed and shoved that after a few minutes we had lost each other in the crowd. The minutes seemed like hours and finally the support act DJ Bobo took the stage and shortly afterwards a voice announced: "30 minutes and you will be a part of history!" We were all so excited because nobody knew what would happen that night! Then the animated film started on the huge screens and HIStory began! In the film, there was a spaceman in a little space shuttle who travelled through different fantasy worlds until he approached a big stadium....then, the film ended and a real rocket came out of the stage. Michael was the spaceman and came out of the rocket – what an entry! When Michael took his helmet off, that was the very first moment of seeing his face in real life. Surreal... All the struggles of the day were forgotten and we just had a huge party! It was over much too soon!

by The Appleheads

08/28/1996 – HIStory Tour Amsterdam/Holland
3 weeks after seeing Michael in Prague, we drove to Amsterdam/Holland to see Michael one more time before he was off to Asia. We drove to Amsterdam by car and got there in only 5 hours. We were so nervous and happy. It will always be hard to describe what kind of happiness you felt, when you were about to see him.
Dutch people seemed to be far more civilized than, let's say, the fans in Prague and so we managed to stand in the 2nd row! We just couldn't believe it, many feelings overwhelmed us. Seeing Michael so close was yet a totally different feeling than just being „somewhere" in Prague.

On the next day we experienced another tour-phenomenon. Everyone in town seemed to be drawn into the Michael Jackson magic and you could see a lot of people with Michael Jackson t-shirts that somehow displayed your pride of being a part of „HIStory". As stupid as this might sound, but having breakfast in the hotel was always a very funny part of being on tour with Michael. Who had screamed the loudest and whose voice had disappeared? Most of the time Michael Jackson fans had this silent understanding for each other that was always comforting wherever we went.

Before we had to head home, we went to Michael's hotel to see what was going on there. Of course it was crazy. Obviously he was about to come out and people wouldn't stop screaming to show their love. It was chaotic, loud and mad and we loved everything of it, because it was our first real „hotel-experience". His vans came out and he tried to make his way through the crowd. Not really knowing what to do, we followed the crowd running after his cars.

Back then we would never have thought that 13 years later we'd still be standing in front of hotels just to catch that so called famous „glimpse" of Michael. You just couldn't help it. He waved to the crowd and only that just felt magical.
On our way home we were all happy, talking about what just had happened, until totally coincidentally his vans passed us by.

by The Appleheads

All we could think of was to hold out a Michael pillow. Funny enough, all we ever wanted was to make him see that we loved him. So we held it out and smiled, we just smiled.

05/28 – 06/01/1997 – HIStory Tour Bremen/Germany
It was time for the HIStory Tour to come to Germany, kicking off the first show in Bremen. We had been waiting to see Michael in our own country for years and our dream would finally come true! In Bremen, Michael stayed at the Park-Hotel which is located at a beautiful park and lake. When he arrived several days prior to the concert on May 31st, it was clear to us that we should try our best to catch a glimpse of him. We were very lucky as Michael was active and in good spirits all the time. There were always a great number of fans waiting in front of the Park-Hotel and Michael came out every day to greet them. He was surrounded by bodyguards and sometimes also TV cameras and whatever he did, the fans would react enthusiastic and even hysterical. Michael came very close, he signed autographs and took some presents from fans. With some of them he posed for pictures. He wore black trousers, black slippers, white socks, a black uniform with gold applications, his black fedora and a black satin mask.

There was also a lot of action taking place at Michael's window. He waved to us, threw down signed papers and watched the crowd.
On May 29th, he visited the city hall of Bremen and met with the mayor Henning Scherf. As you can imagine, talking of Michael Jackson, this meant no ordinary scene. In fact, it was as if the whole city was going crazy about this event. The big square in front of the city hall was crowded by thousands of people. We all gathered behind barriers. Police was everywhere. When Michael and his team arrived and got out of the vans, people started screaming. Michael greeted and hugged some fans who were allowed to come over to him, he signed some autographs. Then, he greeted the mayor and climbed up a small tribune with him to take a look at a very popular statue in Bremen. It was a statue of the "The Bremen Town Musicians", which shows the characters of one of the Brother's Grimm fairy tales associated to this town.

The staff of the city hall then invited Michael to take a tour inside the building and we later learned that he signed the golden book of the city. Then he gave us another very special moment when he climbed onto the balcony of the city hall overlooking the whole place. There was a microphone and Michael addressed some German words to the crowd. When he said "Wie geht es dir?" ("How are you?) and "Ich liebe dich" ("I love you"), he seemed to enjoy himself very much talking those German words and laughed a lot. It made us so happy to have him in our country and he was so sweet to everybody!

The day of the first concert, we queued up early at the "Weserstadion" and waited the whole day for the gates to open up. It was hot and sunny, a perfect day for an open air show! When we were let inside, the excitement grew with every hour that passed. Opening act was the Australian boygroup "Human Nature". Around 9 pm, the real show began. Michael entered the stage as usual in his little white rocket and kicked off an energetic show! There were some new elements in comparison to the shows he had done before. "Come together" and "D.S.", which we had seen in Prague and Amsterdam, were taken out of the setlist. Instead, Michael performed "Blood on the dance floor" from his latest album for the first time live! It was also one of the last performances of "The way you make me feel", which was kicked out of the show just some concerts later. When he put his blue shirt into his trousers, the whole audience went "Uuuuuh!" and Michael laughed. He also still knew his German! When we screamed "We love you" he said: "Wait, wait, wait! I love you more! Ich liebe dich mehr!"

During "Earth Song", the whole stadium was lit up with candles and sparklers. 50,000 people were completely drawn into Michael's show and interacted with every song and move he made, it was amazing. A beautiful firework marked the end of the show when night had already fallen. We were completely exhausted after the show, but just happy. The next day, we drove to the Park-Hotel again to see, if something was going on there. There were around 50 fans, but it was quiet, no sign of Michael, so we just waited.

by The Appleheads

Around 3 pm, people began to get nervous, because we were told that Michael would come out shortly and there was much going in and coming out at the main entrance of the hotel. Two vans were parked in front of the entrance. Then, Michael came out in his brown leather coat, black fedora and black trousers. He came down the stairs, waved and stepped beside the vans to give us a last glimpse of him. Then he got into one van and they drove off quickly.

06/15/1997 – HIStory Tour Gelsenkirchen/Germany
Traffic jam! Oh no! We were already late and now we were stuck in that stupid jam! We arrived in Gelsenkirchen around 3 pm and of course the queue was looooong. Luckily, the distance from the entrance to the stadium was so long that by running a new world record (well, kind of...) we managed to still get into the first row! A little on the left side of the stage, but still we were happy!

Michael was in a good mood! At one point, he read our banner and then pointed at it. Before the Motown Medley started, he forgot to put on his jacket and stood at the microphone only in his shirt announcing "Now we gonna give you..." When Michael Bush (his costume designer) came and tapped him on the shoulder with the jacket in his hand, Michael started to laugh.

07/31 – 08/03/1997 – HIStory Tour Berlin & Leipzig/Germany
The day before the concert in Berlin, we already roamed around the Olympic stadium and the 4 Seasons hotel where Michael was supposed to be staying. We had a little talk with some of Michael's crewmembers, exchanged pictures with fans and decorated an advertising pillar across the street of the hotel with Michael slogans. When we were finished, we realized that Michael's camera man stood at the window of his hotel room and had filmed us.
At 10 am the next day we arrived at the Olympic stadium. We were right at the entrance and were sure that we would be getting a good spot. But when the gates were finally opened at 4 o'clock and we ran, ran, ran... there was suddenly a security guard blocking our way. "This is only an emergency entrance!" he shouted.

by The Appleheads

Michael performing in Gelsenkirchen

What? Slowly panicking, we were looking for the closest other entrance. The quickest way to it was running over a wall, which we did, just to hear another "This is only an emergency entrance!" there. God! So we were running back to the first entrance, where more and more people now had arrived so that the security guard at this time only came as far as "This is only...", then we had pushed him aside to run through. Why on earth can they never do an organized admission? Anyway, we still ended up in the second row so we were pretty satisfied. Afterwards we heard that a fan, who took the same way as we did to the other entrance, fell from the wall and broke a leg…

While waiting, it started to rain… We all sat on the floor with our raincoats on, cursing the weather, when they played Supertramp's "It's raining again" and we all looked at each other smiling. How can you be sad at a Michael Jackson concert? And as if by magic, as soon as Michael was about to get on stage, the sun broke through again. The rain even brought us a special, funny anecdote: After "In the closet" someone came on stage with a brush to dry it. Michael suddenly started to chase the brush and tried to jump on it, which made the whole stadium laugh.

The next day we spent in front of Michael's hotel. Around 1 o'clock, Michael came to the window and waved. Later he even stepped out on the balcony. In the afternoon the vans lined up, he got in and drove away. We could only see him shortly when he stood up and opened the skylight. Then we had to leave, because our travel continued to Leipzig.

Another day, another concert, this time on the "Festwiese" in Leipzig. We were slowly getting used and a little bored by the waiting time, so this time we took pen and paper to play a few games like Scattergories. It didn't last long because at noon people started to get up again. It was always the same at the concerts (except Prague, where we stood the whole time): Everybody is sitting and relaxing until at some point someone gets up quickly and rushes for the gates. Everybody else quickly does the same

by The Appleheads

Michael performing in Leipzig

until the security shouts that they will not let people in until at least 5 o'clock and that everybody please should sit down again. Problem: When everybody's standing, there is much less room for each person. And as nobody wants to take a step back, it's impossible that everyone can sit down again. That little game continues several times until the gates are finally being opened.

We ended up in the first and second row and were really pleased until security asked us to sit down. Sit down? We stood in the mud up to the ankles! In the end, nobody sat down.

When Michael came on stage, he was in high spirits! He said: "Wie geht es dir?" („How are you?" in German) and when we all screamed he made big eyes and asked seemingly astounded: "Do you understand that?" He seemed to have taken a quick lesson in German in Berlin, as he also said "Ich liebe dich" ("I love you") and "Ich liebe dich mehr" ("I love you more").

But then the lean in "Smooth Criminal" didn't work, Michael had to put one foot in front of him so he wouldn't fall. And we all thought: "Oh no, now his good mood is probably gone!" But no, not at this time! Before the Motown-Medley, one of the sweetest scenes of the whole tour happened when there was a little bug on stage which he wanted his bodyguard Wayne Nagin to save. Yes, this scene was cut into the TV broadcast from Munich, but this really happened in Leipzig! After "I'll be there" Michael really started to cry. He just stood there, looked into the crowd and tears ran down his face while everybody was screaming like crazy. That was the loudest audience we have experienced on tour! After "HIStory" three kids came on stage and Michael quickly realized that he couldn't take the "elevator" to get off stage with all three of them. But when they wanted to take one of the kids away from him, he said: "It's ok, it's ok!", shouted: "Good night!" to all of us and walked with the three of them off stage.
On the way back to the hotel we just couldn't stop laughing and shouting "Wayne! Security!" all the time! It was hilarious!
08/10/1997 – HIStory Tour Hockenheim/Germany

by The Appleheads

Michael dancing full out in Leipzig

Sadly, the 10th and last concert in Germany took place on August 10th, 1997 in Hockenheim. We went there with bittersweet feelings. On the one hand, we were so happy to see him one more time, on the other hand, it made us feel sad that it was the last German show for now. During the whole summer, we were living with a magical feeling and the wonderful thought "He is not far, he's right here".

The venue was the Hockenheimring, which is originally build for speed car racing and it is really huge! The part of the area destined for the concert easily took 90,000 people that day. It was the hottest day we ever had on a concert day and while waiting, we were nearly getting grilled up by the sun from above while roasting on the already gummy roadway. The security guards began to pump up fountains of water in the air so that the crowd could cool down a little. Thank God, it helped.

The show started around 9 pm and from the first beat on, Michael had the 90,000 people under his control! He was very energetic that night and real chatty. Before he started the Jackson Five-Medley, he held a little speech and thanked his band and crew members for "helping me build this empire". He also thanked Marcel Avram, "my dear friend" and the security "even though I can't see you".

A funny episode happened when a big zeppelin came flying towards the stage over the massive crowd. Michael looked up, laughed and waved shouting "Hello!!" The fans went nuts, it was just too sweet! Of course, also Michael had to endure the heat that day. In between two songs, he would wipe off his sweat with a towel and drink a lot of Gatorade.

After the show, it took us hours and hours to get out of the concert area. It was that huge and there were so many people so there was no quick way out. We were thirsty and completely drawn-out. When we wanted to buy a drink, they offered us sink-water with grass swimming in it for 13DM (about 8 US-Dollars) which we refused to buy…a little while later we could find a place to buy a can of Coca Cola….we never were that happy to drink Coke! That night, we slept in our car.

by The Appleheads

08/27 – 08/30/1997 – HIStory Tour Copenhagen/Denmark
We already arrived two days before the concert in Copenhagen. We had a great time sightseeing, buying memorabilia and meeting many of Michael's crew members who were very nice! We partied into Michael's birthday in front of the hotel D'Angleterre where he was supposed to be staying but didn't after all. The next day, we arrived at Parken stadium at 6.30 in the morning. We were the first at our gate and the waiting time was cold but relaxed. It was amazing to see how the Danish fans queued in rows of two! At 5 o'clock the doors opened. All went fine until there was a second row of securities that wanted to see our tickets again when the first securities had already taken them from us... After a short discussion they let us through and we made it into the first row again! This time, we even enjoyed the performance of the supporting act "Human Nature"! When you see things for the last time, you tend to look at them differently. When "Ben" started to play, which was always played right before the show began, we started to cry as this was the beginning of the end, the last HIStory concert we would witness!

When the rocket came on stage, everyone started to sing "Happy birthday". Michael kicked against the door, but it opened only a little. We could see him standing inside already, fumbling with his clothes. Then a second kick and the door was open. The white curtain for "Smooth Criminal" didn't go up correctly and for "You are not alone" a really crazy girl came on stage who crushed Michael so hard that Wayne had to come and help him. After "You are not alone", Michael stood near the drums and drank a little, when suddenly a marching band walked on stage. Michael hid behind the people until Michael Bush went up to him and gave him signs to go to the front. So he took his towel to have something to hide and came to the front. The marching band of the Danish amusement park TivoII then started to play "Happy birthday" and the whole stadium sang for Michael. He obviously thought that was pretty embarrassing! He said: "That's a surprise for me! I didn't know that. Thank you! I don't know what to say! Oh no!" They rolled a huge cake on stage and there was a fire-

by The Appleheads

Michael performing in Copenhagen and celebrating his birthday with the Tivoli marching band

work saying "Happy birthday, Michael" and he could only say "Oh no!" again and again and again. He loved the cake, which he thought was "incredible". Then he was asked to put out the candles on it. He tried to wave them out with his towel and then said: "I wish peace and love to the world!" It was a very special moment and Michael was all smiles for the rest of the concert!

Unfortunately the concert came to an end at some point and we were so sad! The summer of 1997 has been a very special one for all of us and we will always remember it as a magical, happy, carefree and beautiful time!

03/28 – 03/31/1998 – Michael in Munich/Germany
After Michael had been in Munich for two weeks already, we had finally gotten our Easter holidays and were allowed to go!
As soon as we got to the hotel „Bayerischer Hof" people were telling us that he would go and see a show at the Circus Krone. We drove there immediately to get tickets and were lucky enough to get in. When Michael came, he showed his son Prince to the people and the crowd was going crazy. He was only one year old at that time and people were so excited to see him. As a lot of fans managed to go in, the whole show was almost a disaster and we felt quite sorry for the acrobatics, because whenever Michael laughed or clapped his hands people would scream and shout his name. Although we were excited, too, it just wasn't fair to the artists. We just kept on watching him. He was so happy to take his son out to the circus, he was like a child himself and it was so cute to see them like that. During the break we decided to go out and wait outside. We took a closer look into the van and fans decided to put presents and letters into it and as his bodyguards did not stop us from doing so, we also put letters onto his seat.
The whole night in front of the hotel was just awesome. Michael was at the window pretty much all the time and threw pillows, toys and bed sheets out of the hotel window. All of it was signed and had messages on it that displayed his love for the fans. He always enjoyed making us happy and Carina was lucky enough to catch a little ball with his signature. It was about 2 am when

most of the fans had headed home. Michael was still awake and all of a sudden, after we did some singing, he leaned out of the window. Instead of screaming we stayed quiet. He managed to say „I...I love you and goodnight". To hear him speak off stage was always a wonderful experience. The tone and the softness, the love and the delicateness in his voice touches you so deeply and somehow hits you with so much love. It is incredible.

The next day, Michael was supposed to leave Munich, so after seeing him wave several times during the daytime, we decided to stay for the night. It was a cold night, but after all it was the last. To get warm, some fans made a small fire. But of course the police quickly arrived and told us to put it out. Well, being cold and shivering was one of the usual MJ-travel disciplines, so we didn't let that demoralize us. Deep in concentration on doing the "step-touch-dance" to keep warm, we only realized something happened when other fans started to run to the other side of the street... It turned out that Michael had thrown a blanket out of his window. "Keep warm!" was written on it. Trying, Michael! He threw down more signed stuff and guess what: It really helped! We were warm! When an autographed red pillow ended up under a taxi and ten fans suddenly lay under the car while the taxi driver irritatedly looked for help, we laughed so hard! Miri caught a signed ball and we were all in such a good mood! We started to talk to "the window" – as we couldn't see Michael. Starting from "We love you's" to doing La-Olas for passing cars to burning some tabloids - which Michael commented by throwing down a message saying "Let's make a tabloid burn!" We invited Michael to play "Truth or dare" with us and it even got more crazy. At one point we suggested he could play "hide and seek" with us. "The window" was still quiet. We didn't care and ran to find a good hiding place. Thank God there were some trees, but it shouldn't have been too difficult to find us when about five of us stood behind one tree. After a few minutes we stepped back on the street shouting: "You didn't find us, we won!" Well, as Michael wasn't reacting but the window was still open, somebody shouted "Michael, if you want to sleep, give us a sign!" and someone else

by The Appleheads

corrected: "No, we are 17 people, give us 17 signs!" We all laughed! Who would have thought that Michael took that comment seriously? A few minutes later one of Michael's bodyguards came down with 17 autographs signed on hotel stationery! Unfortunately some taxi drivers got out of their cars and were given an autograph so that some fans got away empty handed. We also gave the bodyguard, whom we nicknamed "running meter" because he was so small, a little present for Michael. A CD called "HIS-fans" on which were songs that we and some other fans had written and recorded for him. The "running meter" promised to give it to Michael immediately. A few moments later, when we stood a little offside and admired our autographs, something came flying right into our arms. Well, it was probably a coincidence, but some fans interpreted it as a thank you for the present from Michael. Naaah, he cannot aim that precisely! On the other hand, he once had basketball lessons with Michael Jordan, so... In any case, it turned out to be a Neverland T-Shirt which he had signed with "Love, Michael Jackson" twice. And it smelled so good! He must have bathed it in a whole bottle of perfume! All the fans came to smell it – must have looked pretty crazy how everyone put their nose into the shirt.

It was already 4 am now and someone suddenly suggested that we should be quiet for a moment, because maybe Michael would talk to us again. What a crazy idea, we hadn't even seen him for the whole night! On the other hand he must have been watching us and listening, judging from his actions. But if he did, then why on earth hadn't he called the mental hospital?? Anyway, as this had been a magic night already, we all decided to give it a try. But it's difficult to silence such a crazy crowd as us MJ fans! Someone was still talking and another fan jokingly bitched: "Ah, somebody is always talking!" We all burst into laughter! But suddenly we heard a voice from above: "I love you!" He SANG these words. Everybody whispered "sh..." to each other. Michael said "I love you!" again, this time it sounded a little irritated. We shouted back: "We love you!" and he answered: "I love you more!" "Nooooo!" was our reply! For the next half hour, Michael gave an

by The Appleheads

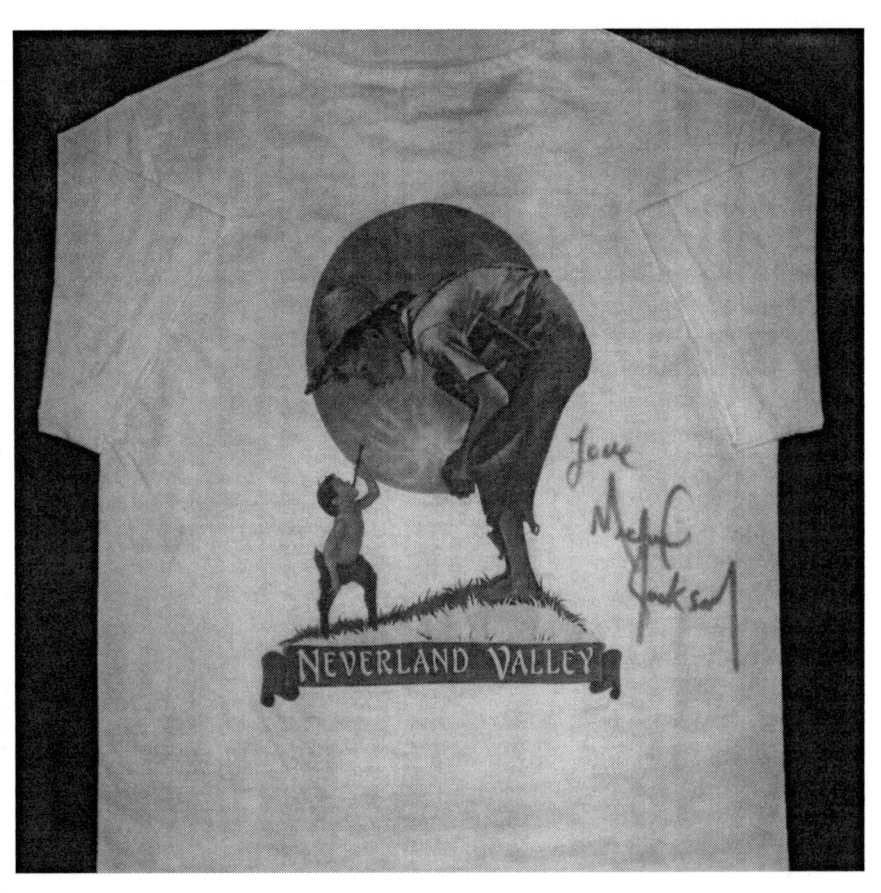

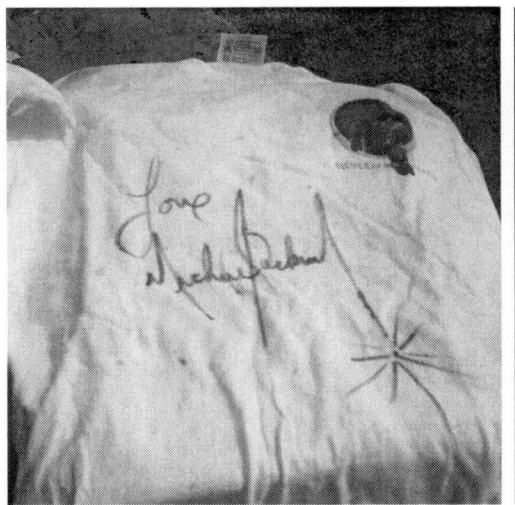

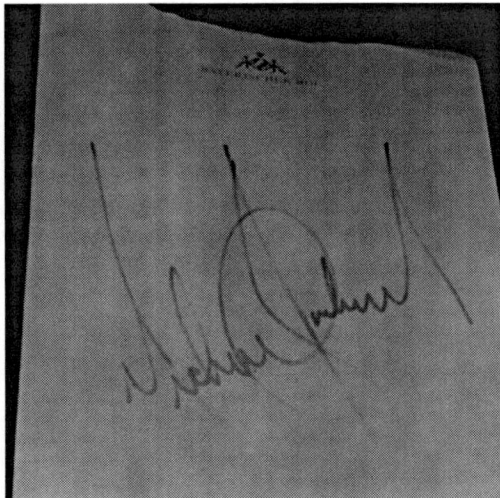

One of Michael's autographs on hotel stationary and the signed Neverland shirt

exclusive little interview to us, if you will. Or he just talked to us like friends who hadn't seen each other for a long time. At least that is exactly what it felt like while it lasted. We didn't see him, he must have been standing behind the curtain at his window. But we heard him loud and clear - except for the times, when a car passed by. After a little while, we always told him to wait with his answer when a car came closer. When he didn't understand us, he said "Pardon?" He was just so polite!

Not in chronological order, at times not word by word and of course incomplete, but this is the conversation we remembered right after it happened:

Us: Did you enjoy our little show?
MJ: Yes, I loved it! You are doing a great job!
Us: How's Prince?
MJ: He's fine! He's with me right now. We're not going to sleep because we'll fly back to America, to L.A., tomorrow to do a movie.
Us: Can he talk yet?
MJ: No, he can't talk but he's walking. (sounding proud)
Us: What about a new album?
MJ: I'm working on it right now. It'll be released in summer.
Us: Do we inspire you?
MJ: Yes you do. Very much! (with a little giggle)
Us: We'll make you No. 1 again.
MJ: Thank you!
Us: What about Debbie?
MJ: Oh, she's in hospital right now…
Us: How is she?
MJ: She's fine!
Us: Congratulations on your second child, Michael!
MJ: Thank you! Thank you very much! …I think we have to destroy the tabloids!
Us: Yes! Fuck the press!
MJ: (laughs)
Us: The word "fuck" is a little too hard for you, but in this case

by The Appleheads

it's ok!
MJ: I, I, I… I hate the tabloids. Don't believe them! (sounding sad and angry)
Us: NO! We wouldn't be here if we did.
MJ: (laughs)
Us: Michael, you should do more "Making of's". We love to see you working backstage!
MJ: Oooooooh! (really surprised)
Us: How about a tour?
MJ: First the movie! …I love Germany and Munich. I'll come back soon.
Us: What about moving to Germany?
MJ: Yes, I'm looking for a house but I'm still searching.
A fan: I've still got the book I wanted to give you yesterday…
MJ: Oh, can I send someone down?
Us: Phantasialand will open again soon. Will you come?
MJ: Oh yes. Sure.
Us: Thank you for everything!
MJ: Thank you! …I may fall asleep now, ok!?
Us: Good night!
MJ: Good night! I love you. I'll miss you! Good night.

Then he waved behind the curtains for the last time and was gone. Wow! Did that really just happen?
We decided to get something to eat in a little café nearby and talk to other fans. What an amazing night!

The next day, Michael departed secretly while we tried our best to hamper the media. After Michael's sad and angry statements, we felt that it really was our duty.

05/31/1998 Cologne/Germany
Well, not all travels were as "successful" and exciting as our last trip to Munich. On May 31st 1998 for example, we made a trip to Cologne after getting phone calls that Michael was there, residing in the Hyatt hotel and working on his new album in the studio in Stommeln, near Cologne. At that time, there was no internet to

by The Appleheads

look up the facts so we trusted our sources and went to Cologne. Quite a lot of fans were already standing and sitting in front of the hotel, but it turned out that nobody had seen Michael yet. Well, we were still in a good mood, met Bryan May (Queen), Ringo Starr (Beatles) and Thomas Gottschalk (German showmaster of "Wetten, dass…?") while waiting for Michael and just had a good time imagining we'd see him soon. The later it got and the more it began to rain, the more fans made their way home, to friends or their hotel. As this had been a quick decision, we had not made any arrangements regarding our accommodation. In the end, we found ourselves alone in front of the hotel, where a doorman asked us to leave the ground of the hotel. But it was raining! We had to flee under the nearby bridge and spend the night there looking up at the window where Michael's suite was supposed to be. We felt so shabby! In the afternoon of the next day it became clear that Michael was NOT in Cologne. We had spent a cold, rainy night under a bridge for nothing…

03/20/1999 – "Wetten, dass..?" Saarbrücken/Germany
How can you draw Michael's attention the best, if you want to make him come really close and talk to you? Just create a box full of presents that is as big as two car seats - and share a small car with four people on a four hour drive.
This is how we started our trip to Saarbrücken where Michael wanted to announce his project „The power of humanity" in the German TV-Show „Wetten, dass…?".
Michael really wanted to see his fans this day and we had a brilliant spot on the fence near the venue for the TV show. We had to balance the huge box on our heads because we had no other space to put it. Teddy Lakis (Michael's "fan advisor" in Germany) was already there informing the fans when Michael would arrive and then called him to let him hear us scream.
A little later he arrived in his van, got out and did a long round to greet all the fans. Thanks to the barrier, which made us feel like animals in a zoo, but which more importantly made sure that nobody ran up to Michael, he could take his time to sign autographs, look at banners and take presents.

by The Appleheads

Michael greeting his fans in Saarbrücken

When he finally came up to us, it was totally expected that he wanted to have our gigantic box of presents. Our first thought: Thank God the travel home would be a little more comfortable! We had some trouble giving it to him, because the fence was really high, but we managed to do it. You could see that our effort had impressed him ;-) Then he took a tape that Carina made for him and when she reached through the fence to give it to him, he asked full of doubt: „It's for me?" - „No, we just realized we had waited for somebody else all the time…" Just kidding! Of course Carina nodded and gave it to him slightly touching his hand. He nodded thankfully, put it into the pocket of his jacket and went on to greet the other fans. It was wonderful to see him again after we hadn't seen him for a year.

Unfortunately none of us had tickets for the show. When a woman working for the TV channel ZDF came out to sell some last-minute tickets, two of us managed to get tickets, we others had to wait outside, which was really depressing! We tried to buy tickets from strangers arriving to attend the show, but of course none of them wanted to sell them. It was frustrating!

While half of us enjoyed the show from the inside and were a little shocked when shortly before Michael arrived, a huge crowd of really crazy fans was let in at the sides of the stage, the other half of us sat outside waiting at the backstage entrance.

After the show, Michael got into his van, which was already waiting there for him. A mother and her two children were allowed to greet Michael. She went really crazy screaming „I shook his hand, I shook his hand!" The van then started to drive slowly towards where we were standing. We realized that the door was still open and we could see Michael sitting inside. He had a little child on his knees which he held protectively. He wasn't wearing a mask this time and smiled his big, bright smile. As we were getting pushed from behind, we struggled to not fall into the van, which seemed to make him smile even more. Then a bodyguard pushed us back and closed the door. But Michael seemed to not yet having said goodbye, so he opened the skylight, stood up,

by The Appleheads

Michael entering the stage of the "Wetten, dass..?" show

looked outside and waved. Shortly before the van drove away, we gave him our banner, which he pulled inside before closing the skylight. Then he was gone...

06/26 – 06/29/1999 – "What more can I give" Munich/Germany
Of course, we had to also be there to attend the concert Michael had announced in Saarbrücken, so on June 26th 1999, we left for Munich. When we arrived, the whole Promenadeplatz in front of his hotel, the "Bayerischer Hof", was already packed with fans. We still found a good space at the barrier opposite the entrance of the hotel. The whole afternoon turned out to be a huge party with fans from all over the world. Impersonators performed on a little stage, the local radio station had set up and we sang and danced to Michael's songs. Later in the evening, Teddy Lakis announced that Michael had just landed. The anticipation grew! Soon his convoy arrived and stopped in front of the hotel. Michael got out and stood on a little platform with his umbrella, waving to the fans. Then he started a little walk along the barrier, pointing to several banners he wanted to have. Unfortunately it was possible for some fans to jump the barriers and run to Michael.
After the second girl did so, Michael retreated into the hotel. We were really angry as they had ruined it for all of us! But the angriness was soon gone, when Michael appeared at his window and so the evening was spent singing and shouting for him. We left the hotel around midnight and drove to the stadium. Our original plan was to spend the night in front of the gates, but it was raining, so we first slept about two hours in our cars and started to queue at 4 in the morning.
We were the first at our gate, but when the doors opened at noon, they only opened a few gates and ours was not among them. Again: Why can't they have a fair and well-thought-out admission? And then saying things like "No worries, you will all get in!"... Come on! Yes, we will get in, but we didn't queue for so long just to get in! After all, we got in and managed to still get a spot in the first row. It was a little to the right side but ok. The show program started soon and there were some great artists we enjoyed seeing (Ringo Starr, Status Quo, The Scorpions, All

by The Appleheads

Michael on the "Bridge of no return"

Waiting for Michael's arrival

Saints, Boyzone, Luther Vandross, Vanessa Mae, Andrea Bocelli... to name a few). But it got more and more exhausting!

At about 8 pm, when the live broadcasting started, Michael finally came on stage. He held a little speech and introduced Andrea Bocelli. Afterwards we fought from one low point to another... Hearing classical music is great, but not while in a crush! And not after already standing for so many hours! Finally, around 10 pm, it was time for Michael! It was amazing to see him back on stage! We were so overwhelmed when we realized he was performing a new version of "Dangerous"! Everything seemed to go just right for Michael until "Earth Song". While Michael performed "Earth Song", he climbed upon a huge bridge that crossed over the length of the whole stage.

A special effect was that the middle part of the bridge with Michael on it was lifted up in the air as high as possible. When it was time for the middle part to be let down and rest at the height level of the rest of the bridge so that Michael could walk off back on stage, the middle part crashed completely down to the ground. It made a huge noise and rushed down in high speed. At first, we didn't realize that it was an accident. We thought it was some kind of stunt. Michael seemed confused as he was standing on the remains of the bridge in the orchestra pit. He managed to climb back on stage and brought the song to an end. There was a long pause afterwards. Then, Michael came back and performed "You are not alone", but he still seemed to be in shock and pain. We could not estimate how bad it actually was for him. Only when we were back in front of his hotel after the concert and were told that Michael was in hospital, we realized that something had gone terribly wrong. In fact, Michael was heavily injured and suffered from back pain until his death. But on stage, he was all professional and ignored the accident until the end of the show to not disappoint the audience. Of course we didn't realize all this on that night and as we were so tired, we just went to our hotel and fell asleep the moment our heads hit the pillow.

by The Appleheads

The next day, thank God, Michael was back. We had so much fun in front of the hotel with all the fans from around the world. We sang basically the whole day for Michael and he loved it, constantly coming to the window and waving. He had his windows wide open to hear us. A few fans had brought gas balloons and tried to let them fly on a string in front of Michael's window so he could take them. We all shouted for Michael to take the balloons. He first didn't understand, because every time he looked out of the window, the balloons were not there. But finally he saw them, took them and rolled up the string around his hand while waving every few seconds, which looked really funny. He was still in his pyjamas and had a hollow needle in his hand – ouch!

As we didn't have a hotel room for this night, we spent it in front of the hotel and later slept a few hours in our car. We were awakened by police men wanting to see our parking ticket. Oops! Well, they were nice and let us get one immediately. We must have looked like a mess the way they grinned. That day Michael was supposed to be leaving. He was a few times at the window before someone said that he had left. We didn't know what to think and just made the decision to drive to the airport and see if he really left. We had no idea how we wanted to find him there but well... Luck was on our side at this time! When we arrived, we saw other fans standing at a fence and joined them. A few moments later, Michael's vans pulled up on the airfield. Michael got out and walked up the stairs to the plane. He stopped on every step to turn around and wave. The higher he got, the sadder we were... we changed shouting "Please stay here" to "Come back soon". Well, we didn't honestly think we could have stopped him from leaving, but still... Then we sang "Never can say goodbye" until he was gone inside the plane. It rolled to the runway, got quicker and quicker, took off and soon disappeared from our views...

03/06 – 03/10/2001 – Oxford & London/UK
On March 6th, 2001 it was finally time to see Michael live in person again. It had been two years since we last saw him and we had dearly missed how wonderful it felt to be in his presence. We

all traveled to London where Michael stayed for about a week. He was busy in promoting his "Heal the kids"-foundation, he met with his longtime friend Macauly Culkin and of course, he took some time for the fans.

When we arrived in London, we first went to the Lanesborough Hotel to check if Michael was there or out in the city. There were a lot of fans, all in an excited mood, so we decided to stay there and wait. An hour later, Michael came out. He wore a red sports jacket, black trousers and a black mask. He was on crutches since he broke his foot at Neverland shortly before the journey. He had his friend Frank Cascio with him and was about to leave for Oxford, where he would read a lecture to the students of Oxford University.

Following Michael, we took a bus to Oxford and got really nervous on the way because we were stuck in traffic over and over again and thought that we would miss everything. But Michael must have been stuck in traffic, too, because we arrived earlier than him. Rain was pouring out of the sky and we didn't find a good spot along the street since there were fans everywhere, no barriers and it looked just like chaos. When Michael's vans arrived, we were surprised that they stopped right in front of us and the door of Michael's van opened for him to get out. But suddenly some fans jumped forward to hug Michael, others followed and so the doors were shut quickly and the vans drove further towards the entrance of Oxford University. We decided to stay behind all this and watch from the distance, but there was nothing to see. As we also were not allowed to take part at the lecture since it was for Oxford students only and as we were already pissed because of these reckless fans, we took a bus back to London. Of course, we returned to the Lanesborough Hotel and planned to just wait there until Michael returned. But suddenly rumors spread that Michael would be staying in Oxford overnight. Additionally it was now raining like never before, our mood got lower and lower and we started to have doubts about our decision as the hours passed by.

by The Appleheads

The Appleheads waiting in the rain in Oxford

Michael waving to his fans in front of the Lanesborough hotel before leaving for Oxford

More and more fans left the place and as we had nothing else to do and still didn't want to give up hope, we at least got ourselves the best spots at the barriers. Then suddenly, at 2 am, hecticness started and moments later we saw Michael's vans coming! He was returning from Oxford! Nobody believed that Michael, who was injured, would really show himself to the fans after an exhausting day like this, but he did. He hobbled towards us and took a look around. We had decided beforehand that we'd rather sing something then just scream as we couldn't imagine him feeling comfortable while people screamed him in the ears. So we started to sing and another group of fans beside us did, too, but a different song. What a chaos, must have sounded like on the fairground!

Suddenly Michael's eyes fell on one of our banners. He quickly pointed at the banner and a bodyguard brought it to him. With the banner in his hand, Michael wanted to retreat into the hotel, but then he saw that there was a fan in a wheelchair waiting for him, so he turned around again to greet the man. It was our luck that the guy was right in front of us, Michael stood near at hand for a while. Shortly before leaving, he wrote a few autographs and we were lucky to get two of them. We were overjoyed and agreed that a few minutes like this made us forget the long and exhausting day with the disappointment from Oxford, our running noses caused by the never-ending rain and the long travel in general. We could not believe how much charisma floated around Michael when he was near. It was late at night, but we all had the impression that Michael glowed in the dark and his magical presence blew us away!
We got the chance to talk to Michael's manager afterwards, who at that time was Dieter Wiesner, a German guy. We told him that we had prepared a funny show for Michael which we'd like to perform for him and he said that we should come back the next day, he then would arrange a meeting with Michael for us. Of course, we couldn't sleep that night and rehearsed our show over and over again. Oh God, was that really going to be the big day?

by The Appleheads

Returning from Oxford

The next day, we came back to the Lanesborough at noon. At about 2 pm, Michael left for UrI Geller's wedding somewhere outside London. We got a glimpse of him, but he was in a rush. We waited the whole afternoon for him and our time to leave for the MJ Day got closer and closer. We set ourselves a deadline – and for the first and probably only time in our fanlives, Michael met our deadline! A minute before we wanted to leave at 6.30 pm, his vans pulled up. Michael got out and started his way along the barriers on his crutches. Unfortunately again, a whole group of fans jumped over the barriers. We will never forget how Michael's eyes widened with fear before he retreated into the hotel. We observed this scene standing on a wall of stone and were angry that these people scared Michael so much and sad that they would always destroy the possibility for everybody to see Michael by jumping at him and causing the sudden end of Michael's presence.

Finally we had the chance to talk to Mr. Wiesner again and asked him if meeting Michael would be possible today. He assured us to get back to him later and that Michael would be fit in the evening to do it.

We then took the underground to the Apollo theatre. That night, the 10th annual MJ Day would be held there – a huge party for fans organized by book author Adrian Grant and his team. They had invited Michael to come there and he had accepted, that's why we had to be there, too. The show was fantastic and several hundred fans reacted enthusiastically. Very talented artists (singers, dancers, a children's choir, a ballet group...) showed breathtaking new interpretations of Michael Jackson's songs.

At the end of the show, Michael hobbled on stage and the atmosphere was exploding. We didn't expect the audience to go THAT crazy, but everybody just lost control. We all jumped up at the same time, stood on the red velvet seats and screamed our lungs out. It was amazing to see Michael on a stage in a beautiful theatre like this, only surrounded by his fans from all over the world.

by The Appleheads

We drenched him with our applause and Michael at first seemed a little bit shy and didn't know what to say. He thanked Adrian Grant and all the performers for the wonderful show and said "I love you from the bottom of my heart." Then, he dropped two phrases that almost brought the house down. He said "I am working on a new album", paused, "Two more months", and everybody went nuts! We could not believe what he had just said and were so excited to hear about the new album [in fact, it took 7 more months until "Invincible" was released in October, 2001]. Adrian Grant, who was on stage with Michael, presented him with two awards for his artistic and humanitarian efforts. The show ended with "Heal the world" which all artists performed together. What a night! We were just happy!
We got back to the Lanesborough Hotel, but Michael had arrived before us and we didn't see him again that night. We talked to Dieter Wiesner one more time who told us that it was not possible to meet Michael now, but that Michael would come to Germany soon and we could meet him there. We were really disappointed that Dieter had promised too much and that this time, no personal meeting with Michael would happen.

After the night at the Apollo, we did not see Michael anymore on that trip. He didn't show up the next day at all (seemingly he felt sick and we just heard that he was spending the day with Macauly Culkin). The day after, we had to return back to Germany. But after all, we were more than happy about the memories we had with Michael!

06/14 – 06/16/2002 – Sony Demo & "Killer Thriller Party" London/UK
Our second MJ trip to London started on June 14th, 2002. We took a "fan bus" organized by a German fan club which drove us to London overnight. We arrived in London on June 15th at noon and now wanted to do our own program.
First, we made our way to where Michael stayed, this time it was the hotel Renaissance. But there was nothing going on since everybody was heading for the first big event of the day: A demons-

tration in front of the SONY headquarter in "Great Marlborough Street". SONY, Michael's record label, had not properly promoted his "Invincible" album since its release in October, 2001. Rumors said that they were trying to set Michael under financial pressure to force him to sell his share of the ATV catalogue, which is a huge collection of licenses for the Beatles' songs and many more artists. Michael was upset and we were on his side for sure. Fans had organized several demonstrations against SONY in big cities, after being on the demo in Berlin, it was now time to protest in London.

About 1,000 fans gathered in front of the SONY building. Hundreds of banners showed our slogans of protest like "SONY kills Michael's music", "SONY can count money, Michael can count on his fans", "SONY is phoney" and chants were sounding through the street. The organizers had also build up a small stage where fans could show their Michael Jackson dance moves and the atmosphere was great and full of energy for Michael's music. We stayed there for several hours and then decided to walk to the Equinox theatre at Leicester Square, because we had to collect our tickets for the second big event of the day: The "Killer Thriller Party". As we were members of MJNI, the British fan club organizing the event, we had managed to get seats in the 7th row and as we were warned to be there on time to pick them up, we decided to leave the demo while it was still in full swing.

While we were waiting in the queue for the tickets, suddenly fans came running, telling everyone waiting that Michael just had been at the demonstration. He drove by standing on an open-topped London Sightseeing bus and took part of the protest. No question that everybody at the demonstration was thrilled to have the mega star at their side! We heard that Michael had climbed over the balustrade of the bus, only held by his bodyguard Mike La Perruque and his make-up artist Karen Faye, to grab several banners held up by the fans. He then held them up himself and punched his fists in the air to the rhythm of the "Sony sucks"-chants by the fans. He also took a megaphone and expressed his anger towards SONY.

Michael speaking at the „Killer Thriller Party"

When we heard these news, we were devastated that we had missed this special occasion! Travelling all the way from Germany and then missing Michael only by a few minutes and a few meters!

But the frustration didn't last long, because the day had only started and now it was time for the "Killer Thriller Party" at the Equinox. The show was really amazing, full of fantastic dancers and singers, highlighted by a boy and a girl who gave an outstanding performance of "Human Nature" and impersonator Earnest Valentino, who danced us to another level. But especially exciting was Michael's presence at the venue for about 2,5 hours. He was seated in a V.I.P. lounge with a balcony at the right side of the stage so he could overlook everything that was going on. He seemed to enjoy the show very much and applauded each of the performers. From time to time, he would eat snacks and he had a lot of friends with him in the V.I.P. section. UrI Geller was filming the whole time. Whenever Michael leaned over the balcony, the fans cheered loudly and he waved to us.

At the end of the show, it was his turn to come on stage. He slowly walked in from the right side to the middle of the stage, a girl gave him a bouquet of flowers. He just looked beautiful with a shorter haircut than usual, black trousers and a black jacket with a white and gold embroidery on the chest. Michael took a microphone and began a long speech. He thanked everyone and then talked about today's music industry and his relationship with SONY, especially that one between him and SONY boss Tommy Mottola. He said Mottola is a devil that does everything to get money. He also said that he owed SONY one more album, just a box set with two new songs that he had written ages ago and then he would leave SONY as a free agent owning half of SONY's publishing. He talked about black artists' position in the music industry that is filled with racism and that many great artists, who gained millions for the record companies, would die broke and alone, because they were just exploited and then thrown away. Michael was very serious, he lowered his voice a few times and

by The Appleheads

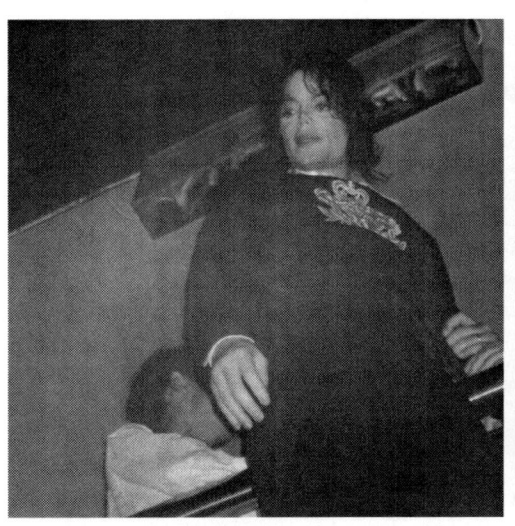

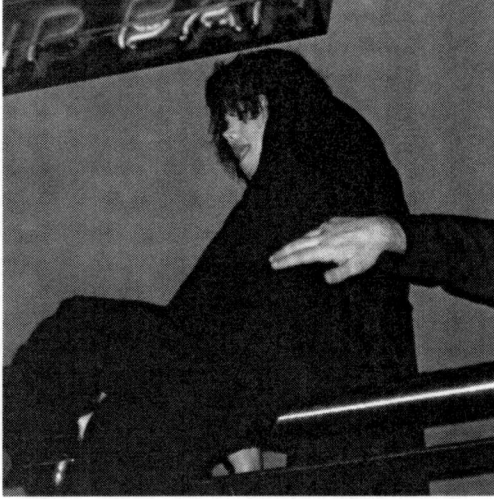

Michael looking out for banners and climbing over the balustrade to get them

spoke very slowly, he paused meaningfully. In between, the fans interrupted him with chants like "Sony sucks" or just applause. We could not trust our ears, we felt that Michael addressed a crowd aggressively like never before. We had never witnessed him talking badly about other people like this. We were really impressed.

When Michael ended and left the stage, everybody seemed to rush out of the building trying to catch a glimpse of Michael leaving. We saw Earnest Valentino still standing on stage and thought we should say hi and especially ask him if he managed to give Michael a gift from us, which we had send him beforehand and which he had agreed to deliver to Michael. In the weeks before our travel, we had rewritten some lyrics to several MJ songs and had turned them into anti-SONY-songs. "Man in the mirror" became "Tommy Mottola" ("We're starting with Tommy Mottola, We're asking him to change his ways, Instead of Pepsi we drink Coca Cola, So if you wanna make the world a SONY-place, Take a look at us now and then make that change…") and "Dirty Diana" was renamed "Phony Sony" ("You'll never make him stay, So take your weight off of him, We know your every move, And every move's full of sin, You did it times before, The world was too blind to see, You try to ruin each star, This time we won't let it be…"). Earnest told us that the CD with the recorded songs was now in Michael's hands as he had met him before the show. That made us really happy! We climbed onto the stage and stood at the same spot where Michael had stood just minutes before to take some pictures. Suddenly, we looked up to the V.I.P. balcony and thought that there was a very common shape of head in sight. Just seconds later we realized, that Michael was still up there, talking to friends.

The few fans that were still in the building had realized him being there as well and when we cautiously called out his name, Michael reacted. He came to the balcony and waved to us, shaking his fist to our chants of "Sony sucks". We all held up our banners which we still had from the demonstration. Michael set his eyes on one

by The Appleheads

of them and tried to grab it. But the balcony was a little bit too high and he couldn't reach out wide enough. So, Michael climbed over the balustrade to get closer! We couldn't believe our eyes! He bowed down, stretched out his arm as long as he could, reached the banner and pulled it up. When he climbed back, he got stuck on the balustrade with his foot and nearly fell. We were all relieved when he was back into safety! Still, of course, we were overexcited that Michael performed such a stunt for one of our banners - amazing!

We then got out of the Equinox and went around the house to find the back entrance where some of our friends were waiting. There were hundreds of fans already and we would have no chance to get a good spot with a view. So we turned back around and thought about already going back to the hotel. When we passed by the side entrance of the building, suddenly we saw a black London cab there and a lot of people coming out... Hello again, Michael! He and some others got in the cab and drove off. We were in such an adrenalin rush as we had not expected him, that we started to run after the cab like crazy, which was pretty hard as we were laughing at the same time. It seemed like a marathon, we ran through many streets, passed squares and monuments. We could see Michael sitting in back of the car the whole time as it was a normal car, no dark windows! His black curls were hanging down his neck over his white collar.

When we already could hardly breathe, the cab stopped at a red light. We approached the cab and Michael was already signing autographs for some other fans. We were just there, when the red light switched to green and they had to continue driving. So much adrenalin was pumping in our veins, so we stayed behind and tried hard to catch our breath. We later heard that Michael was driving out of London to have dinner at some quiet place.

We decided to go to the Renaissance Hotel again and just wait for him. Nothing happened for the next six hours. Only the fans were entertaining themselves with chants and they danced around in the street. There were barriers to keep the crowd under control, but obviously not enough barriers. Fans were already positioning themselves on the other side of the street, where there were no barriers, to jump on Michael's car. As we already knew this kind of situation and even knew how to estimate some of the fans that were standing there, we decided to tell one of the hotel's security to better keep an eye on them. He was pretty bitchy, telling us they were surly in control of the situation. He probably thought that we wanted to tell him how to do his job, but that was not our intention. But Michael situations are always extraordinary and mostly security was not prepared.

This time, it was no exception! When Michael returned at night, his limousine was immediately surrounded by fans. Complete chaos broke out! All the fans that had patiently waited behind the barriers got to see nothing and we were all disappointed! But the worst thing was that one of Michael's bodyguards was hurt and had to be taken to hospital! In this scene, it was a little miracle that Michael had managed to get out of it safely!

A little later, we had to look out for the "fan bus" that was leaving towards Germany and brought us back home. We were full of negative emotions when we left London. And it didn't get any better when the leader of this fan club held a little speech in the bus and praised all the fans for their support for Michael. No word regarding what had just happened! And that, although some of the fans who had started this mess in the first place were sitting in this very same bus…

11/19 – 11/22/2002 – Bambi Awards Berlin/Germany
Michael had announced he'd come to Berlin on November 19th, 2002. He was invited to an award show which was to be a live broadcast. Since we could all get away from work and from school, we arrived in Berlin two days before Michael. It was the perfect way to check out all the places that Michael would go to -well, the places we knew of already.

The day of Michael's arrival, we first stopped at a flower shop where we had ordered a bouquet of flowers decorated with five real apples – after all, we're "The Appleheads". We drove to the

146

by The Appleheads

airport "Tempelhof", where we knew he would land, and talked to some employees there. At first, they weren't very chatty, but we stubbornly asked them about Michael's arrival time and jokingly offered them food and drinks as "a reward" until they just had to laugh and told us it would be either 2 or 4 pm. Satisfied, we went to the part of the airport where we thought Michael had to pass by after getting off the plane and waited. Our assumption seemed to be confirmed when some vans arrived and bodyguards got out. We talked to them a little. They told us they would not stop here and that we should rather go to the hotel. But we let them know that from our experience there was only going to be a huge chaos at the hotel so we rather wanted to stay here. Although they wouldn't believe us, saying there won't be chaos because "that's what we're here for" (never been Michael's security, ha?), they were nice and showed us how to position ourselves so that Michael could see our banner.

But then, there was a change of plan, as the bodyguards told us, and they quickly jumped into their vans to go to another entry. We had no time to think but to jump in our car and make our way to the other entry as well. Luckily, we arrived in time and could line up along a street, holding up a huge banner to welcome Michael.

Moments later, we saw several dark Mercedes vans coming and passing by at great speed. In one of them, we saw Grace Rwaramba, Michael's nanny, sitting. She was pointing at us! The vans suddenly slowed down and stopped a few meters away from us. We slowly approached the vans and Grace greeted us as well as Dieter Wiesner, who was sitting in one of the back seats and asked us to hand in our banner, which we did. Beside Mr. Wiesner, we saw a nanny with a baby in her arms, which we immediately thought had to be Blanket.

When Mr. Wiesner sat back down, we realized that in the third row of seats, there was Michael with Prince and Paris. We welcomed him to Germany and told him, we are "The Appleheads" which made him giggle. We then gave him the bouquet of flowers, which they all found "so beautiful". Attached to it, was a Charlie Chaplin postcard, on which we had also informed him that we had prepared and rehearsed a little funny show which we would like to perform for him and that he should watch out for us at the Adlon Hotel. We did a little small talk, sort of "How are you doing?", "How was the flight?" and he signed us some autographs. We also told him a little about the show, saying that his sister Janet and Liz Taylor "appear" in the show, which he found quite amusing. We just talked too much, he didn't have much chance to get a word in. When Heike gave him a copy of the "Black & White" magazine (a MJ fan magazine) to sign, he wanted to keep it and asked her if he could. When she said "ok" with a heavy heart (sometimes not easy to get back issues…), he asked for her name and then said "Thank you, Heike!"

At some point, Blanket was beginning to whine and Grace said that he was getting cold so they had to move. Yes, it was November and pretty cold in Berlin! As a last good-bye, we sang the refrain of the song "My girl" by The Temptations but replaced the words "My girl" with "Michael", doing a little hand-choreography we had once thought out. All people in the van were laughing and enjoying this little funny episode. Especially Michael! He laughed really hard when we came to the "Michael, Michael, Michael…" part and gave us enthusiastic applause, holding his hands over his head. Wow, the King of Pop clapping his hands to a mini-performance like this. It was amazing! Then we simply turned around and walked away. We only now saw that his bodyguard Mike was standing by the next car. When we passed him he said "Good job", which made us smile. We tried to stay calm as we returned to our car but as soon as we sat inside and had shut the doors, we screamed the hell out of our lungs. We were completely enthusiastic! We had just had our first real, personal meeting with our idol! We were so happy!

We started to make our way to the hotel now and as Michael was on the same path, we soon saw his vans before us. When we arrived at the Adlon Hotel near the Brandenburg Gate, we saw hundreds of other fans waiting there. Nowhere to park for us!

by The Appleheads

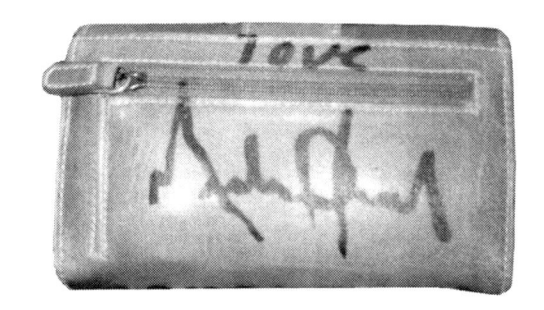

Carina's signed purse

Michael holding The Appleheads' banner out of his window at the Adlon hotel
Picture by Elisabeth Apfel (ElisabethApfel@gmx.de)

Michael's vans drove into the underground parking of the Adlon and before we could really think about it, we drove behind him, right before the gate could come down again. Of course this way we had no parking ticket, which would have cost us the maximum fee of the whole day, if the guard wouldn't have been so nice to us afterwards. We saw Michael's vans stopping at an elevator and we didn't want to bother him again, so we just parked our car and took a different elevator up to the hotel lobby. We sat down there and reveled in our memories. Some minutes later, hectic broke out outside and we saw a black Mercedes pass by and Michael getting out. Obviously, he wanted a bigger entry at the hotel than just sneaking in the basement garage and really greet the fans. Everyone outside went crazy as they saw Michael and started to close in on him. There was chaos and Michael had to retreat into the lobby – but there, he was mobbed as well since the fans were everywhere. Michael's bodyguards managed to get him into a staff area of the hotel and move him up to his suite. We watched this mess from afar and then went out of the hotel again. Moments later, Michael came to the window of his suite. He waved and laughed and showed Blanket – it was the famous "baby dangling incident" which became a huge media scandal worldwide later. To be honest, in reality, it was not half that enthralling as presented by the media. We could see that Michael was holding his baby strongly in his arms and there was no way that Blanket could have fallen down. Although it might not have been his smartest move, he was just a proud father who wanted to show his youngest child to his fans. And the moment didn't last as long as on TV where they always show it in slow motion.

Michael stayed at the window a long time. At times he was waving to the fans and pointing at banners that he wished to have brought up to him, or he glanced over to the left where he had a phenomenal view of the Brandenburg Gate. Then, his nanny Grace came out. She walked around the fans, took presents and banners and then came up to us saying Michael wanted to have our banner, too. Another one? Ok, no problem! We asked her if we could take a picture of her with the banner but she said something about "later" and "upstairs", which we didn't get, then

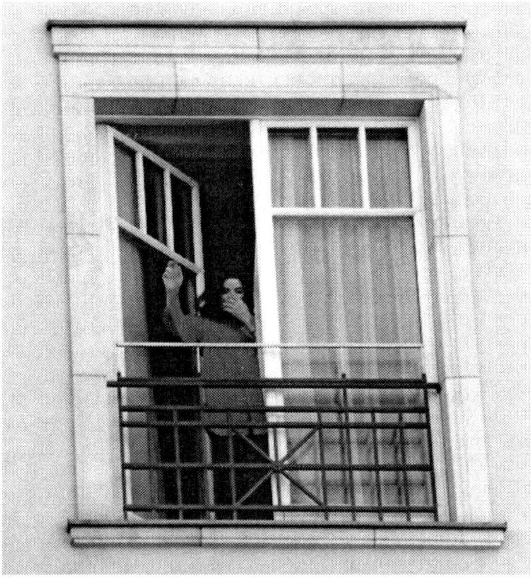
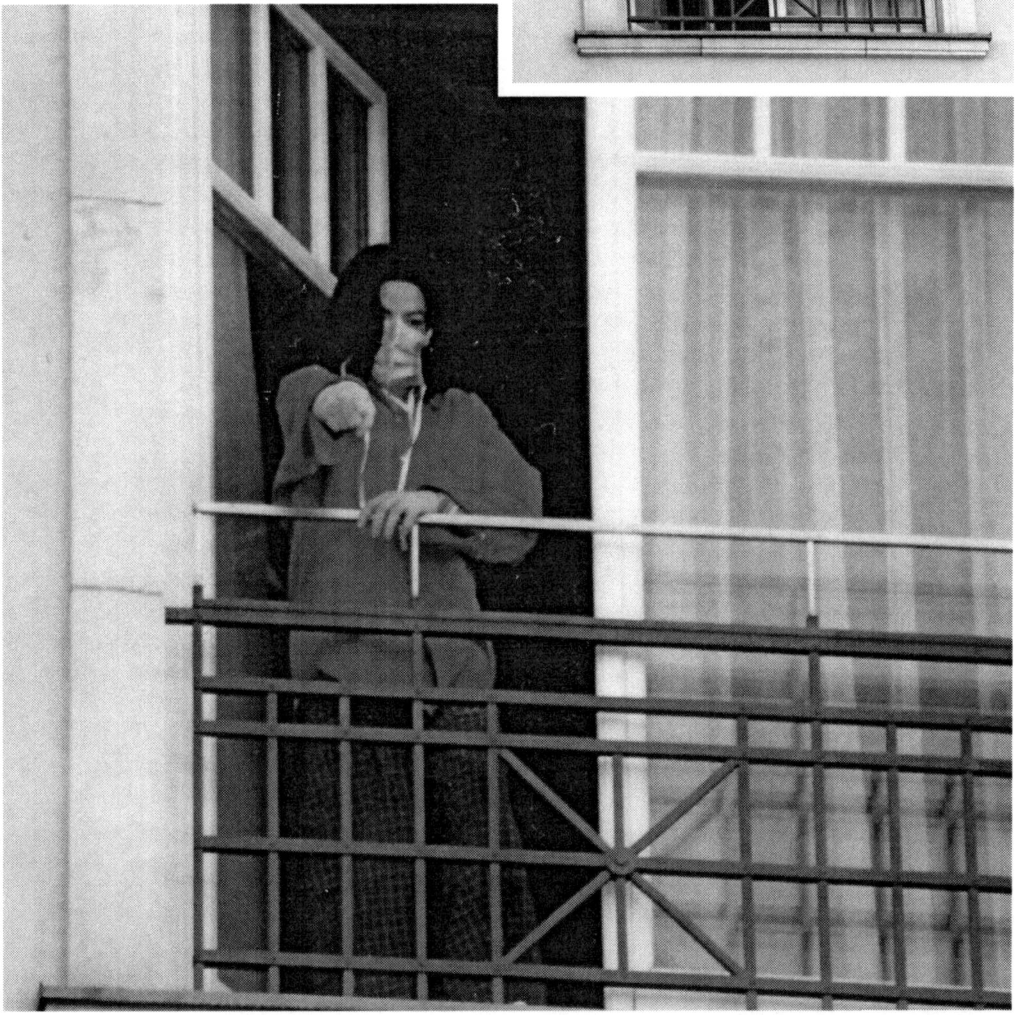

she was gone. We couldn't believe our eyes when minutes later, Michael came back to the window and held out our banner, that showed pictures of Heike's son and Miri's godson and read "The future is in our hands".

But it became even more surreal: Michael seemed to point at us with his hand the whole time and made gestures that we should come up. We thought we were probably only imagining it that he pointed at us. Or had he read our Charlie Chaplin postcard? We looked at him, made a few steps towards the entrance and Michael nodded "yes". Okay, now it was clear, that he meant us. The problem was, of course, that we were not allowed inside the hotel. In that very moment, one of Michael's bodyguards – Chris - came out and said to us: "Michael wants to know if you can do your show for him now?" We were a bit speechless but of course we could do it now! Wow, Michael had read our postcard and directly responded – the meeting at the airport was maybe one hour ago. Chris guided us inside the hotel where we met with Grace again. She took us outside again to give a little speech to the fans, saying that Michael was happy they were there and happy to be in Berlin. Then they took us inside again. Grace was saying "The Appleheads can come" the whole time while we were crossing the lobby, taking the elevator and moving towards Michael's suite. We passed by a lot of bodyguards at every corner.

Our excitement grew! Dieter Wiesner stood at the door to Michael's suite and said we had to wait a bit. So we talked to him and waited. Finally it was our time and we were not even that nervous because we had just spoken to Michael. It all seemed pretty natural. After a few minutes, Mike came out of Michael's suite and we thought "Ok, ready, go!" But then he said to us that Michael had gotten important business calls and the meeting had to be postponed. We were disappointed but they promised us that we would meet him later and so we were still so happy about everything and, of course, believed we could come back later.

We made a short stop in the Adlon restroom and then got back out again. It was quiet around Michael until the evening, no win-

152

by The Appleheads

dow games, nothing, so he obviously had some business stuff to do. We had just settled down on the ground to have a fan-like dinner in front of the hotel as a van was pulling up. We didn't realize Michael was sitting inside until some fans ran there. He wore a white sequined jacket and a white mask and was writing autographs on things that the fans passed him through the window. He also shook some hands. Once he began to write something on the window which we later identified as "video" but it was badly written....maybe Michael wanted a video from one of the fans. When the van wanted to move on, it couldn't because of the fans surrounding it and so the driver blew the horn. Michael thought this was funny and blew the horn himself many times, laughing while doing it. Finally the fans made a way and the van could drive off with hundreds of fans running behind. We stayed behind, we rather wanted to have our "dinner". We later heard that Michael drove only a few blocks away to "Dussmann", which is the biggest and most famous CD and DVD store in Berlin. Michael bought an "E.T."-DVD and met some fans in the store, who had managed to get in, too.

We continued waiting at the Adlon hotel. Later in the evening, we heard rumors that Michael would be going out to have dinner at the "Bar 925" and so we headed for that location. Indeed, there were bodyguards and other fans already. But the windows of the bar were pasted over with foil to shield the clients inside from the press and fans outside. Lisa got a little glimpse inside and saw Michael, his manager and several other people sitting there, eating and drinking. We decided to respect the dinner's privacy – the foil was a sign that disturbers were not too welcome at this moment – and drove back to the hotel and waited on the backside. When Michael returned, he had the light on and we saw him sitting in his van before he disappeared into the garage.

We drove to our hotel and began to realize that we had just had the day of our lives. It was almost too hard to realize everything we had experienced with Michael during only one day. We had to stare at our autographs for hours to believe that we had really

by The Appleheads

Michael surprising his fans by pulling up
in front of the hotel in his van to spend some time with them

met him. We talked for a long time and agreed that Michael was one of the nicest persons you could meet on this planet, a beautiful soul. He had been so nice and open to us that day and yet so humble and grateful for our appreciation....we had not had the impression that we had encountered the biggest megastar in the world....it felt more like meeting someone you've always known. We felt touched by Michael's magic and were so happy that we all had this meeting with him together as true friends. He had brought us together so many years ago and now, if only for a moment, we were somehow complete with him kind of being the long gone member of our group.

On Wednesday, November 20th, another day with big events awaited us. We were up late after such a short but satisfied night. And then we came into a traffic jam! We began to panic as we had to be at the "Metropol" theatre at a certain time to buy tickets for a party organized by fans because we had heard that Michael had accepted their invitation. So we took the bus lane, always pretending to turn right on the next corner and then to realize that it was not that corner but the next - our license number for a different city really helped!... we had a good laugh about it and managed to be at the "Metropol" on time. But whoever was going to sell tickets was not on time and we were waiting and waiting, it got later and later... Then a friend of ours called and said rumor had it that Michael was going to the zoo today and we decided to leave. We then made a short stop at the Adlon hotel to check what went on, but as everything was quiet, we directly headed further to the zoo and waited at the entry. It didn't take a long time until we actually saw Michael's van column coming. The vans passed us by in high speed and everybody ran behind. After a few meters we realized it made no sense. We quickly brainstormed and checked our options. We knew Michael especially loved monkeys so we decided to go to the monkey house and just wait there. But no, no waiting this time! We arrived there from the one side at the same moment as Michael, his kids and his entourage arrived from the other. They had, for the moment, outrun most of the fans and paparazzi so it was a pretty personal moment. As

by The Appleheads

he walked closer we said "Michael, the Appleheads are here for you again". He turned around abruptly and basically screamed in a high-pitched tone "Oh hiiiiiii, I looooove you!" before he went into the monkey house.

We didn't know what to do but as everybody entered the house with him, we did so, too - but were quickly drawn into the chaos.... fans and paparazzi were going crazy and trying to get as close to him as possible. We decided to stay away from that and positioned ourselves in front of the gorilla cage. Michael and his kids were still staying in front of the chimpanzee cage but then they got mobbed too much and had to change place. And guess what, Michael directly walked towards us and stopped one meter away from us. He seemed to be very enthusiastic about the gorillas as his face was glowing and he had his eyes wide open. He tried to explain the monkeys' behavior to his children and pointed to the gorillas' bodies to underline his words. His children were very little back then (it was only Prince and Paris) but they seemed to enjoy their fathers' efforts to teach them about monkeys. One time, the biggest male gorilla came very close to the window of the cage and violently hit against it. It came all of a sudden and made a loud noise. We all startled, but Michael only laughed out hysterically and imitated the sound. He did not seem scared at all....perhaps he was well accustomed to it because of the monkeys he owned himself at Neverland. Unfortunately, the longer they stayed, the more persistent became the paparazzi and some other fans. The bodyguards simply could not hold them back anymore and the situation got dangerous.
Michael, Prince and Paris had to be moved out of the monkey house. Everyone was running behind them and the mob continued outside. It got so rude that we were kicked and beaten by several paparazzi because they thought we were in their way. They tried everything to get pictures of Michael's children, one even got hold of Paris' hand at one point and pulled her away from Michael. We could not believe that this was happening! Michael anxiously shouted "Who's holding her back?" and thank God that asshole (sorry) let her go. The paparazzi also fought

by The Appleheads

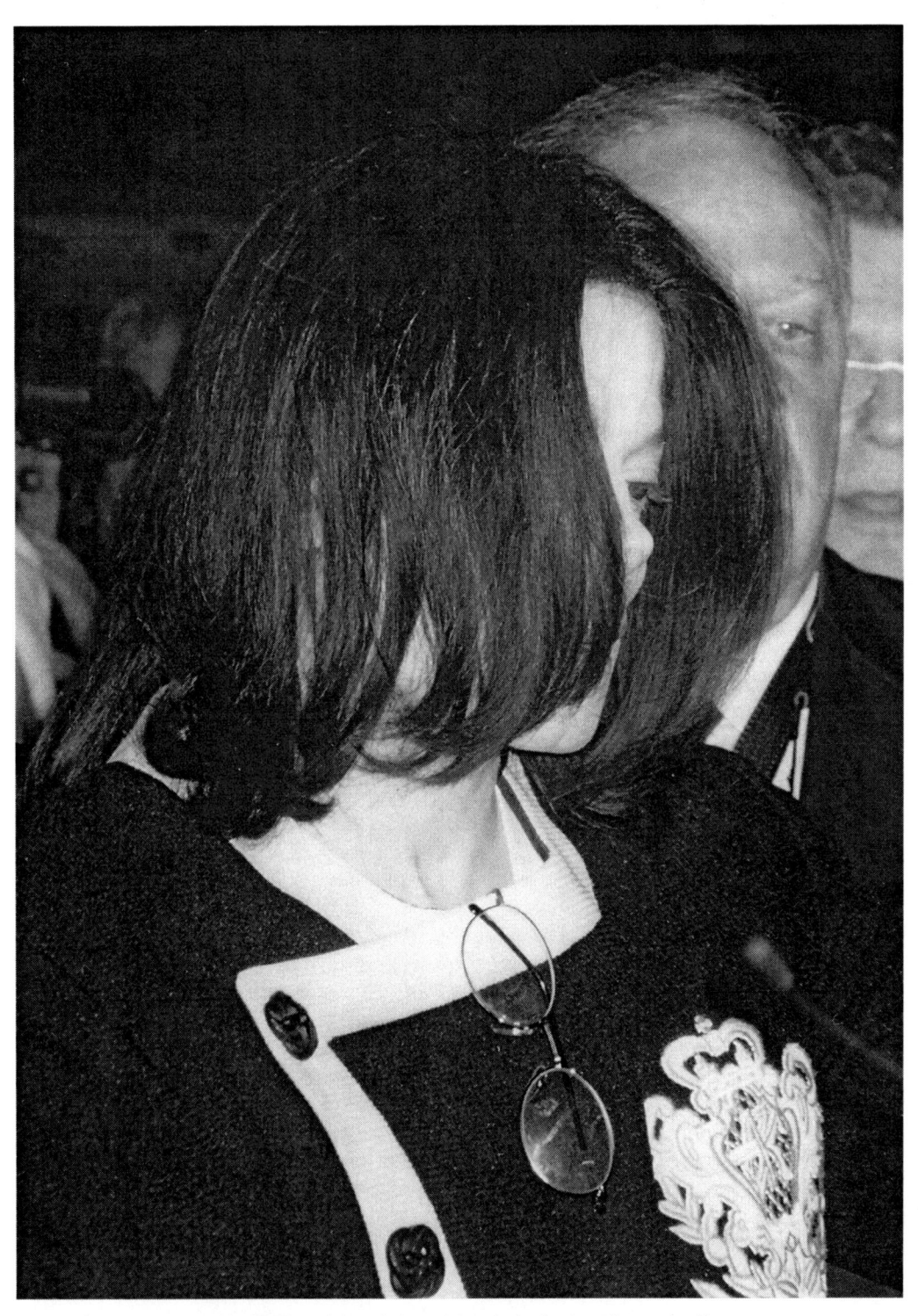

Michael on the red carpet in front of the Adagio after the "Tribute to Bambi"

between themselves and we saw a couple of them tumble to the ground or into bushes. "Nemesis", was all we could think. We had enough of that "zoo visit" and while everyone followed Michael to his van and wherever else he went, we returned to our car.

During the afternoon, we waited in front of the Adlon hotel along hundreds of fans. It seemed like every day more fans from all over the world were arriving and adding to the crowd. There were chants the whole time, a great atmosphere.

Nobody was demoralized by the cold since Michael showed himself at the window many times. He waved and threw signed stuff down. He ordered pizza for the fans, he showed Prince and Paris who were waving and imitating their dad by blowing kisses to us. It was just sweet to see.

In the early evening, we drove to the "Metropol" theatre again, finally got our tickets and waited for the fan party to begin. They were playing Michael's music and we danced for some time, just letting out the joy we had already experienced here in Berlin. But then we asked ourselves "Where's the show?", "Will there be happening anything here?"…with time, everybody started to get confused because no official program was starting, it was just like a Michael Jackson disco. We realized Michael would not be coming. We were disappointed, but there was no time for that when we heard that he was on his way to the "Adagio", a venue where the 'Tribute to Bambi"-gala was taking place that night. Michael wanted to auction the white sequined jacket, which he had worn the night before at "Dussmann", for charity. We drove there as fast as we could and got very good spots at the red carpet, but Michael was already inside. We waited until he came out. It was a great moment, because there were not too many fans there and good barriers.

Michael walked by very close and saw our banner. It had a cute picture of Lisa's sister on it and read "I bet I can make you smile". He pointed at it, said "Ooooooooooooooh" and took the banner right out of our hands. He signed some autographs and then drove away in a black limousine with our banner on his lap.

by The Appleheads

Later that evening, he entertained us fans many times at his hotel window. We stayed at the Adlon until it had become quiet and our whole bodies felt deep-frozen, then went to bed.

The next day was Michael's big day. The "Bambi" awards would take place in the evening, the reason why Michael was in Berlin after all. Michael seemed to be excited the whole day – whenever he showed himself at his window, he was wearing something different and behaving restless. He started by greeting the fans in lavender pajama trousers, then later in a white bath robe, wet hair and towel on his head. Then again, with reading glasses – something we'd never seen before on him and we thought it was cute. It was a wonderful afternoon because many fans had arrived for that one day and it was fun to sing and chant with so many others.

In the evening, we headed for the "Estrell Convention Center", the venue for the award show. There were thousands of people and we arrived seemingly too late to get a good spot at the red carpet. We just stopped at some point where we thought we'd see nothing at all – but would at least be there and enjoy the atmosphere. But then Michael came and his limousine stopped directly in front of us. He glanced out the window, closed the curtain and then came out. He was so close that we could touch him. We could feel the soft structure of his satin jacket still hours later. And he was so beautiful and wore such a cool outfit that we were speechless. He seemed to glow in the dark once more. He then made his way along the red carpet, stopped several times to write autographs and seemed to enjoy the appreciation of the many fans. After he was inside, we returned to the Adlon hotel and parked in the underground garage. We knew nothing would be happening until the end of the show and it was warmer in the garage than outside. We called someone at home who told us everything about the "Bambi"-broadcast and so we knew about Michael's beautiful speech that night after he was presented with the "Millennium Award".

by The Appleheads

When Michael returned from the "Bambi" awards, we first heard it! Many fans were running after him into the underground garage of the Adlon, following him until the elevator.
We just saw him shortly popping out of the car, stopping a while to wave and disappearing into the elevator. Afterwards, he came to the window and showed his "Bambi" award around. He seemed so proud and happy about it. He had friends with him that came to the window with him and they all glanced over to the Brandenburg Gate and the beautiful Xmas illumination of the "Unter den Linden" Boulevard.

On Friday, November 22nd, nothing happened during the daytime. We spent the day waiting in our car to somehow keep warm. All the waiting from the last days made us feel silly and we laughed a lot. In the afternoon, we heard rumors that Michael wanted to visit the castle of Sanssouci. Indeed, Michael's vans came out but when we were halfway to Sanssouci, we got a call that instead he was in some gallery.
We returned to the hotel, parked our car in the garage and finally wanted to get something warm and good to eat after so many days in the pizzeria on the other side. We had just gotten our stuff together, when a van came rushing in. A moment later, Grace came down with the elevator, moving towards the van with Prince and Paris on her hands. When they noticed us, Grace told the kids to say "Hi" and they - being very well-mannered – did so and waved to us. They were so cute. We didn't know where they were going and we didn't even want to know because we wanted our pizza!
We returned to our car afterwards and waited for Michael to get back. He returned together with the kids. He helped them out of the car, giving the sleeping Blanket to Grace. We stayed calm until the kids were in the elevator, then we sang "You are not alone" for him. How corny! But he seemed to enjoy it. He stopped to listen until we were finished and then said "Thank you. I love you!" This was the last time we saw him in Berlin. He was not showing himself anymore and left early the next morning. After this week full of excitement, we were all tired but extremely

by The Appleheads

happy. Although we still hadn't managed to do our show for him in spite of already standing in front of his door, we felt so special as friends and were thankful for everything that Michael gave us.

04/09 – 04/18/2005 – Trial Santa Maria/USA
We would have been happy if the following two travels had not been necessary! But in the meantime, terrible accusations of child molestation had been made against Michael. For the second time in his and in our lives, the world was turned upside down. We will not go into specific details of the accusations or anything connected to it because there has been written a lot about it already. Crucial to the new allegations was that Neverland had been raided and a criminal trial was being prepared. We were witnessing a media hunt against Michael. The media agenda quickly showed a strong tendency towards criminalizing Michael. Opinions and shady statements were being presented as facts. Michael was appointed a paedophile before the criminal trial had even started. The media seemed to have no interest in examining the case that District Attorney of Santa Barbara Thomas Sneddon and his folks were putting together and missed to look into the fact that it was a weak case. To be honest, we were not surprised that all this was happening. It was the way how show business operates.
But we were deeply hurt because it affected and tortured someone that we deeply loved. We knew that those kind of allegations were the worst thing one could do to Michael. He, who believed in the innocence of children and the innocence of love, who trusted children like no grown-up was being attacked and misinterpreted for the wrong reasons.
We knew the trial would cost an immense emotional drain for Michael, we knew it was his worst nightmare. So we felt obliged to support him with everything we could. If nobody in the media and the show business would stand by his side, then we would be the ones to show loyalty and express our belief in his innocence. We had to remind the people of the "Innocent until proven guilty"-right manifested in the US Constitution. But just going to vigils here was not enough anymore at some point. It felt as if our

Beautiful Neverland

ideals, our life philosophy was at trial as well and so we flew over to L.A., where we rented a car to go to Santa Maria.

If the cause of our travel had not been such a sad one, we would have really enjoyed ourselves. The sun was shining, the ocean was beautiful, driving down the 101 was a worthy experience in itself! We decided our first stop had to be Neverland. While we already reproached ourselves for not looking up the exact directions to Michael's ranch and already thought about whom we could ask where to go, coming closer to Los Olivos we saw a huge sign for the "Figueroa Mountain Road". We hadn't thought it would be that easy! The 15 minute drive through the beautiful nature on the Figueroa Mountain Road to Neverland was very enjoyable.

The gate and the surroundings were much smaller than we had imagined. But we loved it from the first minute! As it was evening already and got cold, we got ourselves our jackets from the car when the mishap happened: We left our keys in the trunk and the car locked... Damn it! Well, we thought we just had to call a car service, which would be a little expensive maybe and a long wait until they were there, but ok, we couldn't turn back time so lets make the best of it. But when we wanted to call our car rental, we realized that our mobiles had no reception in front of Neverland. Oh no! We already imagined ringing the bell at Neverland asking for help with them probably thinking that we were so excited to be at Neverland that we forgot everything else. How embarrassing! Thank God there were still some fans in front of Neverland and some of them had American mobiles which worked.

So we called the rental service and it took hours to explain them where we were. I think we spelled "Figueroa" about 20 times, no joke! About an hour later, it already got dark, the car service arrived and it was only a matter of minutes until we had our key back. The guy was really nice, he told us that he had been called to Neverland several times already when something was wrong with one of the cars. He said he uses a secret entrance and also told us that Michael uses that one when he is driving around in his Ford with a flatboard. Unfortunately, these kind of cars were a dime in a dozen there so looking out for it was useless.

Finally, late at night we arrived at the Motel 6 Hotel in Santa Maria, where we spent most of the first night painting our banner for the next morning. We had to get up at 5 am to be in front of the courthouse at 6 am. 20 minutes later the officers arrived and the lottery for the public seats in the courtroom started. We all got little tickets with our numbers on them and when your number was drawn, you were allowed to go in that day. As not many people were there that day, we got in. We had to give our names and our passport number was registered. In return, we got a yellow sticker with our seat number. Afterwards we had a few minutes to bring our stuff to our car as we were only allowed to bring a pen, paper and purse. Inside the courtroom, there were even more rules: No drinking, eating, sleeping or chewing gum. We weren't allow to give any kind of approval or refusal to anything said, not allowed to come close to Michael, his bodyguards or his family, not speak to anybody, especially not from the press etc. A quick last walk to the restrooms and when we got back, the defence and prosecution teams already arrived. Michael got in a few minutes before half past eight. Katherine was with him and greeted us all saying "Good morning" which we answered. Michael nodded his head as a hello. He took his seat between his attorneys Thomas Mesereau and Robert Sanger, while his family sat down in the front rows. Everybody had to get up when Judge Melville entered the room, then the hearing started.
First on the stand was Bob Jones, afterwards we saw Stacey Brown, Dwayne Swingler and June Chandler. Mesereau managed to turn them all into either unreliable witnesses or even witnesses for the defence. It was amazing to see him live! The way he talks, the way he phrases the things he says, the way he asks his questions – it's impressing and even better than scripted hearings you see on TV. He outclassed the prosecution lawyers Sneddon, Zonen and Auchincloss by miles!

Michael mostly sat still, just sometimes he readjusted the flasks, the microphone or the pillow in his back or he wrote little notes for Mesereau.

by The Appleheads

Michael loving the fans' chants at Neverland

There were three breaks every day: 9:45-9.55, 11:30-11:45 and 1:15-1:25. The hearing then ended around 2:30 pm. The breaks could be used to go to the restroom or get something to eat or drink in the courtyard. Beside the restrooms, there was a red line. Behind that line, we were allowed to wave to Michael, who usually went to the first floor during the breaks. He waved back, showed us a thumbs up or the Victory sign.

We always left the courtroom a few minutes before the hearing was over to drive to Neverland and greet Michael there. Usually, everybody behaved really well. We formed a line and when he arrived, he let down his window and we could give him presents, shake his hand or tell him something. He seemed to be happy over each present he got, no matter how small it was! And his hands were so BIG, oh my God! And after shaking his hand, your own hand smelled like Michael for an hour, which was fine with us! ;)

Sometimes he stopped behind the gate and leaned out of the car. One day he even filmed us. We got out our banner and as soon as he saw it, he wanted to have it and one of his bodyguards came up to get it for him.

On one occasion, Michael called the guard house beside the gate and wanted to speak to a fan. This lucky one gave us his messages afterwards. He didn't feel well because his back bothered him which he had hurt during the accident on stage in Munich (1999). He thanked us all for being there and said that he knows what struggles we went through to be there for him but that it helps him very much. He explained that he can feel all our emotions in the courtroom.

Over the next days we saw a long interrogation of Jay Jackson and an even much longer one of Janet Arvizo, who insisted on being called Janet Jackson. She was absolutely nuts! She constantly argued with Mesereau over the questions he asked, pretended to not understand them over and over again, talked more to the

Notes from Janet Arvizo's testimony

Badge to wear in court

Early in the morning in front of the courthouse

jury then to the one interrogating her, cried without tears several times…it made us really aggressive! We constantly wondered how Michael managed to sit there outwardly calm and hear her tell all these crazy lies about no clocks at Neverland, being held hostage there, plans to kidnap her in an hot air balloon to bring her to Mexico etc.

It was a good thing and a bad thing to be there to hear it all live. On the bright side, it was good to see how ridiculous this case was and on the down side, it was bad to see how ridiculous this case was! There was no chance anybody being there and hearing all this to believe it but on the other hand we had to wonder again and again why such a non-case had even gotten that far and why Michael had to endure this torture!

On our last day there, Mesereau finally grilled Mrs. Arvizo! We were lucky to again all get in although over our time there, more and more people had showed up and it was becoming a matter of luck to get in. We even managed to get the best public seats in the courtroom when we told the officers that that was our last day. During the first break we stayed on our seats while Michael had a little talk with his lawyers before leaving the courtroom. As we were among the only people still left there and as we sat right beside the aisle he had to use to get out, his politeness seemed to make it impossible for him to just walk by. But as he wasn't allowed to speak to anybody as well, he put his hand in front of his mouth before murmuring a deep "hello" to us. We said a quiet "hello", too. When he was out the door, we started to laugh because of the surreality of the situation and because the way he said it was so funny.

At the end of the day, a video was shown that was shot of Janet, Gavin, Star and Davellin Arvizo giving their statements for the "Take II" rebuttal video – a video that was made in response to the "Living with Michael Jackson" documentary by Martin Bashir, in which statements had been twisted and wrong facts suggested. The whole family sang Michael's highest praises. Mrs. Arvizo now argued that everything in that video was scripted, even the outtakes that were shown, where she, for example, enthusiastically proposes that they all hold hands like Michael did with Gavin during the Bashir documentary - while a few minutes ago she had told Mesereau she had never seen that documentary. But well, it was all scripted. She excused herself saying that she is not a very good actor on which Mesereau replied "Oh, I think you are!"

It made us even more sad to see that video because it showed what Michael really did for this family and we saw now live what that family's "thank you" for all of that was! It didn't help that we knew we had to leave Michael again on that day. It somehow felt as if we had to abandon him by going home again.
On our last drive back to Neverland to greet him there, we wrote a little card for him, telling him how we felt about our stay. We also added jokingly that the lottery at 6 in the morning was not very good for our nerves. We gave the card to him and had to laugh when later he talked again to a fan and asked her what that lottery was all about and she had to explain him how it worked...

06/01 – 06/12/2005 – Trial Santa Maria/USA
It were only weeks after we got back home until it was announced that the closing arguments of the trial were expected soon. As we had promised ourselves to be there for the verdict, we spontaneously booked our flights and were back in Santa Maria on June 1st. When we arrived at court in the morning a day later, there were a lot of people and fans there! The lottery so went somewhat differently, because most of the fans had to stay outside, us included. So we positioned ourselves at the fence to cheer for Michael when he arrived. We spent the time waiting singing songs like "D.S." and "They don't care about us". When he finally arrived, it was getting really loud. Even from that distance we could see how much he had changed within the last weeks.

We went straight to Neverland afterwards and when he arrived, all the fans there sang "You are not alone" for him – at least we tried!

Michael had his window down and slowly drove past us all.
The next day even more fans were there. We had to line up and the line reached all the way along the courthouse. We were told that the ticket drawn today would also be valid for the verdict as this was the last day of closing arguments. We were not sure if we even wanted that ticket… but at some point Miri said: "I'm gonna get a ticket today!" Everybody laughed! But sure enough, she did!

Thomas Mesereau and Susan Yu came in early that day and started preparing their presentation, trying to project different quotes on a screen, working with huge paperboards with jury instructions. Michael arrived with nearly his whole family. Katherine again greeted us all with a "Good morning". She, Rebbie, LaToya and Janet sat down in the first rows while other family members had to stay outside because there was not enough space. Michael looked not good but took his place with is head held high. Mesereau then continued his closing statement, pinpointing the inconsistencies in the case and in the testimonies of the witnesses. He then went on to explain the concept of "beyond a reasonable doubt". At the end of his closing argument, a video was shown with outtakes from the Bashir documentary. In it, Bashir got not only caught bootlicking Michael but it also showed what Michael was all about and especially what Neverland was all about, as the prosecution claimed that Neverland's only purpose was seducing little boys. Michael talked about the little train at Neverland, which he loved because he used to live near a train track as a child and grew up with the sounds of trains. He got really excited when he talked about a birthday party he wanted to throw for Bubbles in which he wanted to invite other famous animals to join them. It really showed his childlike innocence.

During the first break, while passing the waving fans, he didn't smile, he just nodded with an earnest face. He also didn't spend the whole break on the first floor but was already back in the courtroom talking to his lawyers when the public returned.
After the break, it was Ron Zonen's turn for a rebuttal. It was

Decorated Neverland

hard! Janet, LaToya and Rebbie left the room after his first words. The tension inside grew more and more. Zonen summarized all the arguments for a conviction. He called the witnesses "remarkably consistent", said the JC Penney case (a case the family had brought against the American supermarket chain JC Penney, which turned out to be highly dubious) was "believable, fair and appropriate" and answered the much-asked question as to why Michael did it at a time he was actually under observation with a simple "because he could". He ended with the showing of the video of Gavin telling the police for the first time about the abuse. Then he asked the jury to convict Michael.

Although Michael was calm all the time, one could see during the following break how much he suffered. He had been crying and Susan Yu took his hand to console him while Mesereau talked to him encouragingly.

Lastly, it was Melville's turn to give his final instructions. He allowed Michael to stay at Neverland to wait for the verdict and gave him 90 minutes to come as soon as the verdict was in.
That was the end of the hearings and the jury retreated to discuss the case. While Michael walked down the aisle, everybody tried to show him that we believed in a positive outcome and that everything's gonna be ok in the end.
We all met again in front of the main entrance of the courthouse and waited until Michael came out and drove home. Miri had to give an exact report on what happened inside and she tried but said she was so drained from the tension inside the courtroom that she was barely able to give a full report. We stayed at the courthouse as it was possible that the jury came back with the verdict today, but when that didn't happen, we went to Neverland. We spent the weekend doing a little sightseeing and preparing decorations for the acquittal in front of Neverland. Banners were designed, little flags handcrafted and signs painted. On Monday, many fans met early in the morning to decorate Neverland and the surroundings. It looked beautiful and we were quite proud of us! The next days were spent doing verdict watch in the morning

Tito talking to fans in front of Neverland

Karen Faye and some fans posing with the "Chain of hearts"

and then driving to Neverland in the afternoon. Sometimes one of Michael's people came out to talk to us. One day, Karen Faye (Michael's make up artist) appeared with the "Chain of hearts" fans from around the world had made for Michael. She said he had looked at it and loved it but wanted us to pin it to the fence for everyone to see. But, she continued, look after it, because he wants it back! So together we fixed the hearts to the fence.

From time to time, Michael went to the hospital. We can not imagine how back-breaking (in the truest sense of the word) the waiting must have been for him, when we already had the feeling to go crazy!

On Friday finally the verdict was in – at least that was the rumor for several minutes. Unfortunately it turned out to be just a rumour and Friday went without the end of this nightmare. Our second problem was, that our flights were going back that weekend so we would miss the verdict. We tried everything to postpone our flights, but as the American summer break started that weekend, we had no chance, not even to get a different flight for a reasonable price. We were heartbroken. We even didn't get an accommodation for the last night so we tried to sleep a little in our car in front of Neverland until police came and told us we were not allowed to sleep anywhere in our car. So we drove around the whole night, ending up in front of Neverland again when morning broke. We sat on the little wall, watching all the animals flying and running around, enjoying the peace while fighting back the tears…

We had just returned home when the verdict was in. That was exactly what we wanted to avoid: sitting alone in front of the TV watching that all-important moment… But it was always the outcome that was the most important and as that couldn't have been any better, it was time to celebrate the end of a nightmare and the beginning of something new!

10/09 – 10/14/2005 Michael in London/UK
We heard rumors that Michael would be coming back to London

by The Appleheads

in October, 2005 to work on new music. The thought of him being free to go where he wants to plus him working on new music was enough to keep us glued to the internet for more news. And we didn't have to wait long: Pictures of Michael at the Dorchester hotel and of him surrounded by enthusiastic fans in a parking garage emerged soon. Within minutes, we decided to go there, too. Finally another happy Michael travel. Ok, it was London again…but well… We booked our flights, packed our luggage and just hours later, we were on our way to the airport. It was the most spontaneous MJ trip we ever made.

In London, we went straight to the Dorchester and saw many fans from more than twelve countries waiting there. In the afternoon, a lot of fans left secretly and we later found out that they had followed Michael to Madame Tussaud's. In the evening, there were suddenly three guys on motorbikes stopping by at the entrance of the Dorchester, where we all were still hanging out. They were delivering about 20 pizzas that Michael had ordered – for us. They went around and everybody who was hungry could eat "Michael's" pizza salami. Now what about vegetarians, Michael? ;)

The next day passed without anything happening. In the evening, everyone got so eager, that at some point, we decided to "activate" Michael. As we didn't know which windows were his, we just started to sing and chant on the one side of the hotel. When nothing happened, we crossed the big street that passes along the Dorchester where there is a small stripe of lawn, and tried it again from there. Within moments, a window was opened at the top level! It was Michael! It seemed as if he had only waited for us to start calling him, that quick he was responding! He waved and smiled at us. Then he shortly disappeared and came back with a paper which he threw down in hope of letting it fall to the ground – to us. But unfortunately, it landed on a roof a little below Michael's window and nobody could read what he had written. He tried again but he never succeeded. But he had managed to get us on "his" side of the street now and we all partied like never before. It seemed that everybody was so happy just to see him and cele-

by The Appleheads

brated him with slogans like "We are proud of Michael". To our delight, he brought his children to the window, too and let them wave to us. It was a fun game! We called for Michael and he waved, we called for Paris and she waved, we called for Prince and he waved and we even called for Blanket and we could see his little hand – and again from the start!

The next day was hard. Every now and then, there were rumors Michael would be coming out and fans ran nervously from side to side of the Dorchester to check every entrance possible. It looked and even sounded like a flock of cattle and we couldn't help breaking down laughing. In the afternoon, we gathered at the entrance on the left side, Michael's vans were parking there and we saw bodyguards. As more and more fans came over, it became clear that Michael's safety would not be guaranteed here. Then, we snapped up a few words from some of the so-called insider fans. They were saying that Michael would be going to Harrod's. Immediately, we knew this was our chance because here it would end up in chaos again anyway. We needed to be ahead of time now. We just jumped on the street, stopped the next cab that was passing by and drove to Harrod's. On the ground floor of Harrod's, there was still no sign of Michael. We had to make a plan and decide quickly. If Harrod's would have been a zoo, we would have gone to the monkey house like in Berlin. Since it was a department store, we thought that either the toy section, the electronics section or the jewelry section would be of Michael's interest. Then, we observed some bodyguards coming in. We followed them to an elevator and let them get in. Our looks went up to the display that showed at which level the elevator was stopping next. It was the level with the electronics section. Sherlock Holmes in da house! ;) We quickly took the next elevator up to the same level. As soon as we stepped out, we realized that we hadn't opted for the "less-chaos-situation" as we immediately were inside the commotion that surrounded Michael. Fans and onlookers were following Michael and closing in on him, yelling at him. The department store security tried to keep a distance between the mob and the star. Michael was trapped in. We found ourselves standing right in front of him. He seemed to endure the situation with serenity. We had a hard time looking at him in this chaos since we felt like in a circus, staring at some obscure creature that was exposed against its will. He was so close to us that we could see every change in his facial expression and it made us too shy to really try to interact with him. We felt ashamed that we were among a lot of crazy fans and a part of a mob that just destroyed his shopping visit. We felt sorry for Michael since he had to endure moments like this on a daily basis. It was one of the moments when we painfully realized what Michael really meant when he was talking about his need to know how it feels to be normal and to be treated like a next door neighbor in interviews. Michael himself seemed to be accustomed to situations like this. He just waited for the chaos to settle down and licked on a lollipop that he had in his hand. The Harrod's security guards managed to open a way to escort Michael into a private part for staff only. They passed exactly by us and Lisa touched Michael's shoulder. As the store was closing soon we got out and were shocked when we later learned that many fans had hidden themselves inside to be able to experience Michael shopping.

Then, we lost Michael. Within the next few days, we weren't very lucky. One of the so-called insider fans was still upset that his "secret information" about Michael's visit to Harrod's had become public, so he wanted revenge: He spread the rumor that Michael was going to the famous toy store Hamley's one evening although it was not true. Everyone went there, spent money on taxis just to find out it was a hoax. We didn't understand how fans can be so mean and ridiculous to other fans, especially if you yourself have already experienced so much! That was the level on how we spent the last days of the trip. It seemed like there was a strong competition among the fans and nobody wanted other fans to get a glimpse of Michael, everybody wanted him just for him- or herself. We were happy when we returned home and all this stress fell off of our shoulders. At the same time, we were sad about what had become of the fan community and the fans themselves, many of them having turned to egoistic stalkers.

by The Appleheads

01/28 – 01/30/2006 – Michael in Hamburg/Germany
Rumors stated that Michael had arrived in Hamburg on January 26th, 2006. At first, we didn't believe a word but then we heard he was visiting private friends there of whom we knew of. A picture of Michael's nanny Grace in front of the house of those private friends emerged. As we knew how the house looked like, we were sure now that he was actually there. We discussed if it would be okay to go there because obviously, his visit should have been held private. It only had become public because a stewardess had discovered Michael's name on his flight ticket and had called the press in Hamburg.

We waited another day. In the meantime, press and paparazzi had lined up in front of the house. We ended our discussion by saying that since his visit was public now anyway, it would be okay for fans to go there. At least like this, there would not only be media folks outside the house. And as Carina was living in Hamburg anyway, we could as well do the trip to visit her and get back together.

So on January 28th, we all met in Hamburg. Outside the house of the Schleiter family – Michael's private friends – there were twelve police cars. They were protecting the house against paparazzi and they were blocking the street, too. We heard that was because Michael and the Schleiter's wanted to leave the house at 2 pm. But after all, this trip was canceled – for safety reasons. We felt bad. Somehow we didn't want to be there, it felt so wrong. We walked around a little, then got back into our car and drove around, did a quick stop at Hagenbeck's Zoo, didn't know what to do and then went to get something to eat. When we got back into our car, still discussing what to do, a man in the radio was just reporting live from the Schleiter's house. He said that Michael had collected banners and presents and in return had sent out autographs. So the decision was made: we returned to the Schleiter's house.
In the evening, we all stood at the barrier in front of this private house and still felt strange. What were we going to do here?

by The Appleheads

Everything seemed kind of inappropriate. But of course, there were enough onlookers to "handle" the situations. They were, of course, waiting for autographs and that's why they started to call Michael. We were pretty embarrassed, until Michael appeared at the window only a few minutes later. It was so funny to see: Curtains with flower pattern, a wooden goose as decoration in a completely normal German suburb - and then the world's most famous pop star behind the window. With Michael, you'd always have another surprise! He waved to us and laughed. A few times we could only see his hand as he was hiding behind the curtains. The onlookers now specifically started to ask for autographs. Imagine that it was a normal, small street and we were standing directly at the garden fence. Surely, Michael could hear every word that was said out loud. A little later, Michael appeared at the window with white papers in his hands. We could see him signing them before showing them to us, again. The daughter of the Schleiters, Franziska, then came out and gave out the souvenirs to the fans. We were lucky to get two autographs.

Later in the evening, Michael came to the window to show another paper that was afterwards brought out by Franziska, too. It was a letter that read: "I truly love each and every one of you. I'm so proud to be back in Hamburg. You make me so happy. I love you. Michael Jackson". Knowing this, we were happy that it was okay with Michael having fans around. Franziska also told us that Michael would be going to bed now. As the outside temperature was -10 degrees that night we were happy when we finally got home!
The next day we returned to the house at 11 am. Even more press people were gathering around since Michael had shown himself the night before. Now, they wanted to get more pictures of him. Even a helicopter carrying paparazzi was flying around over the house. But nothing happened. In the afternoon, Mrs. and Mr. Schleiter were coming out and going back in, talking to the police officers, collecting presents and pictures to give to Michael. We were astonished by their kindness to do so. It took a while until they came out and handed everyone back their pictures – signed

by The Appleheads

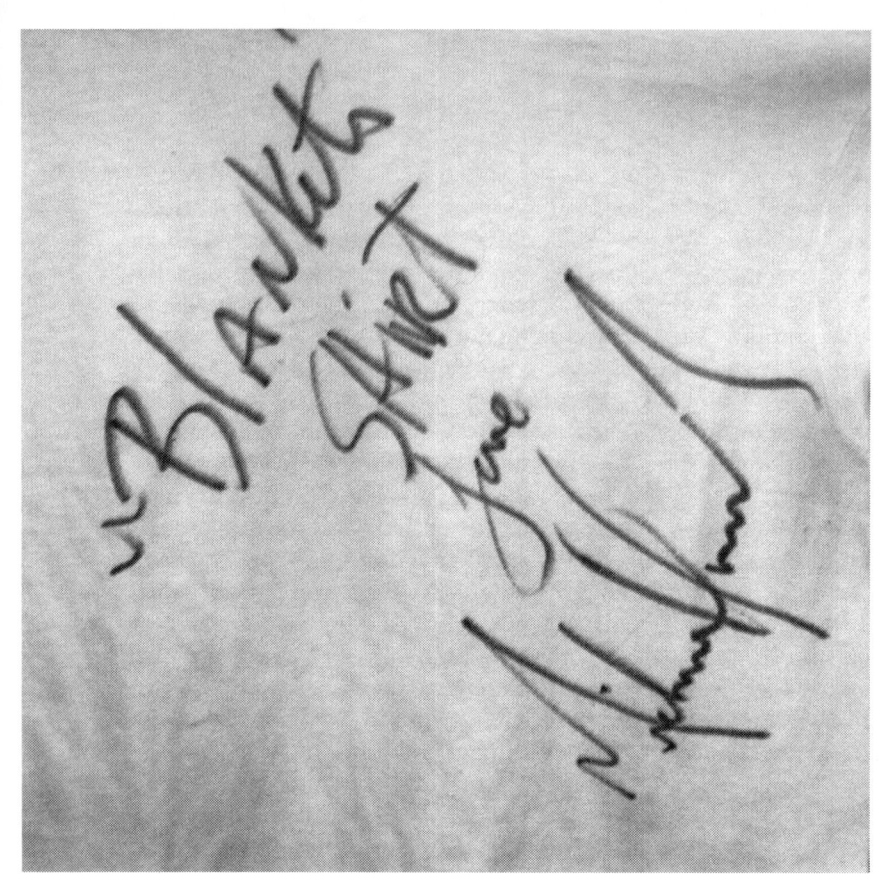

Blanket's shirt Michael offered a fan in return for his cap

Michael's autographs on Carina's picture

an issue of M-files magazine

by Michael. A very sweet episode happened with one male fan: He had given Michael a baseball cap to sign. When Mrs. Schleiter came back, she asked who had given the cap. The male fan said that it was him. Mrs. Schleiter told him that Michael's son Blanket loved the cap very much and Michael would now like to ask if it was okay that Blanket would keep the cap? In exchange, Mrs. Schleiter had brought out a small white t-shirt from Blanket which was signed by Michael. Of course, the male fan joined the deal and we all were amazed how cute that whole story was!

Mrs. Schleiter forwarded some comments from Michael about the pictures that he had signed, stating which pictures he had loved especially. He loved Carina's picture of her with his star in Hollywood and he also enjoyed watching her video of a song she had composed. He also wanted to keep one of the "M-files" magazines we had handed in and we were told that he loved flipping through the pages. That made us really proud as the magazine was being produced by us. We were fortunate to get several autographs altogether that day and were completely happy!

One time, when Mr. Schleiter came out, he was approached by a German television team. They asked if it was possible that Michael signed their microphone protection cover. Mr. Schleiter saw that it as TL television – a TV program with a lot of tabloid elements and he said "He will go bananas!" thinking of Michael giving an autograph to his "enemies". But since Michael was such a giving and nice person, he of course signed it.

Michael ordered pizza for us once more and like always, it was pizza salami. In the evening, Michael came to the window several times to wave to us. It was such a funny night as we sang some German songs for Michael – after all he was in Germany, right? – and rewrote other songs fitting to the situation. It was again one laughing fit after the other!

Rumors were circling around that Michael would leave Hamburg on Monday, January 30th. That's why we got up very early not

by The Appleheads

to miss anything. Arriving at the Schleiter's house, we saw more press people than on the other days waiting there already. With time, more and more fans were adding to the crowd. A police officer then confirmed that Michael would be leaving the house today. We were excited! Within the next two hours, Mr. Schleiter was getting things for breakfast from a bakery nearby (bread rolls, bananas!). Together with Grace, he was also bringing out a lot of luggage (red suitcases!), putting it into their car and bringing it to Hamburg airport. Then, after having waited some more time, real action was going on. The Schleiter's daughter and son were bringing out Michael's children hidden under umbrellas and getting them in a van. Then, Michael came out, his head also hidden under an umbrella. At first, we could only see his black hair behind the van but as we shouted his name, he jumped to the left and appeared from behind the van. He grinned and waved to us, then quickly went back behind the van. Michael wore a red college jacket and black sunglasses. He got in the van and then showed the "Victory"-sign with his hand through the front window. We called "We are proud of Michael" several times and he gave us a thumb up. The van then pulled off and slowly drove through the crowd that had gathered in the street. Michael waved, showed the "Victory"-sign again and opened the window of the car a bit to shake some fans' hands. As soon as the van had driven away, we jumped in our car as well and speeded to Hamburg airport. Unfortunately, we were not quick enough and missed Michael. But we met a photographer who had seen Michael sneaking in. He had taken some pictures and showed them to us – it was a proof, that Michael really was inside the V.I.P. area of the airport already and we could do nothing anymore to see him. We spent the rest of the day together in Hamburg and then everybody returned home.

11/14 – 11/17/2006 - World Music Awards London/UK
News spread around like a bushfire: Michael Jackson would be coming to the World Music Awards in London on November 15th, 2006. There was a raffle on the internet and we were lucky to win tickets for the show. Coming from our different cities as

usual, we met in London. Michael stayed at the Hemple hotel and had come out several times before we arrived in London a day before the Award Show. We had just gotten to the hotel, when Michael came out. It went all so quickly and he was gone. We thought he'd go rehearsing so we took a taxi to Earl's Court, but he was not there. We later learned he had gone to the Guinness World Record office to collect his record certificates. The day went by without anything more happening.

The next day, we had to line up at noon at Earl's Court to get our tickets for the show. Afterwards, we went to Michael's hotel but despite of many screaming fans, nothing happened. The evening came quickly and we queued up again at Earl's Court – this time to get in. Fortunately, we managed to get close to the stage and the catwalk. It seemed like the whole venue was filling up only with Michael Jackson fans. It was clear to see that he was the big attraction of the event and everybody was very excited about it. For days, there had been rumors circling in the media that Michael wanted to perform and make a big "comeback". It caused a huge frenzy about his stay in London although neither Michael nor his management had ever clearly confirmed any performance. On the other hand, neither Michael nor his management had ever denied it and this became a problem. The media was taking the rumor of a performance for real and expected it from Michael.
We missed Michael's arrival at Earl's Court since we were already standing in the packed crowd inside, but this arrival was the point at which the media coverage about Michael in London changed. While walking over the red carpet and shaking hands with fans, Michael was asked what he would be performing that night. He said "I'm not performing". HE himself had to finally deny a rumor that was in the media for weeks around the whole world. Where was his spokesperson? Of course the media reacted negatively to this disappointment!
As we had already expected something like this, we were just happy to see him. But before actually seeing Michael, we had to endure a long and exhausting evening. The World Music Awards were poorly organized. The show started with delay, the host of

by The Appleheads

the evening was an unconvincing starlet, Lindsay Lohan, who had to do every moderation twice because she couldn't get her lines out right. The sound was bad and there were long breaks between the performances of stars like Rihanna, Beyoncé and Nelly Furtado. We were waiting for six hours in that packed crowd until they finally announced Beyoncé who would present Michael with the Diamond Award. The tension in the air was palpable. Everybody had been waiting for Michael to come on that stage and do whatever, but just finally come. And then he came and he looked absolutely gorgeous. He wore a very elegant black outfit designed by Roberto CavallI and he was radiant. Beyoncé gave him the Diamond award for 750 million records sold throughout his career. Michael thanked and hugged her and held a short speech. He said that when he was working on "Thriller" in the Eighties he had no idea how successful it would become. He thanked his children, his parents and his fans for their long lasting support. With every word that came out of his mouth, the fans seemed to scream louder. There was an incredible buzz! For us, it was almost too much to see him on a real stage again after all those MJ encounters in front of hotels. It was simply amazing and we responded with an outpouring of love. Michael disappeared after a few minutes and the show went on. At the very end of the program, a choir with teenagers came onstage and the song "We are the world" was played. We knew instinctively that there was another Michael moment coming. And we were right: Michael walked in from the left side of the stage. The fans freaked out completely – would he perform after all? What would be happening now? We could not clear our feelings and thoughts at that very moment so we all just screamed and cheered like crazy. We praised our king! Michael greeted the choir, took a microphone and began to sing a few lines from "We are the world". But the stupid organizers of the show had taken the version with all the different voices in it. How should Michael be singing live over a playback song with more than fifty voices? Michael decided not to sing the whole song and instead went onto the catwalk. He walked towards the end of the catwalk and stopped several times to shake hands and he threw his jacket into the crowd. It

by The Appleheads

Michael leaving the Hempel Hotel

Hundreds of fans waiting in the rain

was an amazing scene – Michael Jackson finally back on a stage, surrounded by hundreds of loving fans after so many years of silence and trials. We felt happy to cover him with our love and to show that we were still here and he seemed to embrace it all, soaking it up and lightning up. When he left the stage, it almost seemed like he felt bad for it and would have loved to stay there longer. The show was over after Michael left the stage, the lights went on and we got out of Earl's Court as quickly as possible. We ran out and were lucky enough to catch a taxi which brought us to Hempel hotel soon enough to see Michael return! We were so early that we got a good spot right in front of the entrance and when his vans came, he got out right in front of us. He had a huge smile on his face and his award in his hand, which he wanted to celebrate it with us! He shook a few hands before disappearing inside the hotel.

We waited some hours at the hotel, sometimes cheering for Michael but the crowd, although it was big, was pretty lame! Michael came to the window some times but only very shortly and although his windows were only on the first level, we didn't see much.
When we read about the World Music Awards in the media the next day we became very upset. They were writing everywhere that Michael was booed by his fans for not performing. This was not true at all and we knew it since we were there. But the media schemed against Michael and let him look like a fool who lost his talent, his ability to perform and even the appreciation of his own fans. Later, we realized that whatever Michael could have done during the show, he would never have gotten out not being negatively criticized. As constant observers of Michael's activities and his media representation we realized it was one more PR disaster gotten out of control. Michael's public image seemed to be that highly destroyed that it had come to a point where everybody wrote about him whatever they liked.

Nothing was to be read about the poor organization of the whole event, the time delay, the long breaks….Michael was the only

by The Appleheads

thing you heard about the next day and it was him who was overly negatively criticized, not the World Music Awards themselves. On the other hand, we also wondered why Michael had a management and a PR consultant when these people were obviously incapable of handling an event like this and were not able to put an end to rumors – rumors that would be so devastating for his reputation afterwards. We realized once again that Michael was surrounded by inappropriate people.

The next two days, we saw him again at times, coming and leaving, but there was also again a lot of chaos and a lot of disrespectfulness and unfairness among the fans. What we had experienced in 2005, continued here. There was no singing in front of the hotel and just enjoying being there, everybody was just greedy to get a glimpse or even more. Michael seemed to have adjusted to this, he was at the window very seldom, he didn't take any presents or sent his people down to get them, he didn't even seem to care for banners anymore and the barriers looked kind of naked without them... We left the Hempel hotel hours before we would have had to catch our flight because it was no fun anymore... and leaving early when Michael is around means something!

03/16 – 03/19/2007 – Michael in London/UK

While Michael was in Japan meeting fans who paid for it, he let some of them know that he'd be in London afterwards and wanted fans to be there. So we made our way to London again, this time the place of action was supposed to be the Carlton Tower hotel. We saw Michael several times coming and going but unfortunately it was always a huge chaos surrounding him. There were some barriers but they didn't help to hold some of the fans back. The situation tensed when the fans that were inside the hotel could be seen meeting him again and again while other fans waited in the cold and saw nothing. Together with many fans we wrote letters to Basheer, Michael's bodyguard, letting him know that the situation was unbearable and that we wanted stronger security so that Michael was safe. One night when he returned, we were told that Michael would come out to greet us but then he was mobbed in the lobby so badly he hurt his head and understandably didn't come out afterwards. He also didn't come to the window, so the whole travel was pretty disappointing and our will to travel to London to see him slowly vanished after our last experiences...

03/05 – 03/07/2009 – "This is it" Press Conference London/UK
Carina was living in London for a year when we saw Michael there for the last time in our lives. It's still so unreal and hard putting that story together, but we are deeply thankful to have had these moments with him again, because they were unforgettable. Of course it would be London where we'd see him again...we tried hard to forget the past trips that were so disappointing to us.

We all arrived on the day of the press conference and we met in front of the O2-Arena. It felt just like the first time we met to see Michael 13 years ago. We were excited as we knew that something big was going to happen. We couldn't stop laughing. Large screens in front of the O2-Arena displayed Michael's picture and the famous „This is it" slogan. The atmosphere inside was like coming home once more. Fans were going crazy when he finally arrived almost an hour late. Many had tears in their eyes when he made his little speech. He was coming back! To feel his aura was so special in a way that you cannot describe. It was just beautiful to see him!

Still he left us, like everyone else, a little stunned and helpless with his announcement of "the final curtain call", namely ten shows in London...To hear about new concerts was absolutely the greatest thing for us as fans. But why on earth did it sound so minatory when he said "final curtain call" and "this will be it"? It sounded so conclusive as if something BIG was going to end after those 10 shows. We had just heard wonderful news, but we strangely did not feel pure happiness. Now, we sadly know that something BIG ended even before the shows began.

In spite of our confusion, we didn't want to lose any time and went to the Lanesborough Hotel where he stayed. When it comes to the fans it always seemed that London was somehow a little crazier than the rest of the world. Michael could not get out of his car, when he came back from the O2-Arena and he laughed and smiled about it. His bodyguards were a little helpless and very strict, because Michael was not able to take a single step without fans going mad. Although the mood was quite tensed, he was very amused and it made us laugh, too.

On the next day papers said that he would go to the Musical „Oliver". We could not get tickets to get in, but saw him when he arrived at the venue. It was the last time we felt his presence so closely...
Since it was a mess at the venue, because people were screaming and going crazy we stepped away from that chaos and started to think about how we could get close to Michael without being hysterically disrespectful. So we started to talk to Michael's bus driver to figure out in what direction they would leave after the show. He always said he couldn't answer that but when we asked funny 'Yes' and 'No'-questions, he opened up and so it seemed that we got our questions answered. That's what we always did. Be persistent and calm and often you will somehow find out where Michael is going next. We had the plan to wait at a traffic light where he just had to stop on the way back to the hotel. We were quite excited, because we thought our plan was really smart. So we did what we could do best in regards of all our Michael-years: We waited and waited and waited. But: Nothing happened. We decided to walk back to the theatre to check out what was going on. What we saw was rather depressing: No people, no police and of course no Michael. Must have been a last minute change of plans. The atmosphere went back to normal and within a few moments the Michael spirit was gone.
Back at the Lanesborough nothing happened. He rarely came to the window and did not come out anymore. Fans stayed there anyway and so did we.
Saturday, on the 7th of March 2009 at 10:30 pm we were just about to go home when one of us saw Michael standing behind the curtains of his hotel window. We were not screaming or

by The Appleheads

singing and kept on watching him watching us. A perfect final moment that we will never forget. It was the last time...

07/02 – 07/10/2009 – Memorial Los Angeles/USA
Honestly, it still feels difficult to write about the following. It still doesn't seem to be reality. Michael died on June 25th, 2009. Only about two weeks before we planned to go to London to see his "This is it" concerts, he passed away. To us – and we don't mean to be cheesy – it was one of the saddest and darkest days in our lives, a traumatizing day. Before the 25th of June, we were energetic and enthusiastic, full of excitement about spending the summer in London and being around Michael. Since 1997, our biggest dream had always been to be able to "go on tour" with Michael again and the moment we had accepted that this was never going to happen again, it suddenly became reality.

In spite all that, we cannot deny our bitter-sweet feelings towards these concerts. Too much had gone wrong already: The ticket sale, the strange announcement we had witnessed, the fact that suddenly 50 concerts had been announced which we simply couldn't believe was in Michael's interest etc etc. Somehow we felt as if something was completely going wrong!

Still we tried hard to push these feelings away and focus on the positive. We hoped that for the first time after Michael's acquittal in 2005, the world could see what Michael Jackson was all about, that "Michael Jackson, the artist" would be back in the spotlight and outshine "Michael Jackson, the tabloid headline." And we hoped that we, the fans, would help him through his comeback with our support. We wanted to show the world that we were still there by his side and of course, we wanted to light Michael up himself with an outpouring of love. Somehow, we hoped that our applause and delight during the shows would heal Michael's soul and ease his pain from the last years full of trials and accusations. We hoped that maybe he would say afterwards that it was worth the many nightmares that he had to endure because in the end, he would be rising like a phoenix from the ashes. We, too, had endured a lot standing by the side of someone beloved whom the whole world seemed to disapprove at times. We had to take a lot

by The Appleheads

of hate over the years for being so fond of a pop star.

But of course, our own needs, hopes and wishes became unimportant on the day of Michael's death. Reality hit us like a thunderstorm. For us, the world stood still and we tried to comprehend what had happened in Los Angeles that very day. We had a hard time to separate real news from the rest of the media slaughter that surrounded Michael's passing. We nearly went crazy. We had to make a decision: Either we'd stay glued to our computers and televisions, or we'd start to find out things for ourselves. We decided to listen to our hearts. We felt the need to go to Los Angeles and be on location. Plus we felt a duty to say good-bye to Michael personally, to thank a man for everything he'd done to influence, inspire and shape our lives. To us, it felt wrong to stay at home and consume precast media reports that were everything but not what Michael was to us. We did not want to remember Michael's death as something only seen on TV since we had tried to get past that level for so many years. We saw Michael as a real person, a real human being and factor in our lives. We had to be near him one last time.

On June 30th we heard rumors that there would be an open casket viewing at Neverland. Whether we supported those rumors or wanted to see Michael dead in his open casket or not, we said to ourselves that it was time to book flights. Whatever would be happening in the upcoming week, it was the upcoming week that was important. Just two days later, we boarded planes in Düsseldorf and Hamburg and met altogether in Paris, where we went on the same plane to Los Angeles. The purpose of the journey felt terrible, almost too surreal to comprehend. But from the very moment that we had met in Paris, we felt we were doing the right thing: We isolated ourselves from shabby media reports and met with true friends to pay tribute to the man that had brought us all together through his music. All we could do since he was dead was to consciously live our friendship and see it as another dimension for Michael to live on. It was him who created it and it was him who drew us together once again for this journey. During

by The Appleheads

the many hours of daylight, we just stood together in the middle of the plane, reminiscing about our MJ adventures, laughing a lot and comforting each other. When we arrived in L.A., the news situation had changed: No public viewing at Neverland, but a press conference the next day about a Memorial at Staples Center the following week. We rented a car and drove Downtown to the Staples Center. Outside broadcast vans from TV stations all over the world were lining up the streets surrounding the venue, police officers were watching the place. One officer told us that tickets for the Memorial would be distributed via Ticketmaster – the same ticket seller that had sold us our tickets for the "This is it"-concerts. We tried to get some details about it, but we had to wait for the press conference the next morning. As soon as it was said that we needed to register for a ticket lottery on the internet, we jumped up and ran out of the motel room towards the reception where we could have wireless access to the internet. Surprisingly, while we were running, many other motel room doors opened as well and other MJ fans came out running, too, having the same plan as we did. Of course, the website crashed down immediately and we later heard that 1,6 million fans had registered online. It took some time but we succeeded to register in the end. The Memorial was set for the 7th of July. Having nothing to do in L.A. during the next four days, we quickly decided to leave the city and head for Neverland. We thought that no place on earth could be closer to Michael than this. After all, Michael once said in an interview with Martin Bashir "Neverland represents the totality of who I am". We took the Pacific Coast Highway and arrived at Neverland in the late afternoon. The emotional tension grew with every meter. For every one of us this would even have been a special moment, if Michael was still alive. Now we were clenching up, it got hard to breathe and we could not fight back our tears anymore. While we were approaching the last meters to the main gate of Neverland by feet, we could not speak anymore. Sadness overwhelmed us. Suddenly, we had arrived at a place where Michael's spirit was still present, in the trees and the grass and in the sunrays that beamed down from the sky. We again understood why he had chosen to build his home here

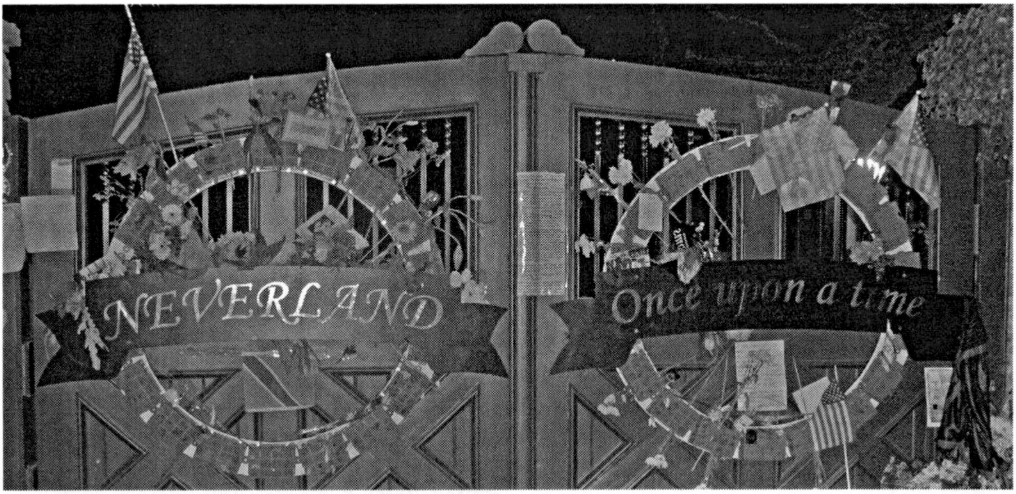
NEVERLAND
Once upon a time

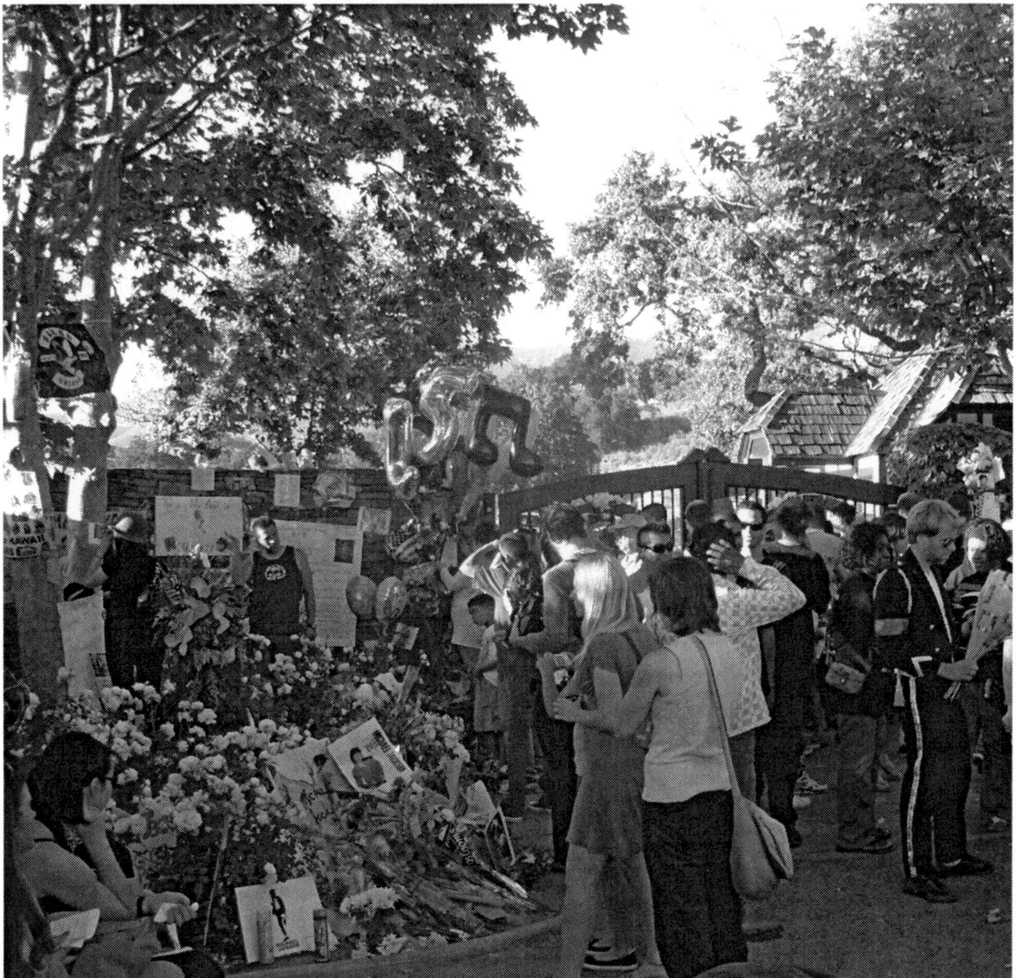

in the Santa Ynez Valley. The place was still magical. We could feel him everywhere and at the same time, we had found a place where his death became a visible fact because of the many grieving fans, many flowers, banners and letters that were being laid down around the gate of Neverland. We were not prepared for all this. We also had wished to be there alone and now we were in the middle of some hundred people. Some people were playing loud music out of their cars, some people were dancing wildly on the Figueroa Mountain Road, others were selling souvenir t-shirts and badges or drinks and food. There were broadcasting vans and TV people like at the Staples Center. We were in the middle of a circus. We had escaped the media frenzy in Germany to land in a media frenzy and souvenir marketplace in California. We could not share the way people grieved there. For an hour we just stood there motionless, crying, strangely waiting for Michael to come out of Neverland. It felt so bizarre and so new to be in a Michael situation but there was no Michael anymore. We had come too late and he was gone too soon.

Then, we searched for a quieter place and drove along the fence of Neverland until it ended. We paused there and listened to the sound of nature, we breathed in all the scents of the vegetation around and suddenly, a beautiful little bird was flying above our heads. He flew in circles and seemed to observe us precisely for minutes. We joked that it was a sign of Michael. Suddenly a car stopped by us. The driver asked us where we came from and what we were doing here in the middle of nowhere looking that woefully and lost. He turned out to be Michael's neighbor who runs the Cricket Canyon Ranch just minutes away. He must have felt our despair, so he invited us to stay overnight at his and his wives' ranch. We gratefully accepted the invitation and followed Lee and Ree to their beautiful home. That evening, we shared some wonderful and deep conversations with the two. It was a real comfort to get to know local people and find out that Michael meant a lot to everybody that was living in that community. We sat on the porch and felt the magic of the area once again. We now knew how Michael felt when he for instance climbed up his "Giving Tree" at Neverland at night to write songs. The area was just so

by The Appleheads

The Nokia Plaza in front of the Staples Center in MJ decoration days before the Memorial

The media stations built these tribunes for their live coverage of the Memorial

inspiring. When we went to bed that night, we had had the lowest low and the highest high on the same day. We slept deeply.

During the next three days, we discovered the area: Los Olivos, Santa Maria (where we stopped by the courthouse and thought of it as a place of horror), Solvang, Buellton, Santa Barbara, the Los Padres National Forest and the Pacific coast. We also stopped by at Neverland every day, each time feeling down again. We went there at day and at night. At night, it was calm and peaceful there and we finally could have some moments "alone with Michael" in spirit.
On Monday, July 6th, we spent half of the day in front of our laptop, because we hoped to get an e-mail saying that we had won tickets for the Memorial in L.A. Actually, we could have gotten two tickets, but since we were five people, we agreed that either all of us should get in, or none. We could watch the Memorial on television anyway. We just had to find out another way to say good-bye to Michael personally.
We returned to Los Angeles in the late evening. First a quick stop at Staples Center where we saw hundreds of people collecting their free tickets – lucky winners. We soon found a motel nearby. Then, we got an insider tip that a Jackson family gathering was going on at Forest Lawn Cemetery in the Hollywood Hills. Although we did not know what to think of this, we did not hesitate and drove there immediately. We parked somewhere and ran to the main gate of the cemetery. The setting was bizarre: There were media people and TV trucks as usual (at least a proof that we had arrived at the right spot) lightning up the dark street with their spotlights. Police officers guarded the gate and watched the fans and journalists waiting behind barriers at every side of the gate. We heard the humming of helicopters in the air. The place was huge and widespread. Behind the gates, we saw hills looming against the moon. We could not figure out what was over there in the darkness, it just felt like standing in front of a mystery forest in a fairy tale. A scenery that would fit in the "Thriller" short film. We were scared. We didn't know how to deal with our feelings. What would be happening now? Would

we even be confronted with a hearse driving in or out? A very depressing and uncanny atmosphere hung over everything. We waited and saw some black cars and limousines passing by, but we could not recognize a Jackson. The more we waited, the more false it felt to stand there and witness the media hunt for pictures of a family's darkest hour. We were somehow relieved when the police officers started to send everybody away and shut down the area. We talked to one of the officers and he said that Michael's casket would be carried to the Memorial the next morning. This was new information that had not been reported in the media before.
We made the plan that since the area around Staples Center would be completely shut down the next day, we would line up along a street near the Forest Lawn Cemetery to see the hearse with Michael's casket passing by.

That's why we really didn't sleep long and got up at 2 am on July the 7th. It somehow seemed that the whole city was restless that night. Helicopters could be heard everywhere, even in the dark and it was really hard to prepare our hearts for all that was about to come that day. While driving towards the cemetery, we already recognized many police barriers that blocked driveways. We parked somewhere and went by foot to reach the gate of the cemetery via Forest Lawn Drive. We already saw police cars at every corner, but we ignored them and went on. Of course, they didn't ignore us and send us away....we had no chance to even come near the cemetery...the city blocked the fans away from everything. We could not believe it and became very angry. Why on earth was it not possible to stand on the street and say good-bye to Michael? We needed a brainstorm. It was clear now that we had to find someplace else. While driving back from the cemetery to our motel, we realized that the Jackson column had to take the same freeway as us to get to Staples Center. We discovered that near the exit that the column would have to take to arrive at Staples Center, there were some bridges crossing the freeway. One of those bridges was just five walking minutes away from our motel. "That's the place", was all we thought. We were relieved to have found out a possibility to get "near Michael" one last time. At the same moment, we became frightened. We still could not believe the whole situation and only the idea that in a few hours, it would become real that Michael was not alive anymore by seeing his casket broke our hearts. How would we survive this moment emotionally? What would come then? A life without seeing Michael anymore was not imaginable.

We went back to the motel and watched the live coverage on CNN. When they showed live images of the Jackson column leaving the Forest Lawn Cemetery (where they had attended a private memorial service), we went outside and walked to the bridge. We felt awfully strange, stepping forward hurt with every heartbeat. On the bridge, time went by slowly. The setting was completely different than the night before but just as bizarre: We were standing on a bridge over a freeway, the hot sun burned down on our heads, made us dizzy and drenched the whole area in its bright and dazzling light. We were having one of our darkest hours in the splendid sunshine. We counted 14 helicopters above our heads, hovering there in wait of the same thing as we did. Below us, heavy morning traffic passed by. Higher up in the air there was a plane that wrote "MJ" and a big heart with white color in the sky. We observed the freeway. After half an hour, the traffic lanes on the left side (leading towards Staples Center) emptied out completely, there was not a single car driving on the freeway anymore. It was quiet for one or two minutes.

Then we saw the motorcade coming. It rolled towards us like a black landslide. First, there came about 30 police motorbikes, followed by police vans and bomb squad trucks, all passing by in high speed. Then, about 30 black limousines and SUV's passed by beneath us – the cars that carried the Jackson family members and close friends. Our hearts stood still. The hearse came next. We saw Michael's golden casket through the windows of that car. We saw the red flowers on top of the casket. We watched the cars slowing down and piling up at the exit to Staples Center. We just stood there and cried and stared into nothingness. It was terrible

Michael's last home in Carolwood Drive

anguish and emptiness inside. It became so real that Michael was dead. We don't even remember how long we stood there, it felt like a whole lifetime. We stumbled some streets further towards Staples Center up until the police barriers. There were hundreds of people, many of them selling souvenir t-shirts and other souvenir items that just disgusted us. How can a person sell souvenir t-shirts of someone who had died two weeks before during a memorial service? We watched the live broadcast of the memorial inside the restaurant "bella cucina". With time, more and more people did so as well and soon the whole place was crowded. The performances and speeches, but of course especially the words that Paris Jackson addressed to the world seemed to tear our hearts apart once again. To us, nothing new was said, we only heard things that could have come out of our own mouths. To the rest of the world, it was apparently a revealing TV moment.... the world seemed to discover Michael as a human being in the moment of his death...

After the Memorial had ended, we returned to the bridge to check if we could see the motorcade once again. But we only saw a bunch of helicopters flying in the other direction. We went back to our motel and fell into sleep immediately. The experiences of the day took their toll and had to be processed in our brains while we were sleeping.

We woke up in the afternoon and decided to visit Michael's star at the "Walk of fame". But it was very crowded over there and we didn't have the energy to queue up for an hour after all we'd been through, so we left without having had a closer look. One single phrase was circulating in our heads over and over again: "Ever since I was born, daddy has been the best father you can ever imagine...and I love him so so much." Paris had touched us so deeply...

The next day, we went to a tattoo shop and three of us got inked with an autograph that Michael had given to us in Hamburg. We also drove to Carolwood Drive in the Holmby Hills to stop by Michael's last residence. The house where he had died. We could not bear to stay there for a long time and so we drove to the ocean and tried to clear our minds. While driving towards the ocean, we passed by the UCLA Medical Center where doctors had tried to resuscitate him. Two days later, we arrived back in Germany. We absolutely felt we had done the right thing by travelling to the United States. But it hurt to return from a "MJ trip" knowing that it was the last one…

by The Appleheads

Epilogue

10 weeks later, when we watched images of Michael's funeral on TV, we were haunted again by the feelings we had when we stood in front of the Forest Lawn Cemetery. The funeral ceremony was held near the Great Mausoleum on Forest Lawn Cemetery. A hot and sunny day had ended, the sunset was beautiful and a full moon appeared early in the sky. We could almost smell the scent of the scenery through our TVs, we could feel the atmosphere over there. It was hard to be confronted with reality again since in between, we all had tried to escape it. Seeing Michael's wonderful children Prince, Paris and Blanket sitting in the front row on the funeral of their dad, was heartbreaking. We nearly turned off the TV because it was too hard, but then we thought we should endure it to be able to get closure someday.

What is left now?
Like no other artist, Michael influenced our lives. The values that he stood for have shaped our outlook on life more than many relatives, teachers or friends have. He was always a good example to look up to. Some may call it "image", but we are sure that these values were dear to his heart! Even if they were not very popular – if he believed in them, he stood up for them! We have always admired the strength he showed by doing that, it will stay an inspiration for our own lives. On the other hand, these struggles have taken their toll on him in the end. He was a human being, he only had a certain level of energy and he had his weaknesses, too.

On the day that he died, we had the feeling as if the good values he stood for had lost the battle. As if OUR values had lost the battle and had disappeared with him. It took us several weeks to realize that that's not the case! "Our Michael" will always be with us and it is now our turn to continue what he has started. To use the grains he has seeded in us to make this world a better place!

by The Applehedds

We will never get over the tragic and sudden loss of our hero. The pain, that he had to leave this earth too soon, will never ease. Like everyone on this planet, we are fortunate to still have his music legacy. Like very few people on this planet, we also have so much more.

We've been following Michael together for the past 13 years. We feel lucky to have lived in the same era with him and to have experienced his "magic". And although our biggest dream, to perform our show for him, never became reality in spite of being so close, we will always cherish the moments we spent in the presence of this special human being.

But most importantly: We became friends through Michael's music. We know that one of the many ways for Michael to live on and to be immortal is through our friendship as itself. Our friendship is the most wonderful gift that Michael could have given us. We'll be forever grateful for that! We share a special bond with each other and whenever we miss him, we at least can remind us that he's still there right between us in a spiritual way. All we can say is THANK YOU MICHAEL for the best times in our lives and for opening our eyes in so many ways!

by The Appleheads

London

by Charlotte Svee Hestnes, Norway

Some years back, rumors said that Michael was going to have some last shows in Las Vegas.
I flipped out when I heard this, and the first thing I did, was to run upstairs to mom to tell her about the great news. My dream for many years had been to get the chance to see Michael live. I just had to go!! I begged mom: "Please let me go, please, please, please, pleeeaseee!!!" I knew that she would say no though because Las Vegas is on the other side of the globe. Anyways, mom and I were standing in the middle of the room upstairs when we talked about Michael, and then she said: "Sorry, Charlotte, I can't let you go to Las Vegas but if Michael ever comes to London, I'm going to let you go so you can get the chance to see him there." I started crying because I really wanted to go, and I never thought he would be coming to London. I lost all my faith in ever seeing him live.
This summer my mom died when our house caught fire. They told me they found her dead on the floor in the room upstairs, exactly where mom and I discussed Michael. A month later, I got tickets for Michael's concerts in London! I knew mom was watching over me and made sure that I got a ticket. Mom once told me that her dream for me was to get the chance to see Michael Jackson, and I was so happy that both of our dreams would finally come true.
But now... now I and the rest of the world won't be able to see Michael at all. We all know that he is in a better place now where he finally gets some peace. At last he can relax. And I know that he will always be here with us, because he will always be in our hearts. God took Michael Joseph Jackson away from us physically, but God will never be able to take him away from our hearts. Michael will live on forever through his music.
He is a legend that will never be forgotten.
We all love you Michael, and we will never ever forget you.

All the magic in your eyes

by Sabine Fritah-Lenze, Germany

I never "met" Michael, though I did dream to meet him one day and I was very patient ... too patient. But I was close to him a few times, and that alone was wonderful. In those moments I wouldn't have been able to talk to him anyway and I was relieved that he did not even look at me.

The first time I came close to Michael was in 1996, in Amsterdam, in the hotel lobby. I went there with my two best friends at that time. Waiting for Michael we stood in the lobby for hours with a whole bunch of other people. We were very nervous and just couldn't imagine that Michael would really go through that lobby. A long time before he finally appeared we were told to stand in two rows to build an alley. There were amazingly many people waiting. Everyone was chatting in nervous anticipation. Suddenly the atmosphere changed dramatically. I didn't see him yet but I knew he was in the lobby, he was perceivably present. All the chatter around trickled away. Then he came around the corner where the lifts were.

I didn't have an eye for what he wore, I only saw him. I tried to sponge up everything he did. At the beginning of the row of people was a child in a wheelchair and Michael bended down and gave his attention to the child. There was so much calmness in him. As he walked further he shook hands, gave autographs, accepted presents, posed for photographs (even though we were told, before he came, not to flash into his face). Everyone waiting there had wishes which Michael was supposed to fulfill. And he did. He gave his best to understand what each one wanted him to do. I never expected him to really take so much time and to try so hard not to let anyone down.

Then for an eternity he stood directly in front of me. I saw nothing but his eyes. It would have been the moment for me to get my photograph of him, which I carried with me, signed. I held it towards him and he took it and put it to the presents he got. Everyone around was shouting at him, I did not. I never got an autograph, not that day and never after that. But I could not shout at him. His eyes were so wide open and the flashes of the cameras around lightened his eyes up all the time. I thought, by now, he must see nothing but red dots. There he stood, my photograph clamped under his arm, busy shaking hands and signing autographs and the only thing I could do was to reach out my hand and caress one of the fingers of his left hand while he was signing. He did not even notice it. For me, it was the closest I would ever come. I did see him after that but never that close.

After he left, I realized that he wore his black mask and his hat, to me all that counted was that he did not hide his eyes. Thirteen years have passed since then and it is difficult to remember every detail, but I still can call back those eyes to my memory and the charisma of him I perceived and the way the other people there reacted to him. Just to be near him was an enrichment for me and for many others, I'm sure.

by Sabine Fritah-Lenze

My little gift's journey

by Dawn Trethewey, Australia

I live in Australia. I knew I would be having a holiday in the USA in March 2005, so I made a „gift" for Michael, with the intention of going to the gates of Neverland, to leave the „gift" for Michael.

All up, my gift travelled over 43-44.000 miles and I never knew if it ever did get to Michael.

This is the mileage my gift „travelled"

1---Brisbane (Australia) to Los Angeles via Taipei by plane

2---Los Angeles to Tampa by plane

3---a 7 day cruise on a ship, via Mexico

4---Tampa to Baltimore to New York City to the Niagara Falls to Chicago to Los Angeles by Amtrak train

5---Los Angeles to Las Vegas by Greyhound coach

6---Las Vegas to Los Angeles by Greyhound coach
I had given myself three days in Los Angeles so I could take my „gift" to Michael. However when I rang the person in L.A. who was supposed to organise the Neverland trip for me, it didn't happen.

7---So my „gift" came back to Australia with me.

8---In late May/early June, a fan I knew who lived in Sydney (Australia) was going to Santa Maria, for Michael's trial, so I sent

my „gift" to her. Alas, the trial ended sooner than we thought, so my „gift" was sent back to me.
9---Finally, a fan in Baltimore, organised a project for Michael's birthday in 2005. I contacted this person and sent my „gift" to her.
As we know by the time Michael's birthday came, he was in Bahrain so I don't expect my gift EVER reached him.

I always have a feeling of disappointment when I think back about it all but the distance my „gift" travelled in my effort to get it to Michael at least made it very unique.

by Dawn Trethewey

© ElisabethApfel@gmx.de

© Heike Arbter

© Heike Arbter

© Alex Gernandt

© Miriam Lohr

© Miriam Lohr

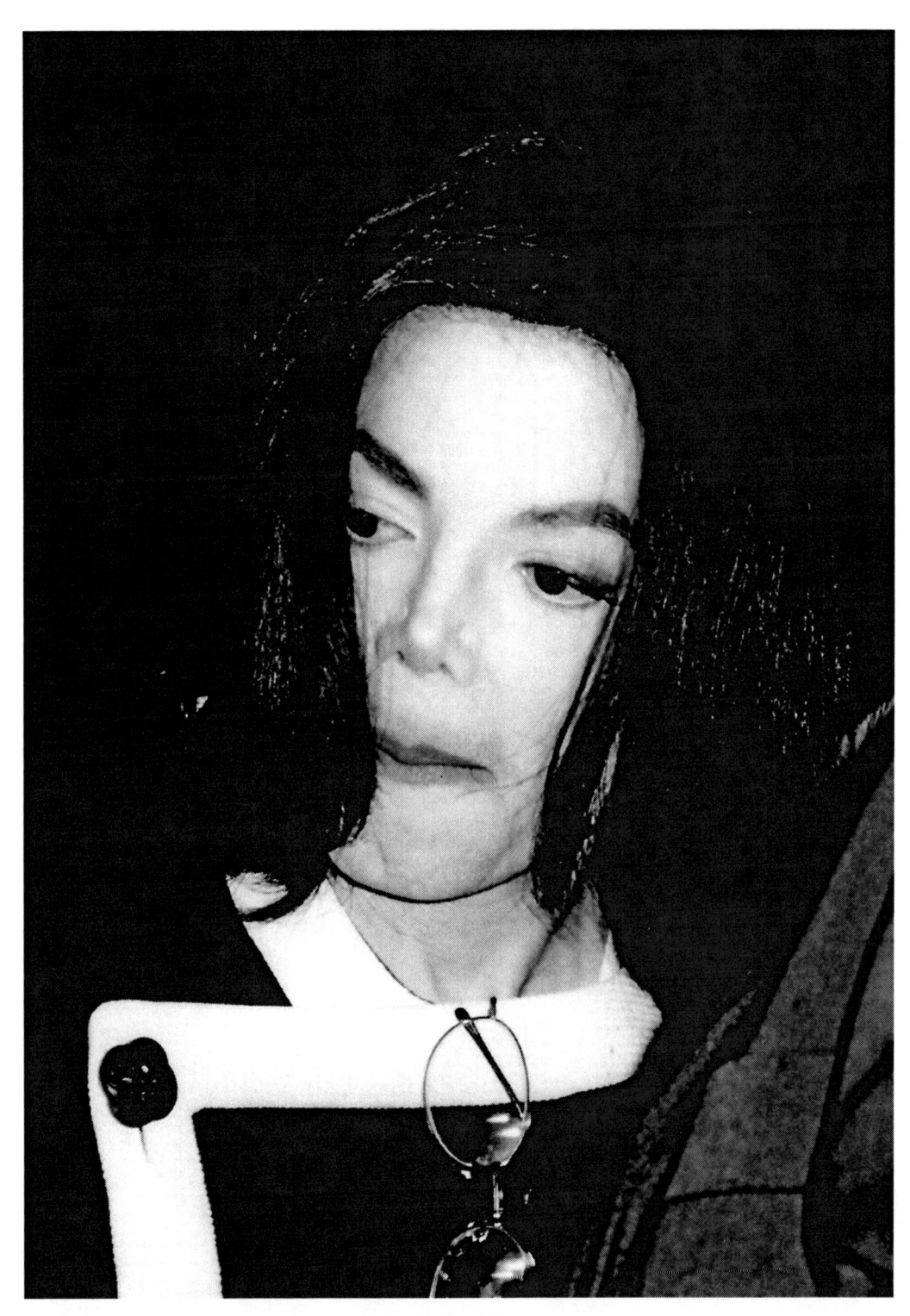

© Miriam Lohr

© ElisabethApfel@gmx.de

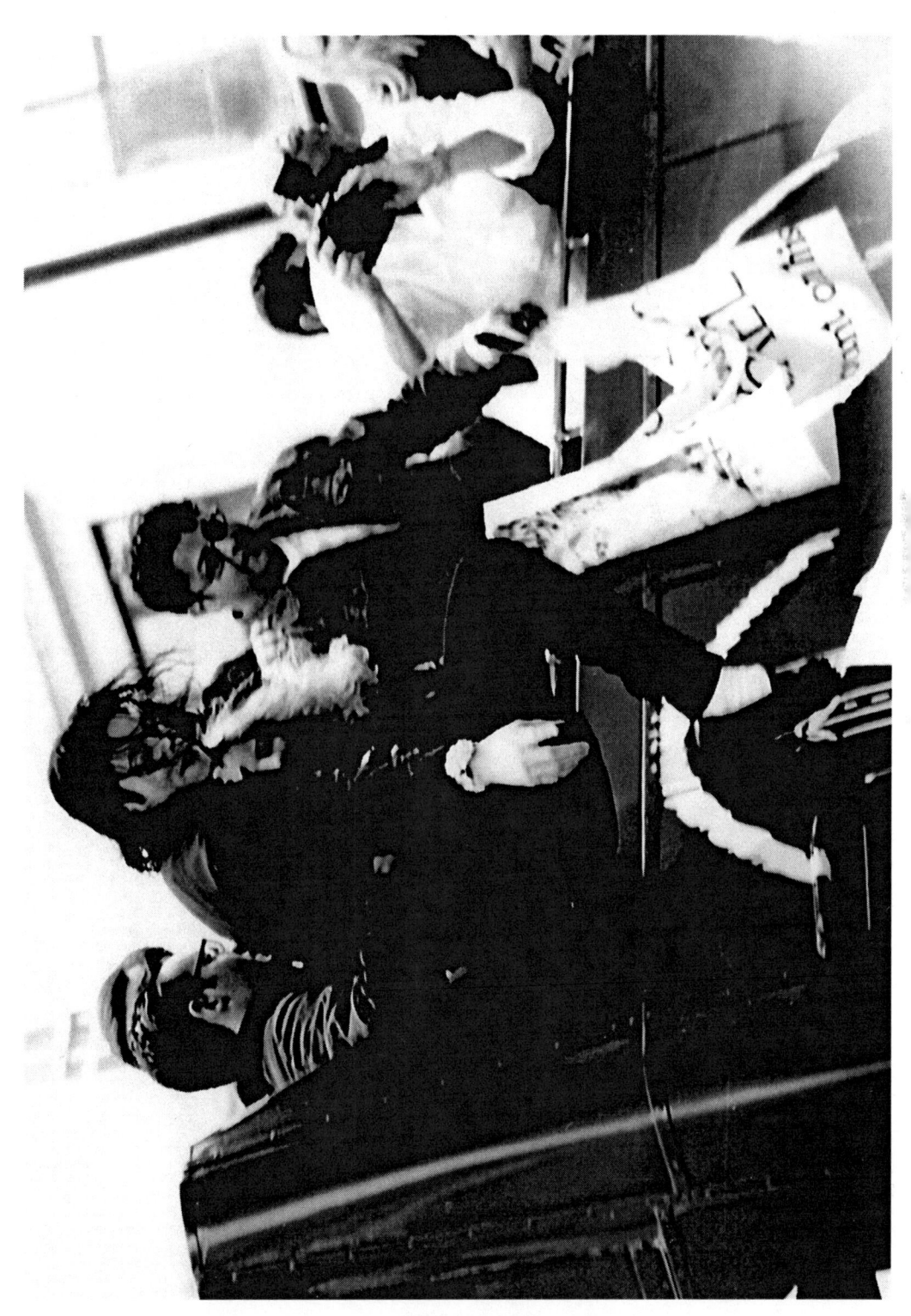

© ElisabethApfel@gmx.de

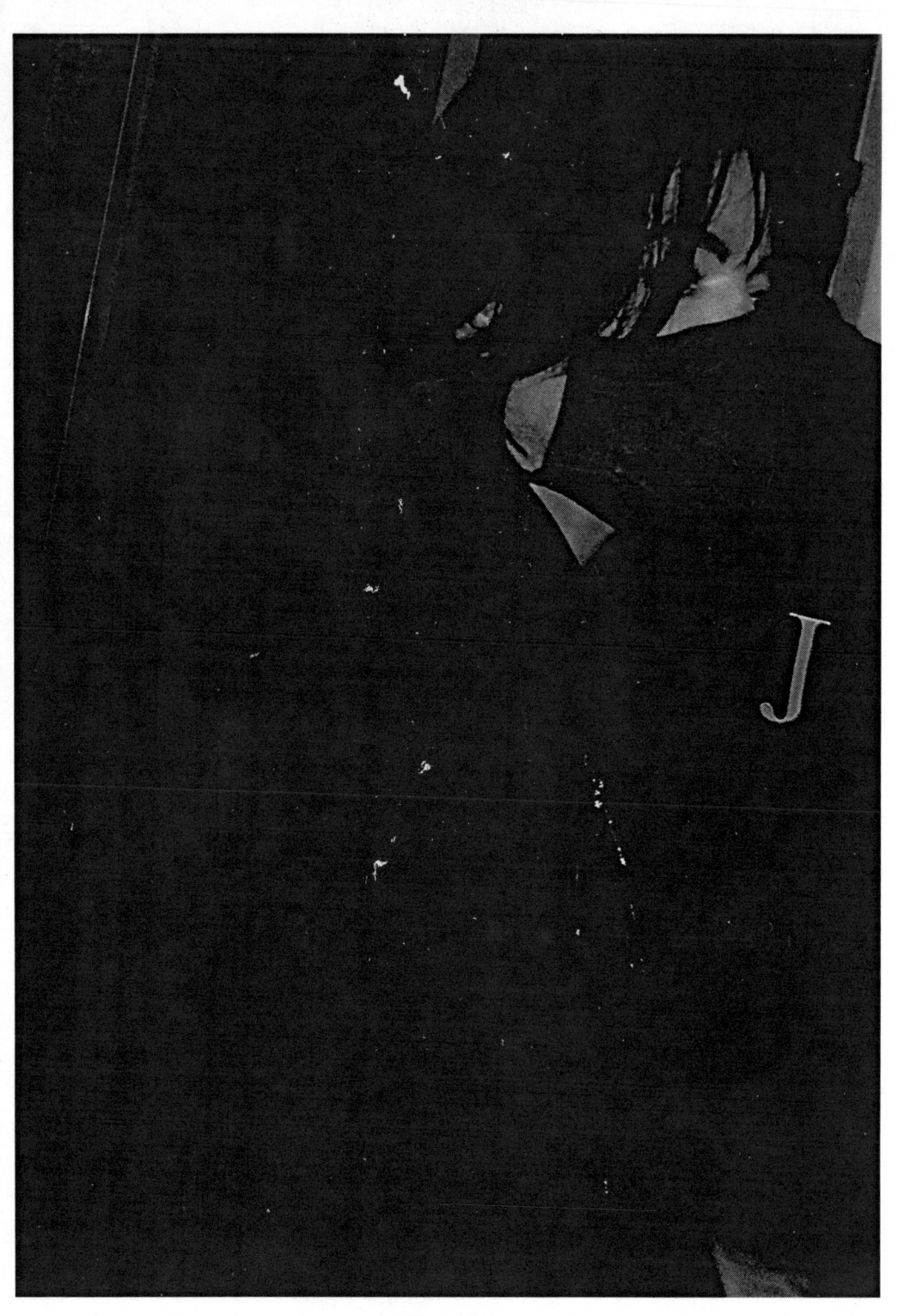

© Kerstin Reinke

© Olaf Haensch

© Anton & Franziska Schleiter

© ElisabethApfel@gmx.de

© Harald Hehmann

© Lisa Hochmuth

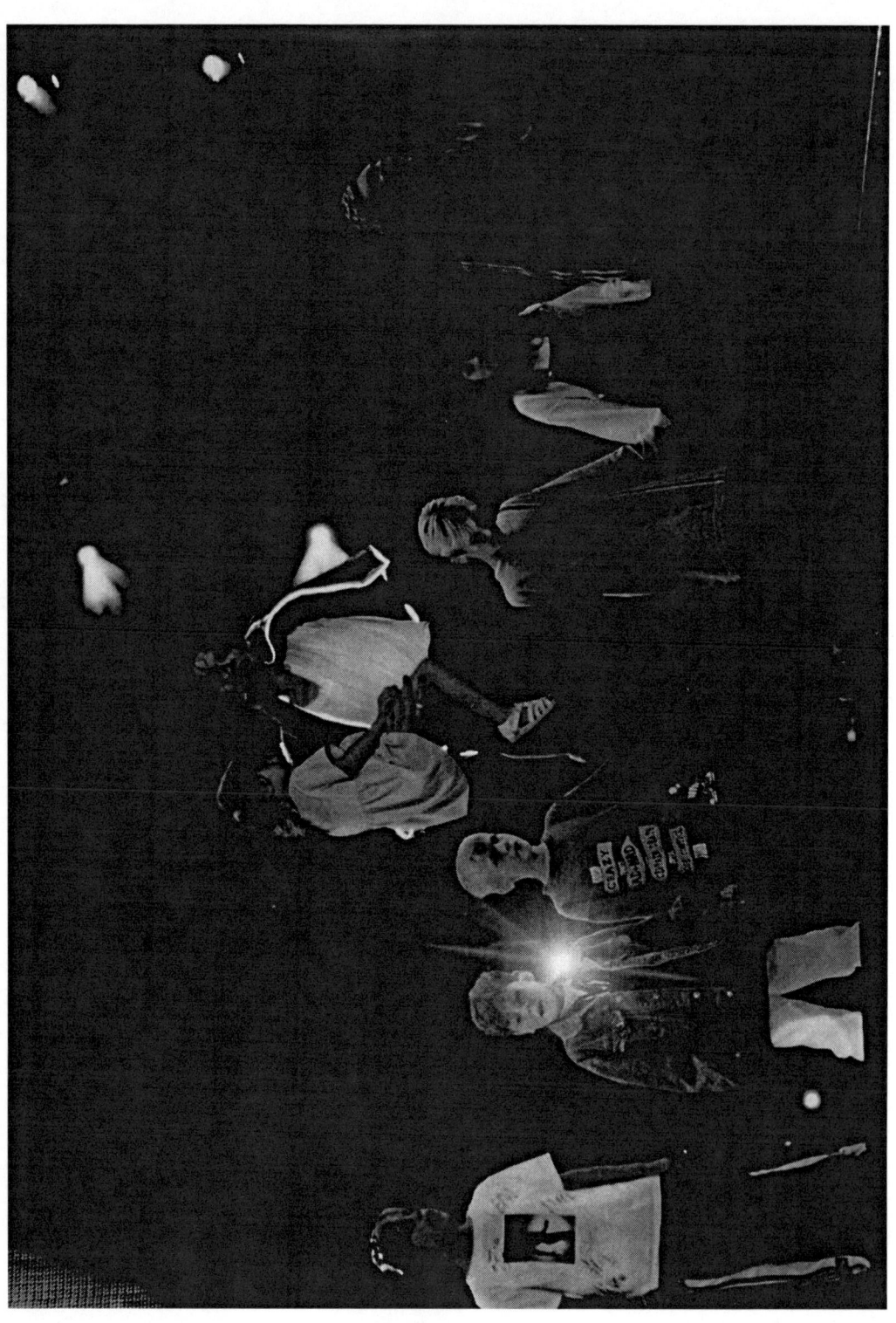

© Harald Hehmann

© Heike Arbter

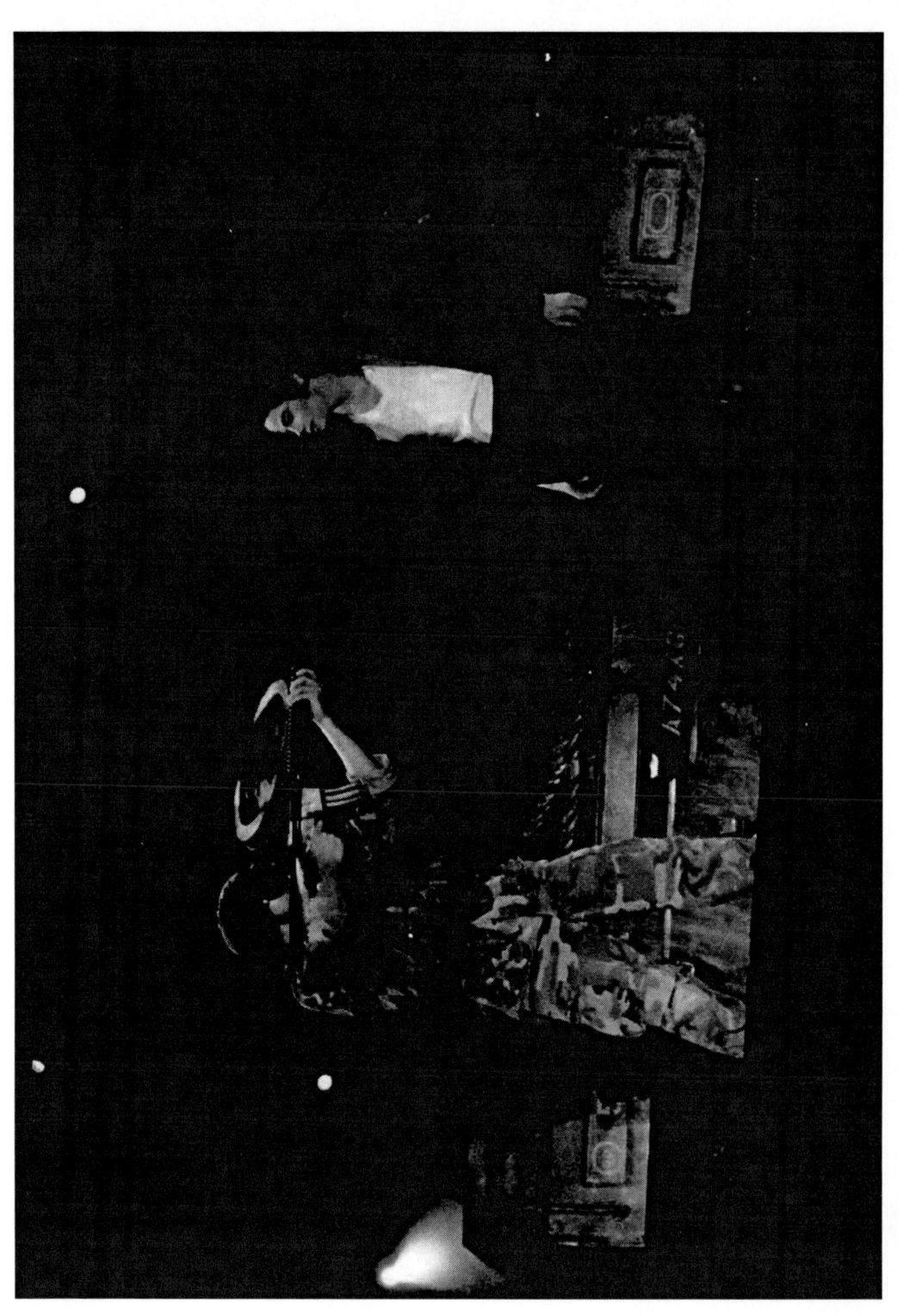

© Harald Hehmann

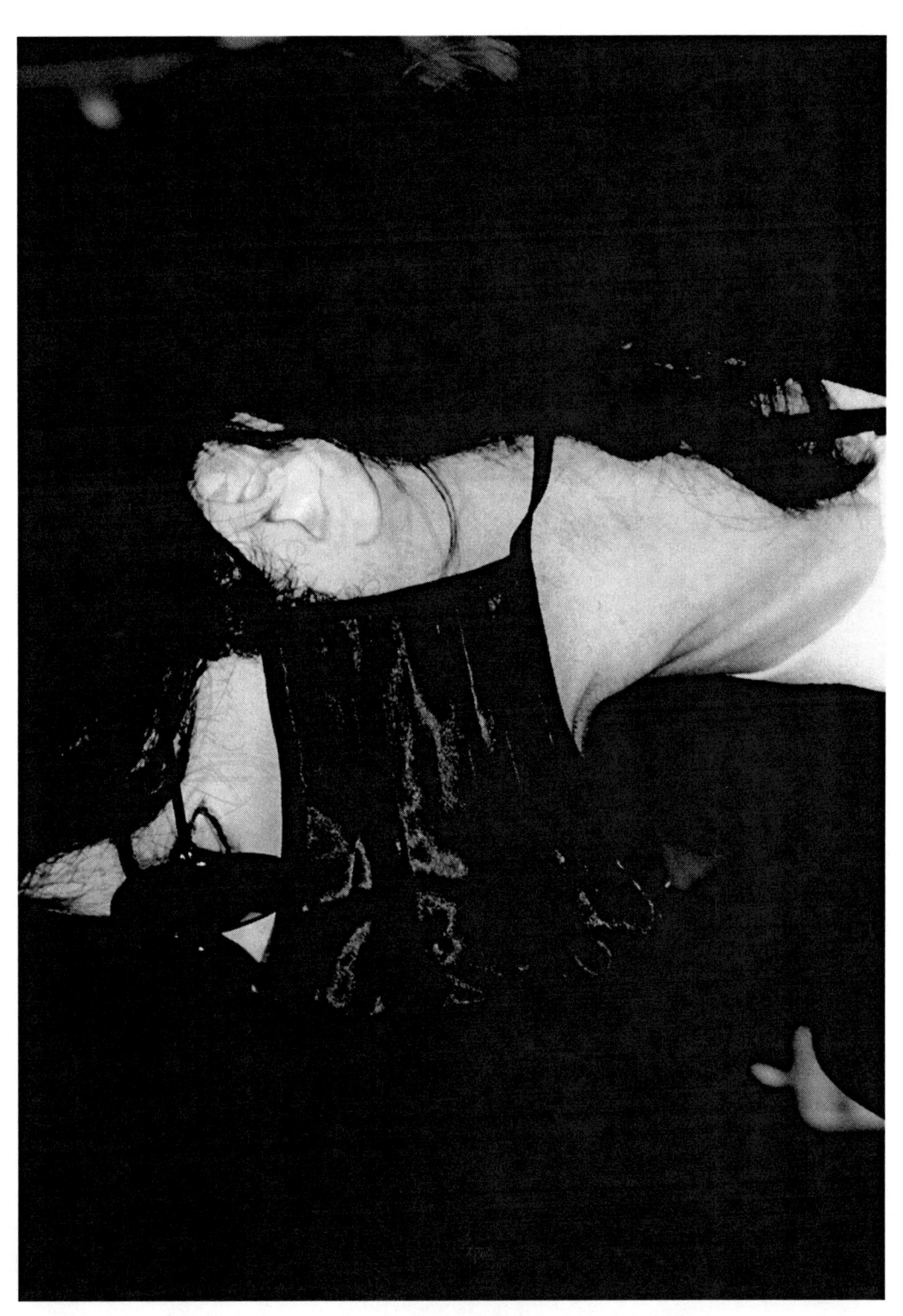

© Miriam Lohr

© Heike Arbter

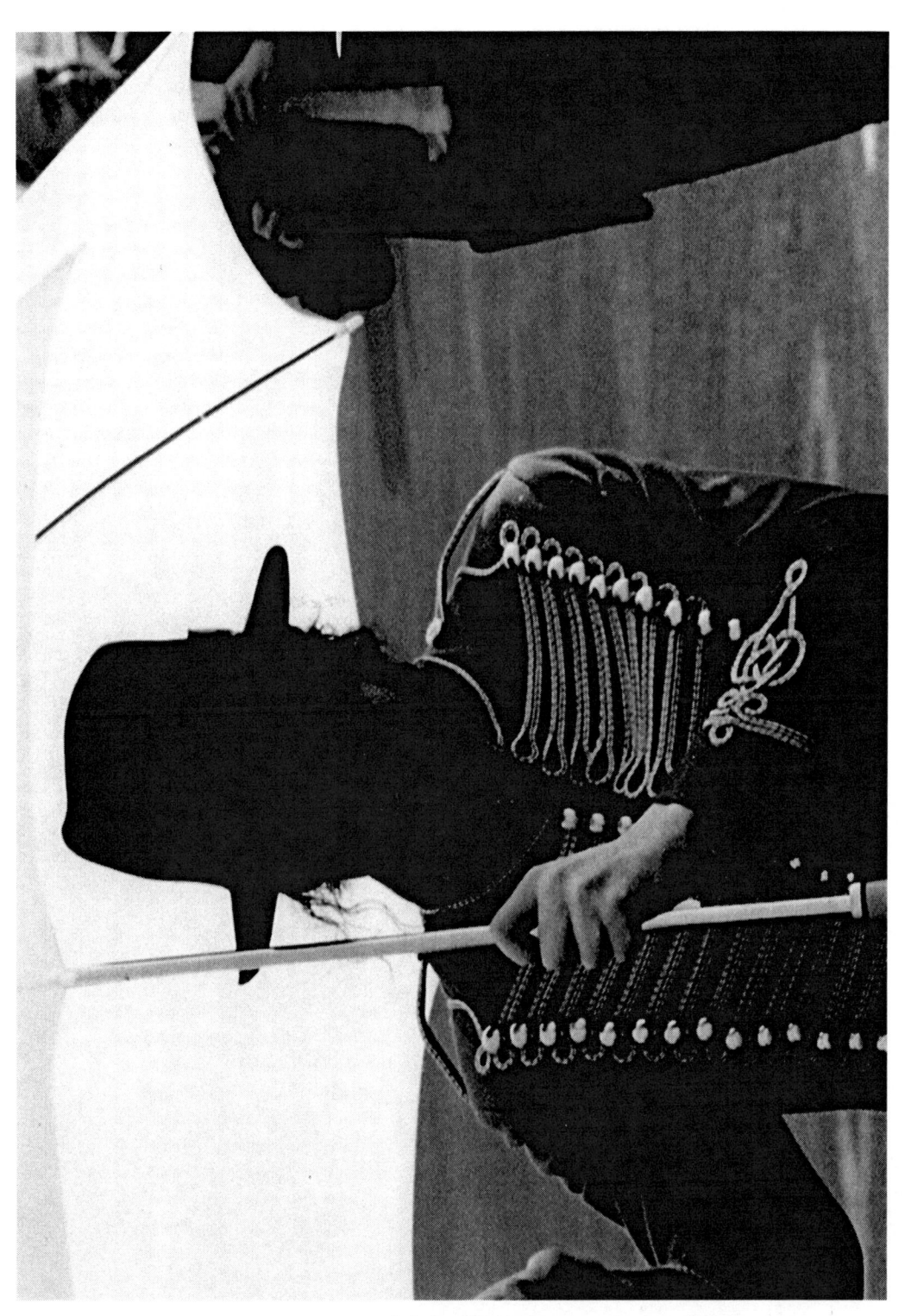

© ElisabethApfel@gmx.de

© Lisa Hochmuth

The "Omni"-experience or "Oh, he's already coming!"

by Sonja Winterholler, Germany

It was August 2004, when me and my friends Gitti and Marina booked our flight from Munich to L.A. to support and see Michael once again. On August 29th his 46th birthday was up to come and we knew that it would be a difficult one for Michael, because it was in the months before his trial (which was only about lies and terrible accusations – as you all know) would start. We had the strong feeling that we had to be there and show him our enduring love and support AND to bring him some birthday gifts from Bavaria!
Arriving at the gates of Neverland was extremely exciting and unbelievably wonderful – each time again.

The days before Michael's birthday nothing special happened. We spent some hot but nice days in the sun watching cows and squirrels, talking and playing Super Soaker with other European fans and listening carefully to some classical music coming out of Neverland from time to time. We knew Michael was there, that was the most important thing for the moment.

Then, THE day had come – it was August 29th. More and more fans from different countries and states arrived at Neverland to celebrate Michael's birthday together and maybe also together with Michael... We had a really good time on and next to the street; we danced, sang and blew birthday balloons, but unfortunately there was no sign of Michael. Hours and hours passed by and all we saw were some unidentified cars and a huge cement mixer driving in. Whatever that meant. We finally concluded, that Michael just wanted to be with his kids on this special day and that they for sure enjoyed theirselves in Neverland... Yes, it was totally okay that he didn't show up or something... It was HIS day, not ours...

Oh boy – why didn't he tell some guards to pick up the birthday presents for him at least???!!! He hopefully knew that we and the presents were here! Hmm, maybe tomorrow.

On the next day our disappointment was all gone – new day, new hope! Again, we and about 30 other fans had some fun in the sun by playing more or less silly games and listening to music in our cars. At this point I have to mention that we didn't always and only listen to Michael's music, for our repertoire was quite big. Our CD-Player had to play The Rocky Horror Picture Show Soundtrack, Bavarian Brass music, a Best of Elvis and some more interesting stuff... We had the tiny feeling that some of the other fans reacted a little bit irritated by some of the tracks that loudly boomed out of our car, what was really funny for us to see.

After a while, a white pickup appeared inside of Neverland. It was the security guards' car that moved towards the gate. Two guards got off and asked us, if we had anything for Mr. Jackson that they could give to him... Of course! At once, everybody ran to a car and after a minute came back smiling brightly and carrying a small (or even large) parcel, a painting, a letter or card, some flowers or something else for Michael. Yeah, finally, we were able to give him our presents! After stacking everything onto the pickup, the guards drove back into Neverland and disappeared behind the tiny hills... All of us were totally satisfied and imagined Michael unwrapping our presents...

Suddenly, we saw another white pickup inside of Neverland

by Sonja Winterholler

slowly driving along the street coming closer and closer… Oh, who is in there??? At once everybody was silent and watched that car, when it stopped at the gate. The gate opened, the car drove onto the driveway and stopped again. In between all of the fans had realized that Michael was not in the car, but who was it? Then, the driver's door opened and out of the car came – a cook. Yes, a cook with one of these big white cooking hats on his head. How funny! The cook walked towards us and said: "I have some icecream and soda for you. It's a present from Mr. Jackson to say thank you for the wonderful gifts!"

Oh, that was soooo sweet of Michael!!! And it was a very prompt reaction, so we guessed that he had already pre-planned it.
Everyone of us happily chose one icecream and a can of soda. I think, I had Ginger Ale and a very watery icecream, but it nevertheless tasted great and somehow also very special. We told the cook to thank Michael on our behalf and to wish him a belated Happy Birthday from all his fans! The cook smiled and nodded. Then, he drove back into the ranch and also disappeared behind the hills.

We felt so happy and went to our car eating the rest of our icecreams. Now, after all that excitement, it was time for us to relax. We laid back in our seats, put our feet on the top of the open car doors and turned on Limp Bizkit's "Rolin'" – very loudly.
While laying there, another car inside Neverland leaped into view. It was a very big white limousine. We watched its approach, but didn't react at all. The only thing we did was to sing along "keep rollin', rollin', rollin'…" and the limousine did. Ha, that was so funny to watch! But, wait! What the heck is this limousine doing there at all?! In the meantime it had stopped a few meters before the gate which was still closed. All the other fans were already waiting in front of the gate, when suddenly Marina shouted: "Maybe we go over there as well!" With these words it hit me at once: Who else if not Michael should sit in such a big limousine that is coming out of Neverland?! Sometimes, our brains were working so slowly…

by Sonja Winterholler

We put our soda cans on the ground, stumbled out of the car and ran to the gate. My heart beat like crazy, when one of the limousine's doors was opened. Kerry, Michael's personal bodyguard at that time, got out and walked towards us. He told us to step back a bit, then the gate opened. Kerry said that Michael would like to meet some of his fans and just a second later, he pointed at three or four people. They should go some steps closer to the car and wait over there. Then, he watched the rest of us again from tip to toe and pointed at another three fans. One of them was Marina, oh my God! But in this very moment, a girl next to her jumped to the group of the chosen fans and that was it. Again, we were too slow to intervene and Kerry also didn't say a word. As he had selected the fans randomly, for him it made no difference which fans were allowed to meet Michael. So, it happened that we were told to go back a little more and the gate was closed again. All we could do now was to watch the small group of six or seven fans meeting Michael. They were allowed to step inside the limousine in groups of two, where they could exchange some words and hugs with him. Oh boy, that was so frustrating! We couldn't even get a glimpse of Michael while the others were talking to him!

After some minutes their meeting time was over, the car door was closed and the gate opened again. The limousine started to move and passed us by, followed by a black SUV full of security guards. Michael opened his window and shortly waved from the distance. In a way that didn't feel fair, because we were only about 30 people, so he easily could have opened the window a bit earlier while passing by slowly... Later we got to know that Michael had his children with him, so he might have acted especially careful. But in this moment we felt a bit dumpish, and at the same time an idea struck our minds. Without saying a word we looked at each other and immediately ran to our car. Marina had already started the engine when Stephanie, a dear friend of us, also arrived at our car. "Willi (her father) went to the grocery ten minutes ago, so I don't have a car! Are you following Michael?" "Yes – jump in!" was our answer. The only problem with that was

234

by Sonja Winterholler

our complete chaos on the forth seat, for we normally didn't need it and therefore used it as depot for all our stuff like food, banners and maps. When Stephanie finally had pushed it all aside, the car was already moving. Half in and half out, she stumbled besides the car until she managed to get in and close the door. Poor Stephanie! Marina sped up leaving behind only a big cloud of dust – well, and our soda cans on the ground. As soon as we came around the next corner of Figueroa Mountain Road, we already caught up with Michael's cars, for our speed was much higher than theirs. Marina had to brake hard to not come too close to the SUV. Our car was a silver Pontiac Grand Prix, a great car with a lot of power!

Alright, we were really chasing Michael – we had never done that before and always thought it was too intrusive to do so, but in this situation it didn't feel wrong and was just exciting. Gitti held our little Bavarian flag out of the window, but after some seconds pulled it back in quickly. At the next crossing, we turned right onto a bigger road that led, as we knew, to the highway 101. At the same crossing another car with some fans from France was already waiting and squeezed in between the SUV and us. That wasn't very nice, but it didn't really matter to be right behind the SUV or not. Then, we realized one more following car. It was a group of two German and one Austrian fan called Claudia, Jochen and Patrick which we knew quite well; we even had their telephone numbers. As we drove onto the 101 we just hoped that Michael was only going to Solvang or maybe Santa Barbara, for we didn't have lots of fuel. We passed by the exit to Solvang and went on and on. We completely switched off the AC to save fuel and Stephanie called Claudia, who was sitting in the other "German car". Oh no, they had the same problem! What should we do?? While talking excitedly somebody had THE idea. Claudia's car should make a stop at the next gas station and then hurry up to catch us while we still would be following Michael. Then, we would make a stop to refuel and catch them again. Ha, what a plan! Michael wouldn't escape us…

by Sonja Winterholler

The Pontiac in front of Neverland

So, Claudia and her friends took the next exit with a gas station sign and we kept on driving behind Michael's limousine, the black SUV and the French fans. After a while, the French fans sped up, changed the lane until they drove right next to Michael's limousine and held a sign against their window. What the hell were they doing? Oh, finally we could read it. The sign said: "We're out of gas!" Then they added their telephone number and seemed to hope that Michael would call them. I don't know if he did…

After that, they changed the lane again, waved to us and took the next exit. We waved back and kept on following with our eyes glued to the fuel indicator. Actually, Gitti and me had a second problem. We had to go to the toilet so badly… Where was Claudia's car? We really needed to refuel! Because of the switched off AC, it got very hot and smelly inside our car and in addition I felt this terrible urge… After some more minutes, we reached the ocean. The sight was beautiful, but there was no way for us to enjoy it. We only thought that now there won't be a gas station for quite a while, for the Pacific Ocean was directly on our right side. We really feared to run out of gas in the middle of the highway, when I discovered a gas station sign at once. It pointed to the left side what confused me a little bit. "Marina! Quickly, to the left lane!" I shouted, when I saw that there indeed existed a left-turn lane. Marina changed to that one as we all realized a tiny space before lots and lots of opposing traffic arrived. "Let's go!" and Marina pushed the throttle. With a rush of adrenalin we reached the gas station. We still couldn't believe that we just had turned left on a highway, but it was all legal! While Marina ran to the cash desk, I started to refuel the car, Gitti hurried to the only restroom and Stephanie called Claudia to tell her that we had to leave the highway. After the tank was full I also ran towards the restroom, but it was still occupied. Oh no, there was no time left! When Gitti came out of the toilet, the four of us jumped back into our car and sped up. To get back onto the highway, we had to risk another left turn over the multi-laned street. And then, we really had to hurry, for we didn't know where Michael's cars went. Claudia's car didn't catch up with them by now, but she promised

by Sonja Winterholler

to call us as soon as she did. The traffic became really heavy as we came closer to Los Angeles, so it was very difficult to pass. But thanks to Marina and our Pontiac, we managed to do so – one car after the other. Long minutes elapsed and with each minute a piece of our hope to find Michael vanished. We already thought about giving up, when suddenly Stephanie's mobile rang. "We've got him! We're still on the 101!"

All our hope came back and Marina pushed on again. A little while later, Stephanie was still on the phone with Claudia, we found out that we must be right behind them, for we could read the same road signs. And, yes! Only a few cars and one big truck separated us. Again, we managed to pass them and at the very moment when we had reached Claudia's car, the limousine and the SUV started to blink right and took the exit to Downtown L.A. Wow, that was close. It would have been much more difficult to find them there! We followed the cars over some crossings and around some corners until the limousine and the SUV blinked to the right again. We had reached the gateway to a basement garage of a hotel. Luckily we immediately found something like two parking spots on the street (I think it was a "no parking"-area) so we could get out of our cars and placed ourselves at the upper end of the gateway. I still had that urgent need to locate a restroom, but I somehow managed to ignore that. The limousine drove down the gateway and then - got stuck in the corner. Ha! It was just way too long! After Kerry had talked to the inside of the car, apparently Michael, one back door opened and Michael followed by his kids got out of the car. Unfortunately, some press photographers already stood next to us, so Michael just waved and smiled shortly and then disappeared into the garage. But hey, he had realized us anyway! Of course, we also had waved to him with the biggest grins on our faces. Now we finally had seen Michael! He wore black trousers and a red shirt as well as dark sun glasses and he looked quite relaxed.

Okay, we knew that Michael went into this hotel – it was the "Omni Los Angeles", a five star luxury hotel. Well, that didn't

by Sonja Winterholler

matter at all, for I was sure to find restrooms in there! So we went inside, still wearing flip-flops and the sweaty shirts from our "un-air-conditioned" journey. Oh boy, I finally could go to the toilet – what a relief! After that and after trying to bring out the best in us in front of the mirror, we went outside again to park our cars somewhere legal. Then, our plan was to "check" the hotel, which means to have a look around and see where the different entrances are and maybe also to find Michael's windows – if he actually had booked a room. Therefore we split into two groups.

Claudia, Patrick and Jochen should go back inside to find out anything like which floor the suites are located or whatever... Marina, Gitti, Stephanie and I wanted to walk around the building and have a look on that. But Claudia and the two men didn't dare to walk around in this elegant building, so we changed the groups' destinations. We certainly didn't look more fashionable at all and I don't know why, but at this moment we simply walked in pretending to be interested in a room or something. Marina was talking with a concierge about the costs and the availability of rooms, when at once a woman passed by that looked very familiar to us. "Look, there is La Toya! Let's see where she is going to!" Stephanie whispered to Gitti and me.
Marina nicely but abruptly ended her conversation with the interesting information that the restaurant and the piano bar are located in the third floor. La Toya went into an elevator and pressed the "third floor" button. Aha! We took the next elevator doing the same. After getting to the third floor, we barely saw La Toya walking around a corner, and so we took the same direction. Just a second later, we found ourselves standing in the middle of the piano bar, trying to behave inconspicuously. The best idea seemed to be to sit down at the next free table and so we took place right opposite the piano. Although we felt like Sherlock Holmes, we didn't exactly know where La Toya went. The restaurant was attached directly to the bar, but we couldn't see her in there. Oh, then we discovered the other, much more likely possibility where she could have been. There was an extra room next to the piano bar, not very far from our table, whose

by Sonja Winterholler

entrance was covered by a curtain. Our murmur was interrupted by a waitress who wanted to take our order. Gitti instantly ordered a Pina Colada, thinking that this was a bar where one should have a "real" drink. Marina, Stephanie and I just ordered boring Coke. We got our drinks very quickly and still had no clue what to do but sit there and wait for, ehm, maybe La Toya coming out again or whatever. The most important thing was to be cool and relaxed, no matter what. We didn't want to attract attention and so we repeated that we are cool and really belong to all these rich people around us. The piano player started to play and it came up a quite comfortable atmosphere.

After only a few minutes, somebody we knew came around the corner. "Oh, he is already coming!" Gitti stated very relaxed. "Who?" asked Marina, who was the only one sitting in the other direction where you couldn't see the people entering the bar. Gitti, Stephanie and myself responded as cool as a cucumber: "Michael". Marina, of course, didn't believe us and said: "Where?" We answered: "Behind of you." Marina turned to her right, the wrong side, where she still couldn't see him and asked again: "Where??!" In the meantime, Michael had walked on and had nearly reached our table, so we said: "Next to you." We were still very calm and serene and Marina now turned left and caught sight of - Michael! Yes, it was really him! The tiny little problem Marina had in this moment was, that Michael was not just somewhere next to her, but directly – we talk about a distance of 30 centimetres maximum – next to her face. All she saw were his black trousers and when she dared to look up a bit, she caught a glimpse of his red shirt. Marina immediately was very ashamed for looking at him and well, especially his trousers that closely, that she just turned to the other side almost laying on the settee and hiding her face. Michael looked at us and for a moment stopped walking. It seemed like he wasn't sure if he had already seen us before and was now waiting for our reaction. Stephanie even heard him say a gentle "Hi!", but as we had practiced before, all of us kept very calm and said – nothing. Stephanie was looking away just like Marina, Gitti was slurping her Pina Colada and

by Sonja Winterholler

I grinned at him stupidly nodding. Oh no, how could we react that silly! And what a sight for Michael! A little irritated, he walked on and greeted the piano player. They shook hands and exchanged a few words, when suddenly Marina burst out: "Maybe we go over there! Come on!" and the four of us managed to stand up and stumbled over our bags and backpacks towards Michael. Some bodyguards which we hadn't recognized yet, lined up in front of Michael, but we heard him say "It's okay" and so they got out of our way again. We finally stood in front of Michael saying "Hi Michael" with a terribly Bavarian pronunciation (except Stephanie, for she's not from Bavaria). Michael repeated "Hi!" and shook our hands one by one. And then Marina's hand again - and again - and again… While they were shaking hands, one of us said something like "Thank you very much for the icecream and sodas at Neverland!" and he said "Oh, you were at Neverland!" apparently delighted.

All of us stuttered "Yes, yes…" and smiled at him. In between a photographer had made her way into the bar as well and started to push and pull on Gitti and Stephanie in order to get a good shot of Michael. But she didn't count on Gitti and Stephanie who vehement urged her back. In the middle of this little fight, Gitti said to Michael "Munich loves you!", which by the way is her standard sentence connected with Michael. Michael reacted on that and started to talk a lot, beginning with the words "Oh, Munich! ….." None of us understood the following words. That wasn't only our fault, for the piano player had started to play again quite loud. After Michael had finished his sentences, I politely asked "Pardon?" and he repeated everything one more time. Marina and me really tried so hard to understand, we even tried to read his lips, but it didn't work. The piano was just too loud! Gitti only understood the last words "…and all the stuff is from you", which surely was a comment on our birthday presents from Munich. Because none of us dared to ask him again and we all hoped very much that someone else did understand more, we all answered with a quite unsure sounding "Yes!?!". Michael immediately noticed that we didn't have a clue of what he had said and so he sighed and started to talk very slow and clearly: "Okay,

241

by Sonja Winterholler

I wanna see you again!" While saying these words, he reached out his hand and pointed around with splayed fingers at each one of us. When he started to talk we had moved our heads a bit forward trying hard to understand him, but when his hand came towards us, we moved our chests backwards. The way we were standing there now must have looked very funny for him! We were very happy about having understood his words and said: "Yes, we also would love to see you again!" And then, Marina turned around to stand right next to him, pointing at our table and saying to Michael: "Look, we sit right there!" Yes, Michael already knew our table for he had just passed it by, but nevertheless that scene looked very cute! Michael politely looked in the direction of our table replying something like "aha" and then waved good-bye to us. Maybe we also did little moves like waving, but I am not sure about that. I only remember that we slowly walked back to our table and sat down, while Michael and his bodyguards went into that separate room. Oh boy, what did just happen? We couldn't believe it and suddenly noted that we totally forgot to wish him a belated Happy Birthday! Oh no! That was really embarrassing, but on the other hand, Michael had noticed right at the beginning of our "meeting" that we were quite confused and – especially slow. So he might have excused that... hopefully.

After a little while, we noticed that Patrick, Jochen and Claudia still walked around outside the hotel! Stephanie sent a short message to Claudia and some minutes later the three of them joined us. At first they were upset, because we had just met Michael and didn't tell them before, but after we had explained how quickly the whole situation came up, they were calmed down again. And, Michael was still inside that room! He had to come out again at some time.

While we sat there, the piano player asked us to wish for a song. Wow, WE were allowed to choose a song! Of course, we chose one for Michael and wished for "I will always love you". Later on, when being asked again we wished "That's what friends are for". It was a really strange situation to sit there in this elegant piano bar and one member of the Jackson family after the other passed by on their way to the restrooms and back again. There were

by Sonja Winterholler

Michael's parents, Jermaine, Randy, La Toya and Janet. Wow! Jermaine and Randy even stopped at our table asking us if everything is fine... Michael must have told them about that strange group of fans sitting there. And Patrick, who also is a big Janet fan, got the chance to see and talk to her! Again, some time later, the man at the piano started to play "Happy Birthday" and all guests in the bar and also some inside the restaurant sang along. When it came to the line "Happy Birthday dear hmm hmm", no one but us knew the right name! So we nearly screamed "dear Michael" and as a reaction we could hear a very loud laughter coming out of the extra room. That sounded very much like Michael! When the song had come to an end, the piano player announced: "Tonight we have some very special guests..." and we wondered if he really wanted to announce the presence of Michael and his family, when he continued "...from Munich, Germany." What??? Really funny to announce US to be the very special guests, while Michael Jackson, Janet Jackson and many more family members were sitting in a room next to us?!? We didn't know what to think, when the piano player started the German anthem. The situation couldn't become more unreal. We were quite ashamed and just giggled while our faces colored. "This cannot not be reality", I thought all the time, but it was. Later, a big cake was delivered to the extra room and we could hear Michael's laughter from time to time. It was great to see that he was having fun!

At once, all Jacksons except for Michael left the room and walked towards the elevators. We greeted them one last time, but kept on waiting for Michael to come out. We waited and waited, but nothing happened. At some time we paid our bill and also went downstairs, for the extra room seemed to be totally empty. In the hotel lobby we saw two of Michael's bodyguards and innocently stepped beside them. Stephanie could overhear a telephone call, in which Kerry angrily talked with someone working in the basement garage. "It must be there! It is a BIG white limousine!" Oops, they couldn't find Michael's limousine! How could that happen?! We didn't know what to do now, but after standing around and being watched by Michael's bodyguards as well as the personnel

by Sonja Winterholler

of the hotel, we decided to go outside and wait there. Nothing happened. The whole family except for Michael (and his kids) had already left the hotel, so we concluded that he might stay for the night. We thought about staying here or driving back to Buellton near Neverland, where we had a motel to sleep and where we had left all our luggage.

We finally, again, split into two groups. Marina and Claudia drove back to our motel and the rest of us stayed here, in front of the hotel. It already was very late and Marina had to drive for about two and a half hours, but she somehow managed that without falling asleep. Patrick, Jochen, Gitti, Stephanie and me sat in the second car the whole night, watching Michael's black SUV that was parked in front of the hotel. If it moved, we had to watch out. What a night! I think no one of us could sleep at all until the next morning. And still, nothing had happened. Gitti and I had some kind of breakfast by eating our salads that we had left over the day before. We waited for about three more hours until noon, when suddenly the driver got into the SUV. We crossed the street to see where it was going and found it being parked next to a side exit of the hotel. Then the white limousine, that obviously had been found again, was driven directly in front of the exit door, so that Michael would only have a very short way to enter his car.
Unfortunately, these press photographers were also there again and tried to get the best spots around the limousine. And then, one of Michael's guards, I don't remember if it was Kerry, told them to step back. He allowed us, the fans, to stand in the front while the press had to move to the back. Great! That was just amazing!

Gitti and I had some little things for Michael, namely a card on which we thanked him for the meeting in the hotel and also told him that we had wished those two songs for him, as well as a "Calling Michael" CD. "Calling Michael" is a song that fans wrote and recorded for Michael to show their support at that time, when Michael needed it for sure. It is a beautiful song and we had promised the producer to give our best handing it to Michael.

by Sonja Winterholler

And then, Michael came out of the hotel waving and smiling and stepped into his limousine, again followed by his kids. Once inside, he opened one window a bit to shake the fans´ hands. That was our chance to give him the card and the CD. And, yes, we managed it. He took the things immediately thanking us. We also could see Paris and Prince sitting next to their daddy watching us with big and beautiful eyes. They were so cute! And Michael really was in need of a very good vanishing creme, for his hands were so dry. He might have had a good one at home, since his stay at this hotel wasn't planned at all. He also still (or again) wore the same clothes as on the day before. Ha, now he also had to sit around in sweaty clothes, not only we had to! When the limousine started to move, we shouted "We love you!" (Gitti, of course, said "Munich loves you") in Michael's direction and then quickly ran to our car. Patrick, Jochen and Stephanie had also managed to touch Michael's hand and so all of us were really happy. Patrick drove the car and again we followed the limousine and the black SUV. We were not sure, but hoped very much that they would go back to Neverland.

In the meantime, Marina and Claudia who were hoping just the same, had bought some sun flowers as well as some other things to decorate the gate of Neverland. There were still our red hearts put onto the gate, but Marina and Claudia wanted to have some more decoration. Michael should see and enjoy it when coming home – hopefully.
Once we drove onto the highway 101, Stephanie sent Claudia a short message that we and Michael are on our way and we think that it will lead us back to Neverland. "We and Michael"? They weren't sure how to understand that. Were we sitting inside the limousine next to Michael? That would have been great, but later on they saw that we were all sitting in our own car.

After following Michael for a while, we finally got rid of two cars from the press. They were driving very dangerously, just to get close to Michael's limousine. Crazy! About one and a half hour later, we thought about passing Michael to already stand at the

by Sonja Winterholler

gate of Neverland when he would be driving in. But we had a problem – that crappy car! Marina drove the Pontiac and we just had an old Chevrolet... Now we understood quite well, why Claudia and the others took so long to catch up with Michael again the day before. That car didn't speed up at all. So, we crawled onto the left lane and tried to pass by the limousine. Gitti had prepared a sign that said, of course, "Munich loves you" and held it against the window. Finally we had reached the limousine, but the passing process seemed to never end... We waved and smiled to the darkened windows and got more and more embarrassed. Patrick had pushed the throttle to the ground and some looong seconds or even minutes later, we were in front of the limousine. And wow, there already came our exit! We turned right and didn't get our eyes off the limousine until it was sure that it also took that exit. Now, we tried to speed up as much as possible. When we arrived at Neverland, a big smile was glued to all our faces, for we really had managed that journey and went all back safely. Marina and Claudia had just welcomed us and each of us quickly had taken one of the beautiful sun flowers, when Michael already arrived. We held up the flowers as well as our "Munich is here for you" banner and we could see that Michael had already opened his window. When passing by, he completely laid out of that window showing one of his brightest smiles! He looked so happy and gorgeous at that moment, it was just fantastic! Wow, we actually made him smile.

A second later we screamed "Watch out Michael! Your head!", because the limousine had reached the gate which wasn't that wide and Michael could have bumped against the doorside if not watching out. In the last moment he pulled himself back into the car still laughing. He might have been aware of the upcoming gate, but we don't know for sure...

With that little shock our journey to L.A. and back again had ended, but what didn't end yet was our Michael-trip. We didn't really see him anymore until we had to fly back home, but we had the big honour to visit Neverland two times! It was amazing!

by Sonja Winterholler

We could drive with his trains (there was a small and a big one at Neverland), go on all the rides in the amusement park and watch some of Michael's live performances inside his cinema. I especially loved the "Sea Dragon", a big swingboat and the "Spider", a wildly turning carrousel, although me and Marina nearly got sick on it! And there is one thing we are very confident of: He made his sentence "I wanna see you again" true, while watching us in Neverland…

Neverland was so beautiful and I'm unbelievably sad that it doesn't exist like this anymore. The loss of Neverland somehow marked the beginning of the end…

Michael, I want to thank you for all the wonderful experiences and especially my dear friends I got to meet through you! In our hearts you live on forever. I love you, Michael!

by Sonja Winterholler

Neverland gate decorated by Sonja and her friends

Blue Skies, August 29, 2004

by Sandra Mojas, USA

Blue skies on a full moon night.
Mountain peaks sketch a heartbeat
and angle like the high kick of a cheerleader,
as the moon sits on her vanity
reflecting back my own enchantment
and dilated sense of potential.

"Yes Mother, leave the door open a bit"
and revive the luminous child.
Bathed in disneylight, I am myself
again…

My meeting with Michael

by Dagmar Herrmann, Germany

It began in London. To be exact, on the trip from London to Exeter in the Royal Car. There I delivered my parcel on June 14th 2002 to UrI Geller, wrapped in red-roses-wrapping-paper (inspiration by Carla), with all sorts of things and the most important one: my Art Work Book with my painted, drawn and collaged works of art dedicated to Michael.

After an unforgettable stay (Michael „got on the bus") in London I already returned home on Sunday while Michael and many other fans still stayed there. On Monday, I received a call from our dear Claudia, another special thanks to her, who informed me that Michael had sent out his assistant to keep an eye out for a certain Dagmar Herrmann, for me, in front of the hotel „Renaissance".

This way the contact came about between me and Mike, not Michael, but this „loyal Eckhard". I sent photographs of my finished art works for him to view, to find out if they would find favour in the eyes of the „Almighty". In this case I would be welcome to deliver them at the next occasion. Well, I do not want to go as far as to say it was a matter of life and death, but his decision ¬ would certainly influence my fate in a way. After all I was informed that yes, they found their approval and, yes, even Michael himself was very impressed. OH MY GOD!!!

Berlin was the right opportunity, of course! Does anybody have enough fantasy to imagine what was going on inside of me when I started the trip, right by my side the wonderful man in my life for the moral and organizational support as well as two rather big plastic bags, in which the precious pieces, which would hopefully open the door to paradise for me, and which now had to wait patiently for their presentation as well as me, and all the other stuff that you need for such a trip. We arrived at our destination without hurting anybody seriously, including ourselves, all safe and sound.

After Michael and his people had found residence in the hotel Adlon , I contacted Mike after an adequate rest time, who gave me a date in front of the hotel for Wednesday between noon and 2 o'clock, when he would pick up me and my freight. Like everybody that was present knows, it was freezingly cold, and I almost froze off my butt as I waited two and a half hours for admission - in vain. Completely nothing happened until a police loudspeaker exclaimed the catastrophical message for me: "People, you can go home, Michael Jackson has just left the hotel through the back exit."

I lost all hope, an almost frozen off fingertip was only a tiny little problem. I threw myself into a taxi and drove back to my hotel, trudged up the stairs with lead in the legs, fell onto the bed and cried, cried cried. The world ended!!!!

Nevertheless there was still this wondrous human being, the real existing patron of Daggi, who with touching and encouraging words again raised me up and basically ordered me to call the „true Eckhard" Mike via the hotel phone to ask once again why they had stood me up. Everything was good! Michael simply wanted to visit the Berlin Zoo with his two elder kids as long as it was still daylight outside and so he was now there next to the monkeys and giraffes, but had by no means forgotten DaggI with her paintings.

So, have another go. Come to the same place within the next half hour. Since I didn't want to expose my endangered fingertip to further cold influences, on my arrival at the hotel I directly

by Dagmar Herrmann

asked a hotel employee for the reception clerk, to whom I had already described my awkward situation when Michael zoomed off without telling a word to me or to the others. This guy, a helpful human being, gave me the permission to wait for Mike in the foyer.

Ha ha, folks, actually the whole story gets much too long, if I also tell you, how it has been in the lounge. Man, woman, children, simply fabulous!!! Hey, one can certainly understand, why the rich men and prominent persons do not want to appertain to the primitive miserable people with small earnings. Therefore, the cappuccino costs 6 Euros, but that was worth the thing, too. It came with several delicacies, that one commonly refers to as cookies; and this waiter that I directly confronted with the fact that this is not my price range, didn't grimace, not even batted an eyelash, a real pro. Afterwards he even bestowed me with an understanding smile, I almost felt as if I belonged there. *g*

However, you certainly don't want to know all these details. Let's get to the main thing. And now it gets celebratory and my heart feels strange. I have to take a small break to wipe away my tears.

It only took a short while, then I saw Mike coming up to me. "Hi, Dagmar", he pronounced the "Dagmar" simply perfectly. "Hi, Mike." "Do you have your paintings?" What a question! In between quickly a few words regarding my state of mind. You will not believe it, after all the excitement and the supposed catastrophic disappointment I had been very calm, totally calm, as if I had at least taken two Valium. Therefore, I did not stumble behind Mike, but went very upright and composed as if I had done that every day, simply delivering two paintings in Michael Jackson's suite.

We went upwards with the lift into the… was it the third floor? We walked along a corridor that now after all, seemed never-ending to me. Some people of the security came in view, so I had no doubt to be right there. Mike carried one of my paintings, „Po

Daggi's painting "Popmozart"

pmozart", into the suite; when I unpacked it and gave it to him, he said: „Wow". That, of course, felt good to me and then I had to wait again. Yes, still outside on the corridor. How would you have born that? And it lasted at least a quarter of an hour.

In the meantime bodyguards and hotel personnel passed me by, once I saw Karen Faye coming out of Michael's room, and I heard loud laughing and screaming children. "These are not ours", a bodyguard said. Therefore, I combined, other children were still in the suite, which was the right assumption. Suddenly, the door opened and a German couple came out with two very fair children. They passed me by as if they had seen the Christ-child and perhaps they really had. Later it turned out, that it was the Wolf family from Meissen, victims of the flood catastrophe in Eastern Germany.

Well, now it was my turn. Mike beckoned me to come closer. After I entered the suite, I had to wait again in a kind of anteroom, where I could already catch a glimpse into one of the rooms. There was Michael's jacket, which I always call the wandering preacher jacket, casually flung onto a table. Suddenly, from next door, wonderfully intoned sounds of a piano could be heard, at first something classical, baroque, and after that I guessed Gershwin. I was surprised and wondered, whether Michael can play the piano so brilliantly. I still don't know up to now, although I had intended to ask, but it didn't come to this. Suddenly a sweet midget with highly raised head marched past and gave me only a glimpse after my „Hi", before he put his fair small head through the door into the hall. There he was immediately shooed away by Mike and was sent back into the room. Well, you can already guess it, it was nobody else but Prince, the heir to the throne - and I had made no formal curtsey. ;)

Until now I had heard no word from Michael, several voices spoke and the children romped aloud, laughed and shouted with a man that obviously played some wild game with them, but whose voice was not Michael's. But suddenly, my heart almost stopped

by Dagmar Herrmann

beating, I heard him speaking with Mike. Unfortunately, it was impossible for me to understand what it was all about. Perhaps my senses somehow didn't function correctly anymore. But then, it obviously was a question about me: "Whom do you have next for me, Mike?" It sounded a little resigned and Mike answered: "Now comes the artist!"

Goodness gracious! Mike opened the door and by nodding he made me understand that I should enter. THE BIG MOMENT!

The room I entered was the bedroom! I would gladly have turned around again and left, because seldom I have felt so wrong, so invading, so stamping into the real privacy of another person. I realized that so sudden that it hampered my step. I stood rooted to the ground. On my right, in front of the bed, Prince and Paris played with a man with building bricks or something like that. I could absorb everything with an enormous clarity, the children are delightful, like dolls, so pretty to look at.

The room lay in dim light, the curtains were closed, the nightstand lamps as well as some other indirect light was on and Michael rested on the bed in half-seated position. He wore a pyjamas top or house jacket, anyway, it was red and black striped. I managed to move some steps closer to him, so that I could at least lean my bags with the paintings against the bedposts. Now I stood there again, SPEECHLESS. Okay, yes, I believe that I had said „Hello" when entering, but that was it. He looked at me with a searching look, searching, yes, he just looked, neither friendly nor unfriendly. But I returned his look, still silently. Then he helped me out of this kind of awkward situation when he raised the hands for the Indian greeting. What a relief, I answered him in the same way and at the same time I bowed deeply.

Now the ice was broken. After initial difficulties with the English language, I said: "my name is…", "shall I call you Mr. Jackson or ..?", and Michael very nicely answered: "Say Michael". I talked about how I came here, about London, the art work book,

by Dagmar Herrmann

Daggi's dedication to Mike, Michael's bodyguard who helped her meet Michael

"Cool!" Michael screamed when he saw this artwork

"you have chosen theses works, now I am here to deliver them..." blahblah. The „Po pmozart" painting was next to him on the double bed and I said: "You have already seen it". I then explained what I want to express with it, "to compare you with the genius Mozart on the field of pop music". He said, already more lively: "Oh, thank you." I continued to tell him more about it. He asked: "Oil or acryl?" –"Oil". Then: "May I show you the next one?" –"Of course!" He said that with an emphatic accentuation, what was already much better. My heart made a small hop! Oh my God, I now must unpack the piece, considering 60 x 70 cm, from the plastic bag and it was also wrapped in wrapping paper - rip-rip - throwing the paper on the ground. While doing that I could wonderfully take a look at Michael's feet in white, ribbed socks and his totally wore out slippers. lol

Done. I held the painting in front of his really well-shaped, although, like everyone knows, very slim nose, nevertheless everything hunky-dory. And now, I still can't believe it, he straightened up in the bed vertically and gave an enthusiastic „COOL!", „Invincible", Michael murmured; that's what the painting is called, it says „Invincible - Michael in Knight's Armour".
Curious and apparently encouraged by the emotion of his „employer" (?), the ominous man, who was sitting on the ground with the children so far, now also raised and started to praise me: "Great, wonderful! How long did you work on it?" And I answered truthfully: "Four months on both." Yes, you hardly believe it, but nothing at all could shake me in this moment.

Fortunately, while unwrapping my updated Art work books came back into my mind. I got them out saying, "one is for you and please give me an autograph on the other" -"of course". Michael pulled out his marker and started to write elegantly, then paused and asked: "What is your name?" Okay, I had already said it, but I thought that this time, I make it a little easier and said: "Please write simply DAGGI". He wrote, raised his head and said "Dawgi?" (like "saw"), "no, Daggi, D a g g i". We have tried it two or three times in phonetic language, he even placed the finger to

by Dagmar Herrmann

the larynx while saying "oh" and to the breastbone while saying "ah" in order to find out the correct sound (that was somehow worthy to make a movie about it, but so sweet that he tried so hard), but at that time the little accident had already happened. I saw it only later, Michael now renamed me to "Dawwgi". Now, that is the way it is written on my Art Work Book for all times: "Love Michael Jackson to Dawwgi", sweet, isn't it?

The presentation of my paintings, because of which I had initially been granted the audience, was actually finished. Now I still should get rid of my missions, but the situation was simply too intimate and delicate. So it was impossible to bother Michael with some complaints or wishes that other ones had given me to pass on, especially since Mike had told me at the beginning: "Only some minutes". Those were gone for a long time, if I still could judge that at all; I already mentioned the loss of my senses…

I still managed to stutter whether I may unpack a couple of gifts. With these words I gave him the video-cassette of Mirko with some explanatory words. Then I asked if I could put my small presents, "chocolates for the kids" and a Praline box in gold paper and with a blue organza bow "especially for the Lady, who is caring for your children", onto the bedside table. "Oh yes, of course, thank you, that's so sweet, so sweet." He really said this all the time while I was stacking the stuff there.

Now, the moment of saying good-bye had come for me. I had not even touched him and just wanted to sneak off discreetly, stepping back one or two steps without turning around - just like you proceed with real kings, when something incredible happened, which I didn't expect anymore. He arose in an incomparable kind and manner. I'm wondering all the time, in which video clip or where else I had already observed him doing this movement. He almost floated from his resting place in a way I have never seen a human being to stand up and … hugged me. (Now it's all up with me. Drying tears…)

This embrace was not fleetingly, but tender. Indescribably homely warm - I can't express it in words any better - and he smelled as good as honey or honey cake. I don't know how else to describe it. And I always thought I would be taller than him, but we were

258

by Dagmar Herrmann

Michael, your are my inspiration
Look at the result

art work dedicated to Michael Jackson
the greatest pop artist of all times and one of the warmheartest human being on this planet
done by Daggi and others

Daggi's artbook with Michael's dedication renaming her to "Dawwgi"

almost cheek to cheek and I whispered: "Michael, we love you, we never leave you."
You must be satisfied with this, because it is just impossible to describe it in words. Then I left the room the normal way, namely grabbing my bags, slipping the paper into the hands of the dear, good spirited Mike, turning my back on Michael and leaving the room while the delighting kids called after me in unison: "You're beautiful, you're wonderful, incredible, we love you so" (a chanting the fans continuously started to sing under Michael's hotel window). I still managed to turn into their direction, to do the peace sign and call back: "I love you, too." With that, the "audience" was brought to an end and I was in real life again.
The wonderful, polite Mike said to me: "Thank you, Dagmar." I do not know how I arrived downstairs again, anyway, I went out of the hotel and looked into the faces of the waiting crowd - it was like a dream.

by Dagmar Herrmann

Make that change

by Hoda Karamzadeh, Sweden

Ever since my mother was pregnant with me during the war I was kicking in her stomach to his music. My parents probably knew how healing music could be for us. I'm originally Persian, we moved to Sweden when I was only three since my mother's family lived in Gothenburg and some of them in Vienna since the 70s.

One of my brother's first birthday gifts in Sweden was the Thriller LP. The album was and still is a true ambassador of what pop music can be. Michael Jackson and his music truly made me believe in magic, his love was magical, everything he did and everything about him was magical. I can proudly say I have been one of his biggest fans all my life.

One of my best memories is from his "HIStory Tour" in Gothenburg, Sweden which was the greatest. Some of my friends had been sleeping outside the stadium for days so they could be in the front row. One friend actually came all the way from England. I remember when he started to sing "Heal the world", some of my friends looked at each other and said: "This was our dying wish - to see Michael perform live right in front of us!" What a feeling, he is the King of all Kings. I said: "I bet he is still going to have concerts 10 years from now and we are all going to have front row tickets to all of them!"

Well, I was wrong! A tragic in-door fire disaster took place on the 29th of October, 1998 at a discotheque in Gothenburg. Nearly 400 youths attending a Halloween party were inside the building when the fire started, killing 63 people and another 213 were injured. More than 50 sustained serious and life altering injuries. Many of my real close friends died in that fire. Some of them were MJ's biggest fans; they were those friends standing in front of me at the HIStory concert.

During that period I started to listen to every word Michael had to say and I listened to his music 24/7 because it was so healing for me. I was thankful for being ok and that one of my brothers, who also was at that party, was ok, too. My brother had lost almost all of his best friends since they were the people who organized the whole thing.

We all had one thing in common: the beautiful message Michael gave us through his music that changed our lives. He truly changed my life, he made me become a better person through his messages. He made me open my eyes so I could see how people were suffering and all I wanted to do ever since was to help. I started to donate money and my time to some charities. I even wrote letters to companies so they could participate in helping children who were suffering. I started to help lonely child refugees by bringing them gifts and giving them my time. Well, I know I could have done much more, that is why from now on I will try to get as many as possible involved in charity work a great start will be to donate gifts to children's hospitals.

I really looked forward to see Michael perform again after so long. His upcoming "This is it" tour with front row tickets was the only thing I had on my mind.
The sad part now is that I'm on my way to London, not to fulfill one of my dreams, but for paying tribute to a true king that I have looked up to all my life on the day that was supposed to be his birthday. I can at least wish and hope that one day maybe I could meet his family or children so I could explain how much their beloved son, brother or father meant to me and what an inspiration his humanitarian work was.

I am so proud that I had the privilege to grow up with Michael's music. He tried in enormous ways to help heal this world, he was an international icon and a great humanitarian. I can only imagine how great this world would be if we all tried to imitate his good work. There is one thing that can still bring a smile on my face, it is that I know he is Moonwalking for the angels now.

by Hoda Karamzadehw

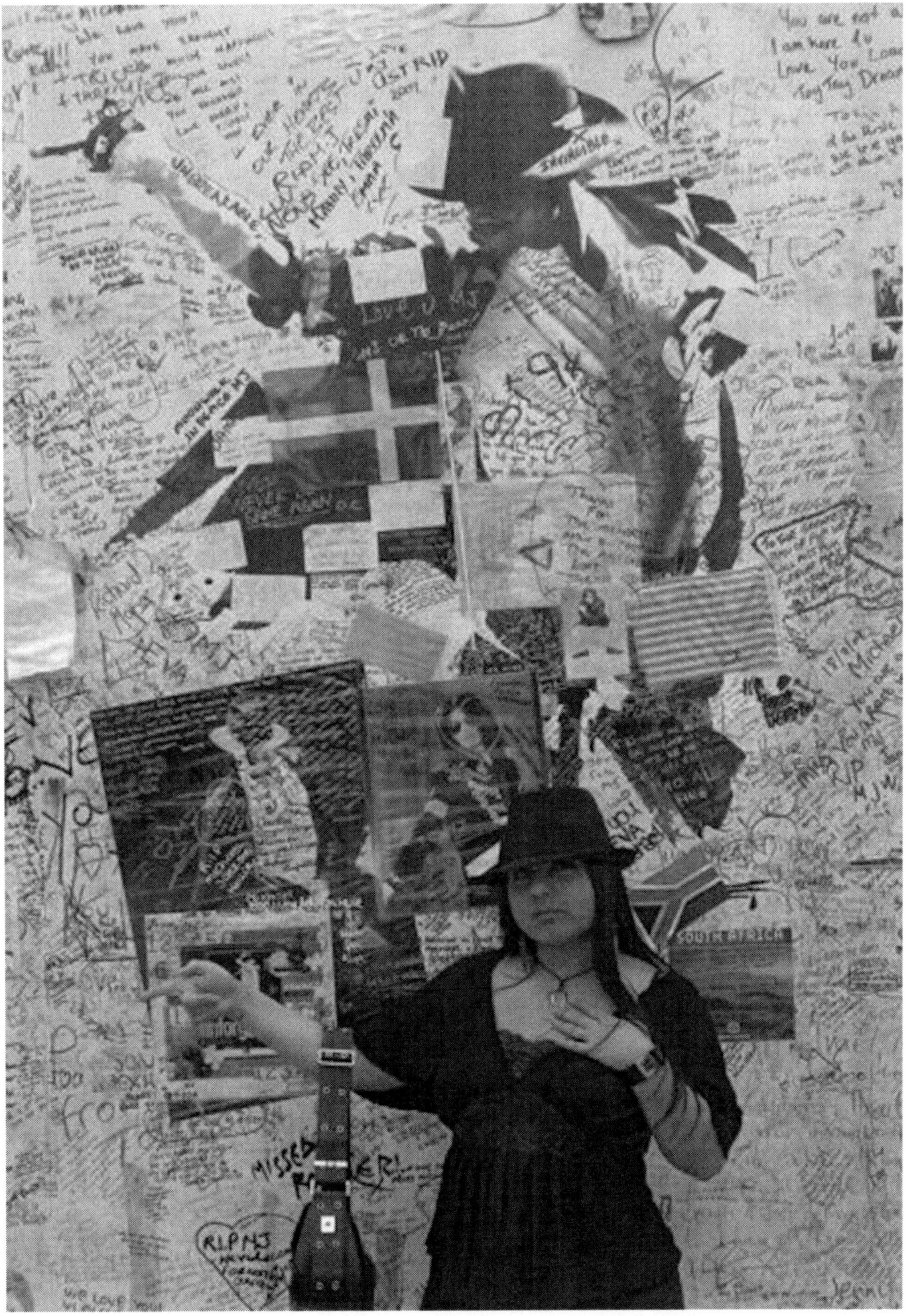
R.I.P MJ

American Bandstand 50th Anniversary

by Marjorie De-Faria, USA

Place: Pasadena's Civic Auditorium
Host: Dick Clark
Date: April 20th 2002

I had my bags packed and everything was ready to go by 7:30 that evening, Friday, the 19th. My mind was racing and the anxiety levels in me were pretty high. Driving to Pasadena would only be an hour's drive; just waiting for everyone else to turn up was making me nervous.
Finally everyone showed up as scheduled and finally we were on our way to see the "King of Pop".
To ease my nervous tension I put on the radio station to Dick Clark's oldies but goodies just to get us all in the mood for the show.

The evening was warm, and we had the windows open and we were singing our lungs out to the tunes playing on the station. Nancy and Anne were in the back seat singing to the Jackson-Five's "ABC." They were singing so loud that the car next to us began looking at us strangely, causing us to laugh.
It was as if we all had entered into a time machine where we could once again be teenagers having fun without a care in the world.
Driving late in the afternoon wasn't bad, considering Los Angeles traffic. We by- passed all the working crowd and made it there by 11 pm. Everyone was really tired, so we hit the hotel, showered and all went to bed.
Saturday started out rather cloudy, but it wasn't long before the sun came out and the day warmed up nicely.

I was rather tired, all night long the body wanted to sleep but the mind was on Michael Jackson mode. We got up, got dressed and set out to find the Pasadena Civic Auditorium. Finding it wasn't all that bad, but knowing exactly which entrance to go to was, as there were many other functions going on that morning.

Security was pretty much everywhere and I asked which entrance was the one for the American Bandstand show. The guard rather chuckled. I asked him „what's so funny?" "Oh," he said, "nothing," and pointed to the other side of the stadium. Now I saw why he was laughing, fifty fans had already been camping out and eating some breakfast, chatting with one another and just waiting. This was as early as 8 am I asked one of the girls if they were there for Michael…the group replied YES!

Seeing the crowd, I got an anxiety attack and decided that we all better go back to the motel and get changed. It looked as if the lines would get bigger if we waited any longer. We were gone only an hour when already the crowd had increased to around seventy-five more new people. The young man who was the page told us we had to get in the back of the line. There were fans from China, Mexico, Japan, USA, Spain and even Sweden lining up everywhere.
It was now about noon, and it was warmer, like around 90 degrees, too early for summer like weather and most of us wore black and wished now we didn't, because the sun was baking us.
There were plenty of Cher's fans lining up as well, but fans of Michael's outnumbered Cher's.

None of us had any doubts about the show being cancelled, as some fans knew that Michael would definitely be there, as if they had some inner connection with him. For me this was a whole new experience.
In the very front was the group of fans from France. One of them came over to us and said: "Michael Jackson will be arriving soon and we are trying to gather up as many fans as we can to show him our support. He would really like this. So would any of you

by Marjorie De-Faria

like to come with us and do this for Michael?" Who was going to say no to that really? So some of us went with this group while the others maintained our space in line, while we followed these fans to the other side of the auditorium where Michael was to arrive.
Most of us were dressed up in fancy dresses, and we had to run over to the other side of the building. Everyone started running, and in high heels, I hiked up my dress and ran. Believe me I thought I was going to fall flat on my face.

In the meantime, photographers, like hungry buzzards waiting for their meal, were watching us closely, as we all lined up against the mechanical fence. Then all of a sudden they started pulling out banners about Sony and Tommy Motolla. They told us when the cameras start to roll, yell out "Sony sucks" really loud. Some of us didn't think this was nice and we didn't say anything at all. Then the shouting started. "Sony sucks, Sony sucks, Sony sucks".

All of a sudden the head of security came over to us and said, "You are entitled to your opinions, but if this continues we are going to have to tell you to move or you will not be allowed into the show. There is going to be press and lots of publicity," he said, (something I think he shouldn't have said,) "and we don't want this type of stuff going on." We said: "Yes okay, we won't do it." Then he told everyone to put away the banners.

Once we all settled down, and had our gifts in our hands they began taking pictures of us. The leader of the club made sure that I was in the picture. He pulled me right in front with him. We held up our pictures and other gifts for Michael and the camera men snapped with glee.
Within minutes of this, the cars drove up and then Michael stepped out. The fans began screaming and shouting towards Michael: "We love you Michael, we totally support you, Sony sucks!" "Oh God", I said to myself, "I'm going to be arrested or something and end up not seeing the show at all."
But then we caught Michael's attention and he slowly got out of

by Marjorie De-Faria

the car with his bodyguards holding an umbrella over his head. Michael then turned to us and began waving. The photographers had a field day. Michael came a bit closer to us; someone handed him a white poster with children and babies on it, Michael nodding as he accepted it. Michael slowly worked the crowd of fans. And then suddenly he was in front of me. I didn't know what to do, I thought I was dreaming really, as much as I tried to tell myself to keep control, I couldn't. Like a silly girl I began to cry, tears rolling down my cheek, as I reached over and gave him my artwork I had made especially for him. He gladly took it. I reached out my hand to shake his hand, nodding back to him, as if addressing a Royal King. Michael's hand was so huge, it was soft and silk like and it wrapped around my entire hand. Little did I know then, you "don't" shake hands with Michael. You hug Michael. Yet Michael didn't mind.

I wasn't prepared for what was to come next. He pulled me over to him, and he hugged me, and through more tears, I whispered, thank you. He held me tight, and whispered to me: "You should have stayed home, you look very sick." (Let me explain this part. I was just receiving chemotherapy at the time, and my face was pretty swollen, not to mention discolored, and the hot day didn't help out much. This is Michael, concerned and considerate of others feelings above his own.) All I could mutter to him was: "I know, but I will be okay", and thanked him again.

He moved away and I felt good, yet empty without his touch. I was overwhelmed and in disbelief. Me... a silly girl from Boston, who has been dreaming of meeting Michael for eons and never been to any concerts and here I am right in front of him and he held me. Cry...oh my ...the water gates were wide open by now.

Once again the chanting started up. But now Dick Clark had to get Michael out of there and into the center to begin the taping. During that time, I was photographed with Michael, but little did I know then, that unless he took your name, the photos don't get published. An artist friend of mine from the UK tried to buy it from the photographer, but he wouldn't let it go.

by Marjorie De-Faria

Meantime, Michael went back to the restricted area where other dignitaries and press were waiting for him.
I thought to myself, "oh here we go", the security was running towards us. I got really scared. But suddenly the pages loudly announced that they were moving the lines and if we didn't get back in line we'd lose our spaces and won't see the show. As much as I hated to move away from where Michael stood, I didn't want to lose the chance of seeing him perform. I got to meet Michael and I was still in shock and awe.

All of a sudden the crowd dispersed like mad, running in all directions. I had to remove my heels in order to run. One Japanese girl, who was beside me, gave me some socks to put on, she told me to hold up my long dress to my thighs and we both started running. Giggling and laughing as we did.

Then someone shouted: "Oh God, not this way, quick, down the stairs and up the other way." All of us were running and jumping over small gates and down stairs to where the line was. I was laughing so much. Never in a million years did I think I'd be doing this kind of thing and loving every minute of it. I was so afraid I lose my step and fall down the stairs or something worse. By the time the two of us were back to the original lines we were breathing pretty heavily. We rubbed each other's back and drank water to get back to norm. This was the best part of being here. These fans were so warm and friendly and just fantastic to one another regardless of our ages.

It was now 2:30 pm; the lines started moving slowly in the direction towards the security checks. Those fans that brought cameras began ditching them into the bushes and handing their cell phones to their friends to put into their cars, while others stuffed their cell phones down their pants. It was rather comical to view in a way, as pages went up and down screaming: "No cameras, no cell phones, no food are allowed into the auditorium."
Once the lines began moving the French fan clubs began trying to cut in front of us, begging us to please let them in. The security

by Marjorie De-Faria

guards were really beginning to be ticked off and told them flat out: "You either get in the back of the line or get out of here." The French group replied in their language angry, but went towards the back of the line. The minute the security guards left, the girls worked on the pages and some of them got up to the front, the rest had to remain at the back of the line. This was making most of us, who had been waiting a long time, quite angry.

Once we got to the security checks, we found out they weren't all that serious; we went through them rather quickly actually, like cattle we were all herded into another line. No one even checked out our IDs. Groups with mailed passes went to the left. The rest of us with the paper-computerized printed tickets went off to the right. We seemed to have stayed there for quite some time and not going anywhere.
We could hear the music and we all assumed we weren't getting in or were being bumped off to the next show.

Suddenly I got brave and decided to ask one of the pages what exactly was going on. "Oh they're rehearsing; they moved up to the show to 3:30 and the lines will be moving in about 20 minutes." Another ten minutes went by; finally we all began to see movement into the building at last. This was it, the time had come, and we are going to see Michael. Oh my God it's for real. I kept telling the girls I was with to keep pinching me, I thought I was dreaming, and we all giggled.

One page was holding a counter, I thought "oh God, please don't let me be the one who gets bumped off because there's no room". Once I gave my paper ticket to the page I knew I was okay. I heard her say: "Okay, that's it for the bottom floor, now let's start with the balcony." We were just three people away from being separated and being bumped to the balcony.
Running now and not walking, another page told us to quickly find any seat we wanted as long as it was empty. Once again we all start rushing down to isles watching that we didn't hit our heads against cameras or trip over the long electric cords which

by Marjorie De-Faria

were laying precariously all around the floors towards the center of the stage.

The front center rows were filled with the former dancers of American Bandstand. The next two rows D, E, F, and G were filled with The King of Pop Fanatic members.

We sat in row J; people were nice to let us slide into the rows to sit. Many of us were so grateful to be just in and to be able to sit down at last.

It was all so fascinating to me to see. I was like a child who just entered Disneyland. The center stage had the logo "50th Anniversary" off to the right side of the stage, and to the left, a small screen showed clips of the American Bandstand's old shows. Center stage was a large screen showing more old clips like Diana Ross singing "Baby Love", and then Marvin Gaye, but it was silent, you didn't hear the music at all.

Above the entire set was this huge lightening system that looked like a space ship, hanging ominously, occasionally flickering off its lights, like a prop out of the "Alien" movie. To the bottom left and right, smaller lights that first looked like dark miniature space men began slowly coming alive as their leader told them to bend and flip and shine their colors. The lights were blinding white, yellow, pink and blue. The heat from them all was intense, but the sides were even more intensive as they stayed on for some time.

Finally, Dick Clark came out from the right side of the stage and he received a warm ovation. He looked really good, even better than what we've seen on television, still quite the handsome man he always was. With him he carried his infamous white microphone, as he began welcoming us all to the taping.

Mr. Clark explained the taping procedures to us all, when to applause, cut it off and then rise, for Cher, who was the first guest up, "when you hear the director end with the number four I want you all to stand and give her a warm welcome".

Mr. Clark began reading the prompt, this big television screen in which I was sitting in front of, was rolling his script. "Sonny

by Marjorie De-Faria

and Cher were unknowns, but tonight we are going to make history…"

"Let me introduce you to Cher." We all stood up and gave her a standing ovation. She then broke into her song. The audience all clapped and danced, following the beat of her music, as the swirling two cameras, like eagles swung down and through the crowd and over our heads through the entire performance. When she finished, we all gave her another long standing ovation. Dick Clark went over to Cher and they both hugged one another, Cher thanked him and then exited off the stage. There was a break and the stage crew ran busily around the entire set setting back screens up for Michael and checking the pyrotechnics, lighting and other things.

The moment I had been waiting for was about to happen. Dick Clark returned back to the side of the stages and once again explained to us how this performance was going to work. First he said: "We are breaking this into two, as it is very long. So don't worry over not seeing the complete act. Once the tape is spliced together you will be amazed at how they did all this." The producer told Dick Clark to read the prompt again, but this time end with the Cher ovation and begin with Michael's introduction. Dick tried four times to read the darn prompt but kept making mistakes. He started laughing and said, "This isn't even funny enough to put into my Bloopers show."

Once he got it right we were told to do a basic clap, which ended Cher's tape segment and now we were onto Michael. But every time Michael's name was mentioned, there was some girl he kept referring to in a red dress, that he was getting upset with because she would shriek so loud, it ruined the tape. Dick Clark said to let him get through the introduction, and then you all can go berserk all you want. The producer goes: "Everyone get away from the screens."

These were the screens with the logos on them and the stage hands could be seen as shadows, especially when they were taping, and this made the director and Dick Clark angry. "Okay,

271

by Marjorie De-Faria

audience ready, everyone quiet, get off the stage if you don't belong there and roll, one, two, and three" ...and he point to us... "clap ...", we all did it."
Then this girl in red down the front row screamed again before the producer could finish counting. Dick Clark by now was totally pissed off. He said, "Would someone get a straightjacket for that woman, would you?" We all laughed.

Also Dick Clark spotted a cameraman running around near the base of the stage and said, "Hold it, are you one of us? I don't remember seeing you?" The producer told Dick to calm down, that it was one of his people getting extra shots. Dick Clark was being very protective of Michael Jackson. He threw out the "Entertainment Tonight" reporter and camera crew.

Meanwhile we all could see the shadows of Michael and his dancers getting themselves ready on the stage. Loud squeals could now be heard from the front rows. "Hold on now," the director said, as Dick once again began reading the intro of how Michael began his start on his show... "Michael Jackson is my long time friend... he has practically grown up on this show... Now for the moment you've all been waiting for... Michael Jackson!"

The entire auditorium came alive, as fans screamed with sheer excitement, and shouted. „We love you Michael," could be heard throughout the Civic Center. Outcries from the balcony above of love and adoration could also be heard everywhere. Fans began crying all around me: "Oh, Michael, we love you so much." As the music to Dangerous began, its vertebrae began jolting the entire floor; the fans enhanced it more by stomping their feet in the balcony above. The loud beat sent chills throughout my body causing tears to build up in my eyes. Every pulsating note, caused gyrating, screams, and chants of love as Michael flipped his dancer on his back.
He was dressed in a bright red leather looking shirt, black jacket and pants, wearing his infamous spats and fedora, tape on his fingers, giving us the solid stare... divinity in motion is all I can

by Marjorie De-Faria

say. The tears were streaming down my face as I clapped and danced to the beat, watching the dancers orchestrate their dynamic moves across the stage.

The audience even played with him by shouting, "Dangerous", he shouted louder "Dangerous"… about three times, each time getting louder and louder.
The well-choreographed segment was performed with precise movements that brought the crowd to total hysteria.

Then his female dancer dressed in a dagger style body suit, slithered over to the center to antagonize her man, Michael. Michael moved in behind her and began grinding his groin like a smooth criminal, dangerously she tossed one of her daggers down to the sound of broken glass and then a loud boom, a flash and then smoke …sent us all further into adulterer frenzy.

The cameras on either side swooped down across the front and off to the sides and above our heads, sweeping the audience and returning back again. You could hear the cameras snapping, photographers twisting their bodies to get the perfect shot of Michael each time he moved.

The added dimensions of the pyrotechnics enhanced the act and mood. Michael then slipped into a minor moonwalk, twirled around and then flipped his hat out into the audience, grabbed his crotch and tilted his pelvis out and ended with his arm out stretched, striking a pose, and ended the song. We all gave him a wild long-standing ovation for this.
Mike knew he had us all in his grips now and he wasn't going to stop there. He turned to all of us and threw us a kiss and then walked over to Dick Clark and hugged him, telling him he loves him and slowly exited off the stage.

While screams of adoration still could be heard all around, club fans began gathering at the base of the stage with bunches of bouquets of flowers. The pages took them and went back towards

by Marjorie De-Faria

the front of the auditorium, where they went I don't know. Meanwhile, Dick Clark reminded us that if this was up to Michael, he would like to stay and do this all night. A squeal of delight was heard by all in the crowd when he mentioned this. But I didn't want Michael pushing himself, because he had a weak ankle and he was really pushing it. But Michael, being a perfectionist, wanted to do a second segment of the tape. We all screamed and clapped with delight to the sound of this. So there was a fifteen-minute break while the pyrotechnics fixed things and the stage crew cleaned up and set up again.

Michael wasn't quite done with us and the second taping was even better than the first one. More intricate dance steps and it ended with the infamous stage light shining solo on him. The roar of the clapping had Michael standing closer in front of us this time. He seemed so grateful and pleased that we enjoyed his performance. He threw us all kisses, put his two hands together as if in prayer and bowed to us slightly. Once again, he walked slowly to Dick Clark and hugged him, and slowly walked towards the exit. He then turned to us all and waved just one more time before disappearing out towards the side of the stage where some blonde woman was waiting for him. He totally left us all ...speechless! The tremendous support for Michael was just so wonderful by all of the fans and non-fans as well. It was truly unbelievable.

While everyone was leaving for their break, the producer requested those fans that were still in the audience to gather right up front towards the stage so he could get some extra footage of us. He told us to scream and jump and act excited, while showing us Michael's picture. Then once again the side cameras all swung into action getting wide eyeshot of the audience.

Then we all went for our break. The talk and chatter over Michael's performance was heard all throughout the main quad of the auditorium. "Man, I didn't think he could still do these things", " No one can perform as good as Michael, he's a top entertainer", "He's totally amazing, I've never seen him perform

by Marjorie De-Faria

before live, I knew he was good, but man this guy is beyond good. He's out of this world", "No one can say Michael is all washed up, no way, he's got much more tenacity going for him", "He is invincible", "Fantastic."

Dick Clark was seen having a photo shoot with his former dancers from his show. I thought this would be a good time to speak with him about Michael Jackson. So I asked one of his dancers if I could speak with Mr. Clark. So that's when I asked about Michael and how he truly felt about him. Mr. Clark said: "Michael is and always will be my dearest friend. Michael considers me as a father figure, someone to look up to and respect. He is one of the finest entertainers in the business. He learned from the best and is still learning. No one could ever do what Michael Jackson has done over the years. I was so happy he did me the favor of coming tonight and I'm so happy the audience was so responsive to him as well." I thanked him and shook his hand.

I'm so glad to have had the chance to meet with Michael, see him perform and meet with such wonderful people from all over the world. The love was truly there in the audience before the show began and maintained for a long time after the show had ended.

by Marjorie De-Faria

Munich 1998 or Let US entertain YOU

by Brigitte Bloemen, Germany

I'm not really sure what day it was, but it was in the middle of March 1998. I was sitting at home doing some homework for school, as I heard the guy on the radio mentioning Michael Jackson. That caught my attention, just like it had done almost exactly a year before.

On a rainy Sunday afternoon, I was watching TV, when they showed an advertisement for Michael Jackson's HIStory World Tour coming to Germany in the summer of 1997.

Of course I knew that name. Growing up in the late 80s everybody in grade school knew and loved Michael Jackson! Under "Who is your favourite singer?" we all wrote "Maikl Jäksn" (English lessons started not until high school) in each others friend books, my Dad even copied me the BAD MC (yes, we did have music cassettes back then) from our local library.

Of course, I knew the name, but that was basically it. My awareness of Michael Jackson ended after 1990. I loved the BAD album, but didn't know anything else about him, I didn't even know Thriller nor that he had toured the world in 1988/1989. I was only seven years old back then, how could I possibly know about who he was and what he did?

I couldn't. So entering the teenage years I lost sight of him. Hearing his name on TV then was like hearing voices of the past somehow. To be honest, I wasn't even aware at that time that Michael Jackson still lived on the same planet as I do.

Gitti's ticket for the HIStory Tour show in the Olympic Stadium in Munich

Suddenly it HIT me. Wow, would it actually be possible to go and see Michael Jackson live? Next thought was, hell, yes, and I HAVE to get a ticket! In a rush I grabbed the phone and dialled the ticket number they showed on the TV ad. After solving some "worldly" problems I hadn't thought of before calling the number, like being only 16, not having a credit card nor enough money to buy a ticket (well, parents have to be good for one thing, don't they?), I ultimately received the ticket in the mail just three days later.
Sooner than I thought the day arrived, July 4th 1997, Olympic Stadium, Munich, would be the first time I ever saw Michael Jackson.

I couldn't really put into words what I felt during the show, I was simply blown away. The show, his dancing, the music, all that was amazing, nothing I've ever seen before can be compared to that. But what hit me the most was his aura. He was about 40 metres away from me, but still I could feel his energy, his love, his passion, I could feel HIM, the person he was.

After getting that glimpse into this man's soul I desperately needed to know more about this Michael Jackson. Who is he, really? I grabbed every piece of information I could get, I joined a fan club, I bought the Black & White magazines and everything else that contained info or pictures about Michael. Through the wonderment of "penpals" I got to know many other fans from around the world.
I read some fan stories about meeting Michael in several magazines, but never in a million years would I have dreamt about seeing, not to mention meeting, Michael Jackson myself. Maybe, I thought, when he comes on tour again in a few years, maybe, but only maybe, then would be a chance to see him again.

But there it was..., March 1998, the too good to be true message from the radio guy saying Michael Jackson had landed in Munich to visit his friend and tour promoter Marcel Avram.
It was a private visit, but everybody knew he was staying at the

by Brigitte Bloemen

hotel Bayerischer Hof where he had already stayed during his tour a year before.

Although I read about some fans who once met Michael in a hotel or while he did some shopping, I just couldn't imagine something like that happening to me, right here in the city where I live nearby.

Next day, right after school, I took the train to get to Munich. About 20 minutes later, I exited the train at Munich's central station and after another 20 minutes and asking several people for the right way, I finally arrived at my destination, the hotel Bayerischer Hof.

It was 2.30 pm and all looked pretty normal. There were only about five other fans sitting and standing around right across the street from the hotel where there were some nice trees, grass and green benches to sit on. Not knowing anybody, I first sat down on one of the benches a few metres away from the others. I began to wonder why in the first place I had gotten here and what I should do now. I didn't know what would happen, if anything would happen at all nor if Michael was still here or had already left Germany. So, after a while I decided to go and ask one girl who was holding a picture and was quietly screaming "Michael" from time to time. Obviously she was here because of him, so I asked her if Michael was still here and if yes, where was he and if she had seen him already. She immediately showed me the row of windows up on the 4th floor telling me that all those windows "belong" to Michael. Okay, I thought...and now what? She told me she had already seen him at one of the windows. Still, my brain somehow didn't make any connection at all, I simply couldn't imagine just SEEING Michael Jackson at this hotel window here in Munich.

A while later a girl from Munich I knew from writing some letters back and forth with her, arrived. She hugged me and immediately began to talk and talk and talk...soon, others joined in and within an hour I got to know every possible story surrounding Michael and those particular windows at the hotel Bayerischer Hof. Many of the fans had already seen him there in 1997 during the HIStory tour. Despite hearing all those detailed "window-

by Brigitte Bloemen

stories", I still couldn't get a grasp on it, those were normal windows, it is a hotel, people staying there usually have better things to do than look out for fans on the street. I just couldn't paint the picture in my head: Michael Jackson, that legendary artist, the King of Pop, waving out of a normal hotel window.

Meanwhile we were about 15 fans, and it turned out, I didn't have to paint anything anymore in my head, because the next moment the picture was real. While all others were screaming, I could only stand there and look up at the windows with my mouth open. There he really was. You could see a white t-shirt, a black hat and black mask, all hiding behind the white curtain. So, some might say you couldn't really see ANYTHING, but we all knew it was him. Why? You could just FEEL it. Even though I had only seen him once before on stage and he was about 30 metres away hiding himself behind the curtains, I just knew it was him. I could feel that incredible aura again, such a warmth and feeling of familiarity. It was magical in a way. I felt this bond, this happiness, this love that you normally only feel for people you are very close to, your family and good friends. At the same time it was more intense, it really felt like love at first sight, but not like a physical love, more like a spiritual love, I could feel his soul. Never before and never after, have I felt anything like that. At that moment there was nothing else in the world, it felt like the world had stopped turning and it seemed like forever to me. In reality he waved and was gone again ten seconds later. I felt like I needed a pinch. But there was no time for that for there he was again, this time without the mask. You could see his smile through the curtain and him having fun waving at us. This time I managed to not only stare open-mouthed, but also scream "Michael! I love you!" He smiled again, waved once more, closed the window and disappeared back into the room.

My brain jumped in again and I remember thinking, why would a person like Michael Jackson want to wave out of his window to US? I'm sure he has many other things to do, important things and there is nothing in it for him, so WHY is he taking the time to

by Brigitte Bloemen

do that? We are just wet and freezing, non-important school kids staring and screaming at him while he is privately staying in his hotel room, so why should he care about us? Why isn't he mad at us for disturbing his privacy, but instead was happily smiling and waving at us?

My head packed with all those strange thoughts and feelings, I had to leave early in the evening to get back home by train and bus. So, I said goodbye to the other fans. "See you tomorrow". Although nobody knew if Michael would still be here, I planned to come to the hotel again after school the next day. I just had to.

Well…it turned out to become my daily ritual for the next two weeks.

Being younger, I was 17 then, you adapt so fast to new things. After a few days, it became kind of normality to be at the hotel every day, to see the other fans, get to know new people, to talk, have fun, make new banners for Michael and of course see Michael every day. Not a day passed that I didn't see him at the window. It was daily routine. Normally Michael didn't "do" anything, meaning of course at the windows, until early afternoon. So, the timing was perfect, school in the morning, then rushing to the hotel to see Michael. And at the weekends I was there all day long. It began to feel like a second home with all the other fans you knew and had a good time with. Who cared that we often froze our hands off, stood in the snow or rain for hours only to see a hand. It was all so worth it. Sad thing is nobody understood it, parents or school friends made fun of me telling me how stupid it is to spend weeks like that. The only ones who felt the same were the other fans. So, we initially bonded, sharing the same love for Michael, having the same irrational thinking, being crazy and loving every minute of it. It all seemed as if it was bound to happen, like it was simply meant to be. It was all matching so perfectly, like it has been put together on purpose, Michael and the fans, that immediate feeling of happiness, friendship and knowing.

It would be a whole book on its own to write every detail that

by Brigitte Bloemen

happened every day while Michael was in Munich in March 1998, but I'll mention a few of my most memorable moments.

Like most other fans that were there, I first had to "evolve" so to speak. From the first three or four days I only remember seeing him at the window in various clothing's, shapes, sizes or shadows. And every time someone or something moved at one window I just screamed, I couldn't help it, it all was still too unreal and I guess letting it all out by screaming helped me to realize it and somehow hold and remember that moment.

The fear that all this magic could be over any day remained, but after a while most of the fans slowed down a little, realizing this is real and he might stay here a while, so we should just enjoy each moment and not spoil it with screaming.
From now on, most of us waved and smiled back, held up some banners, pictures, cards or letters when Michael came to the window. When the window was open we also quietly shouted "We love you!" or began to sing for him.

"I just called to say I love you", the old Stevie Wonder classic and many other songs were changed as we saw fit to sing them to Michael. "We just came to say we love you, we just came to say how much we care".

He immediately liked the singing a lot better than the screaming.
One afternoon, two days before Michael left Munich, we started singing a lot of his songs the best we could. Well it didn't sound too good and the clapping to "Billie Jean" was a bit out of the actual beat, but Michael seemed to like it or was amused by it. Either way, he was sitting at the window for about an hour listening to us singing his songs. So here we were, WE performing for HIM in front of a hotel. Could it get any more surreal? In any case, we ALL had so much fun doing this together. Michael also filmed us one time from his window and was on the phone quite some time, every once in a while holding the phone out of

by Brigitte Bloemen

Michael doing window games
Pictures by Elisabeth Apfel (ElisabethApfel@gmx.de)

the window to let the person on the other end of the line hear our performance, too. Later we got to know he was talking to Debbie Rowe in California who was highly pregnant with Paris back then.

We basically communicated all the time, Michael wrote signs and held them out the window, saying "I LOVE YOU" or "GOOD NIGHT", he sent down bodyguards to collect gifts or banners for him, he made evening "light shows" for us every once in a while (light out/on/out/on), he even showed his little son Prince at the window a few times who also waved down at us. He threw out all kinds of things, messages he wrote on pillows, cloth, autographs, he even threw out a blanket once and wrote on it "keep warm" and bathrobes to stop us from freezing at night. It was like friends who cared for each other. He didn't have to care about us, but he did.

It seemed we made him happy for a while, seemed he liked being entertained by us.

We all knew the tabloid press is making up stories a lot of times and Michael was their favourite target, so one day a fan brought a banner saying "Stop filthy press" which Michael got and held out of the window a few times. We, in return, screamed "F+'* the press, Michael is the best!" to which Michael always held his fist up to show us his consent.

Michael also loved it when the streetcar that was passing by right in front of his windows got right between him and us. Some fans were so focused looking up to his windows that they didn't notice the streetcar coming and once it stood directly next to them as the streetcar driver rang his bell. You can imagine what a shock that was to us every time again and again. Of course Michael was laughing like crazy every time that happened.

One day I will never forget was Friday, March 27th 1998. Since it was weekend, I was allowed to stay at the hotel longer at night. It was quiet that evening, Michael only waved one or two times, but it wasn't raining and everybody had fun talking amongst

by Brigitte Bloemen

Michael communicating with the fans via banners and balloons

each other, eating, writing a letter, just doing the things you do while waiting in front of Michael's hotel. It was already dark, as around 6.30 pm the wooden door to the right side of the hotel's main entrance opened and a few men stepped out. It took a while until some of the fans got a closer look and recognized Michael amongst those men, who turned out to be his three bodyguards. It was pretty hard to see all that since it was dark and everyone was dressed in black, including Michael who also wore his black hat, mask and sunglasses. They walked a short distance on the pavement in front of the hotel until they were surrounded by fans and bypassing people, all in all about 35 people. Despite the pushing that was going on, Michael stayed very calm and polite to everyone. Pictures were taken and Michael signed a few autographs and took some letters. After approximately 10 minutes, the bodyguards pushed Michael along with some fans back inside the door they had just come out.

I don't know why, but two other fans and me just looked at each other the second Michael disappeared and ran as fast as we could through the opposite side entrance of the hotel. I remember running through the whole hotel lobby right between the guests waiting at the check-in and a group of dressed up girls and boys who had their dance school ball that evening. After getting through that crowd, we came to the stairway leading up to the suites where Michael was staying in. There he still was, standing on the maybe 8th step of the stairs. Beneath him his three bodyguards, Wayne, Skipper and the one with the greyish hair whose name I forgot. In front of the stairway about 15 fans.

Again, Michael very calmly and openly took gifts and signed pictures and cards people gave him. I had a Black & White magazine with me, in it that cute picture of him holding little baby Prince. I took out the magazine and gave it to Skipper, he passed it on to Michael who looked at the picture and smiled under his mask (you could see that from the side since the lower part of the mask was loose). After he signed it, Wayne got a little confused not knowing whom the picture belonged to. I said, it's mine, it's mine,

by Brigitte Bloemen

Michael meeting fans on the staircase of the Bayerischer Hof

but for some reason he didn't believe me, I don't know why. After a little screaming Skipper finally turned around, took it and I got my signed picture back. I was so relieved. I shouted "thank you" towards Michael who looked at me, or at least in my direction (couldn't see it with his glasses on) and gave me a thumb up. The next minute, two girls and a little boy were allowed to go up to Michael and hug him and got autographs, too. They also talked to him for a few seconds.

Finally, after another ten minutes, Michael moved upwards very slowly, putting his hands up, pressed together to gesture a thank you. We all shouted "We love you" and "Thank you" once more and then he slowly moved up the stairs. As he started moving we all applauded and started to shout "F+#* the press, Michael is the best" again. Michael looked at us once more, approved it by nodding and blowing kisses. You could see him walk up all the stairs, while he kept on waving down and holding his thumb up.

After he disappeared, we all stood there a while not realizing what had just happened.

When some hotel personnel asked us to leave, we continued our staring, talking, smiling or crying outside, in front of this now so familiar hotel. Every once in a while somebody screamed a "Thank you" up towards THE windows.

We tried hard to comprehend what we all just witnessed; HE came down to meet us. Why? We didn't know. Thinking about it was just overwhelming. Michael must feel such a huge love for people, especially his fans that he wanted to say hi personally, say thank you and give some love back. He not only appreciated us being there the whole two weeks, he seemed to need it, the love the fans showed him. Just amazing.

While thinking about all that, it became really late. Who watches the time after something like that just happened anyway. So, I missed my last train home.

Luckily, one friend living in Munich offered me to stay at hers the night, so I called my parents at home who agreed to let me stay overnight.

It must already have been 2 or 3 am that night, only about five

by Brigitte Bloemen

fans were still there, when suddenly a window opened and a towel flew out on the street. I don't recall the full text, but one sentence Michael wrote was "See you at the circus tomorrow, Good night".
Bewildered why Michael did tell us that, but assuming he wanted us to go there, otherwise he wouldn't have told us in the first place, we shouted up to the windows asking "Which circus, Michael?" After a few shouts he opened the window, only to close it again after a few seconds of waving and smiling. Then he turned out the light. Okay, that was the sign he wanted to sleep, well, so did we, but how should we know which circus Michael meant and when would he go there?
All those questions in mind we couldn't sleep a minute that night. So after talking and trying to figure out what he meant, we went back to his hotel around 8 am

On the way we grabbed something to eat from McDonalds, take away of course. We really were in a panic to miss something at the hotel, as always.
Eating our bagel, it suddenly came to us: the only permanent circus in Munich is the "Zirkus Krone". It has a long history and is one of the oldest and biggest circuses in Europe. It seemed obvious Michael meant this circus. We went to a ticket shop and checked the playtimes of "Zirkus Krone" this Saturday. They had two shows, one in the afternoon at 3 pm, the other one at 8 pm in the evening. So, now the question was to which show Michael would go, IF he actually meant that circus which we didn't know for sure.
Back at the hotel, we met a few other fans and talked with them about the "circus problem". Once the clock showed 2.30 pm, there was still no sign of Michael leaving or doing anything else. We had to make a decision though, if we wanted to arrive in time for the afternoon show at the circus. A moment later we jumped into a taxi and drove to the circus. Arriving there around 2.50 pm we ran towards a doorman and asked if Michael Jackson was already here. He just stared at us, laughed and gestured as if we were nuts to ask such a thing. It seemed he wasn't here yet. The

by Brigitte Bloemen

show should start in five minutes, still no sign of Michael's vans. Nevertheless, spontaneously, we bought tickets and went inside. The circus started. We looked around trying to find Michael hiding somewhere. After a while we made out one person sitting in the third row wearing a hat. We could only see him from behind. We talked forth and back and finally we were sure: This had to be Michael! We were already planning how to get down there, to get a little closer to him, when finally a light went on and a group of people rushed down the stairs about two blocks left from where we were seated. We could see the bodyguards, a few kids and Michael. So, what about our infamous hat-wearer in row number three? Well, "he" turned out to be an old woman.

As usual, Michael came too late, we should have expected that. They seated him with his entourage in a box reserved for the circus owners and special guests about 30 metres left of our seats. The whole circus now was watching him, people were talking and yelling and taking pictures. We ran down a few stairs to be as close as possible, waved, screamed "We love you" and blew kisses like crazy, until we noticed the whole circus was now watching us. As the whole audience was calming down again we went back to our seats as well. We couldn't stop watching Michael, though, who was wearing his hat and a mask, no glasses this time. He looked over to our side and waved back a few times. After another few minutes and the constant bids for silence from the circus' "ringmaster", the show finally resumed. But that was only until Michael lifted a cloth and unveiled his little baby son Prince. He was sitting on his lap and sucked peacefully on his bottle. Now the whole circus applauded the little Prince. Finally the audience' attention shifted towards the show again. I couldn't tell what went on at the show the first minutes, I was too busy staring at Michael. But I do remember some great trapeze artists, whom Michael applauded enthusiastically. Since Michael came so late, the show lasted only about another 20 minutes until the break, in which he was pushed outside again. We didn't follow. Later we heard he went to a private room where he talked and took photos with the circus owners. After the break, Michael, you might have

by Brigitte Bloemen

1. PLATZ

KRONE Der Circus, den die ganze Welt kennt

1. PLATZ
unnumeriert

28.

00586

März 1998
Nachmittag

Samstag 28. März
NACHMITTAG 15.00 Uhr

Keine Haftung für Personen- und Sachschäden.
Ton-, Film- und Videoaufnahmen nicht gestattet.

Fronhofer, Regensburg

Michael enjoying Circus Krone

guessed it, came back in a bit late. The show act with the lions had already begun. The noise caused by Michael re-entering the circus made the lions pretty nervous, they were jumping against the fence and roaring angrily. The trainer even had to leave the cage for a moment. They asked the audience to quiet down again, so that the show could continue without anyone being eaten.
To make a long story short, Michael enjoyed the show, as did we.
Right before the finale we headed towards the main exit where we saw Michael walk by, back to his van, a few minutes later.
Back at the hotel we shared the circus experience with some other fans that had just arrived.

At that time I didn't fully realize it, but there were so many fans travelling to Munich during these weeks to see Michael from all over the world, it was incredible. I saw people from England, Holland, France, Czech Republic, Austria, Switzerland, Spain, Italy and many other countries there.
That is probably one of the most awesome of Michael's many achievements, bringing together the most diverse people from different countries, religions, skin colours or ages. All joined in this common sense of love, his love.

Two days later, Michael left Munich to fly back to California, where he just made it in time to be there for the birth of his lovely daughter Paris.
He was gone, but he did leave a few things back in Munich, some only temporarily, some to stay forever. To name just a few, Michael left the hotel Bayerischer Hof short of a number of towels, bath robes and pillows, a few slightly ripped curtains and a garage wall full of written fan-messages of love to Michael.
Fans left their messages all over the place; the formerly green benches in front of the hotel now were plunged in black ink. The grassland opposite the hotel windows had little flattened spots which fans had claimed their beds during Michael's stay. Dogs were angrily screamed at when seen trying to relieve themselves there. Taxi drivers, waiting in line in front of the hotel, right under

by Brigitte Bloemen

Michael's windows, could relax again. They didn't have to fear any "apple" attacks from above anymore. Michael used to wrap an apple inside some of the towel messages to give them more weight before throwing them out of the window. Some of them hit a taxi car roof from time to time, which led to about 20 fans jumping onto the taxi fighting for the towel.
The streetcar drivers' job got back to normality, too, as did my life. At least it seemed that way. No more standing in front of a hotel every day after school, no more screaming, freezing or drawing banners all day long, no more excitement, no more Michael.
But he left me changed forever. He left us all a very special gift that will last for the rest of our lives, a lot of love and a lot of friendship. In these weeks I got to know many great people and found the best friends one could ever imagine. After 1998 we travelled all over the world together to see Michael, meet new people, see new places, feel incredible emotions, run through city streets behind cars, catch flights, miss buses, wave flags, hold signs, sing songs, dance, sleep on the streets, share a double-bedroom with six people and some cockroaches, go into courtrooms, ... we laughed, we cried, sometimes both at the same time...but all those are stories of their own. A lot of incredible, crazy, sad and funny memories that could fill a whole lifetime already, but still I would have wanted more of them.

I will cherish the last 12 years forever and will be eternally grateful to Michael for making me who I am and for giving me the time of my life. Those moments will stay with me forever, HE will stay with me forever. As will the most beautiful gift he left me with, best friends.

In this sense, I would like to dedicate this story to those best friends and Michael of course.
"To all the adventures that still lie ahead of us, to Michael who will always be with us, to the future, to love and to life!"
THANKS, YOU KNOW WHAT YOU DID!

by Brigitte Bloemen

Ain't no sunshine: Goodbye gloved one

by Pranav Dixit, India

My first encounter with Michael Jackson was in a small, rather dusty little town called Narayangaon, about 80 kilometres away from my hometown, Pune in India. I was running all around my uncle's house, a tiny lad of six, when I chanced upon a large, dust-covered rack full of audio cassettes in a dark corner of the attic. The rack contained classics like Madonna, ABBA and Boney M, and a lot of old Hindi music. It also contained Michael Jackson. I don't know what inspired me to pick up Michael's tapes. Looking back, I think it was the two dark, intense eyes with the prominent Jheri curl staring back at me that might have influenced my decision.

I took the tape out of the moth-eaten plastic cover and popped it into the brand new stereo player that my uncle had just purchased at the time (cassette players still existed in those days, you know. If yours came with a radio built in, it was supposed to be relatively high-end!). Thus commenced a brand new relationship, one that would see me through all my growing years, right to this very day.

I think it was the perfect, pounding rhythm of the song Dangerous that did it for me. Or maybe it was the gritty, clenched-teeth vocals in Jam or the simple yet heart-stirring lyrics of Gone Too Soon. It was the definitive moment, when the phenomenon called Michael Jackson assailed all barriers, crossed the pastiche walls of genre and carved a niche for himself in a deep corner of my six-year-old heart - and I have been hooked ever since.

I call him a phenomenon, not because of the millions of hysterical fans that swoon at his every public appearance, not because of the thousands of accolades that have come his way, not even because of how much excitement and controversy he manages to generate with just about anything he does. He is a phenomenon because of his rare gift of effortlessly making a place for himself in the hearts of millions of people, irrespective of age, gender and even nationality. He is a cultural icon of our times in every sense imaginable.

How many artists have the distinction of being known by over three generations? My seventy-eight year old grandfather, who knows as much about Western music as I know about African vegetation, often smiles and taps his feet at the familiar strains of Billie Jean blasting through the home theatre. "There's your guru", he smiles at me with a twinkle in his eye whenever there's a snippet about Michael in the newspapers.

My mother, a die-hard Marathi music aficionado hardly ever listens to anything with a hint of English in it, but she still managed to write a Marathi poem, inspired, of all things, by the soulful and veracious lyrics of Man in the Mirror. Of course, her favourite music video happens to be Earth Song, which is screened without fail every year at the beginning of the environment classes, which she takes in the college where she teaches.

My father, who is as typical and conventional as a simple, middle-class Marathi married-man-with-a-single-child can be, and who has trouble distinguishing between Aishwarya Rai and Katrina Kaif (thanks to his total I-am-a-happily-married-Marathi-man-who-has-nothing-to-do-with-pop-culture-whatsoever-attitude) recounts the days when Michael had played in India for the first (and only) time.

"What a spectacle that was!" Dad gushes. "They were broadcasting the event on national TV and we Maharashtrians were at our wits' end trying to figure out how in the world did Bai Thackeray end up being pals with this alien-looking creature who was about as far away from Hindu culture and Marathi pride as you could get!"

I was too little to remember anything about Michael's concert in India when it happened. But I made up for it by feverishly downloading every concert video that was ever put up in cyberspace as soon as I was old enough to get online. Soon, I was downloading

by Pranav Dixit

and devouring everything MJ – Michael Jackson music, Michael Jackson movies, Michael Jackson interviews, Michael Jackson documentaries, Michael Jackson e-books, Michael Jackson music videos, Michael Jackson acapellas, Michael Jackson lyrics, Michael Jackson pictures and even Michael Jackson parodies. I have stacks of DVDs full of things of everything Michael Jackson. Stuff that is easily available, and stuff that is extremely rare and hard to find - I have it all. I even have the outtakes – all the songs that Michael recorded over the years that were never published, simply because there were too many to fit in a single album.

I have a vivid memory of jumping up and down in ecstasy when I bought a copy of the excellent biography, Michael Jackson: The Magic and the Madness by J. Randy Taraborrelli at a tenth of its cover price at an exhibition in Mumbai.

Of course, being a fervent fanatic of Michael is like being a social outcast in some ways.

"What, you like Michael Jackson???"

"Eww...what has he done to his face?"

"Do you know he takes female hormones to keep his voice high-pitched? I heard he also sleeps in an oxygen chamber. And oh, just what in the world has he done to his nose? Tsk tsk..."

"Michael Jackson? Yeah, I used to like him...or her (snigger)."

"Why do you like him so much, man, he's a %!@&*# paedophile, man..."

"You ever listen to any Pink Floyd, dude? Metallica? Iron Maiden? You know, like, some real music?"

"Michael Jackson? Yeah, I used to listen to him when I was about five years old. Then, you know, I moved on."

Over the years, I have always heard out my detractors and explained calmly that I tend to separate the person from the personality and the man from the genius. Trying to get to know Michael so closely over the years has only made me intertwine the strands of my life with his in an almost subconscious manner and there are occasions when I will suddenly point out something that happened in Michael's life and how similar it is to something that is happening in my life at the moment (these are also the occasions when other people think I am a complete freak,

by Pranav Dixit

which, incidentally, is not much different from what they think of Michael, in the first place). Yes, of all the people in the world, I can, somehow, sometimes, relate to Michael Jackson.

I guess it is these enduring bonds, which Michael and I both share that make it so hard for me to let go. A part of my mind refuses to believe that the sprightly young boy who grew up to be a shattered, lonely individual hunted by the baleful gaze of the public eye exists no more. There will be no more moonwalking or bursting onto stage in a mighty explosion of blinding pyrotechnics. No more fans fainting at the sheer excitement of seeing Michael in person on stage. His high-pitched, clear voice will no longer reach the astounding heights to which it once did. There will be no more albums to look forward to. Nor, thankfully, will there be any more fodder for the news-starved tabloids to publish about Wacko Jacko's latest bizarre feat.

Michael's soft voice lilts in my head as I struggle to come to terms with the loss. Michael, broken and profoundly lonely in the last years of his life, not unlike Charlie Chaplin, whose pathos-lined classic „Modern Times" inspired the legend to write the sweet, yet melancholic Smile.

„Smile, though your heart is aching. Smile, even though it's breaking. When there are clouds in the sky, you'll get by. If you smile through your tears and sorrow, smile and maybe tomorrow you'll find that life is still worthwhile – if you just smile."

„I have to remind myself that some birds aren't meant to be caged", says the great Morgan Freeman in the timeless classic, „The Shawshank Redemption". „Their feathers are just too bright. And when they fly away, the part of you that knows it was a sin to lock them up does rejoice. Still, the place you live in is that much more drab and empty that they're gone."

Michael's flown away too. And whatever anyone may say, for me, moving on is simply not an option. I miss you, Michael.

by Pranav Dixit

Crazy Times

by Heidi Laurito, Germany

To me it all started in 1987 when I was 11 years old and Michael was thrilling the world with his BAD Tour. At that time Michael was extremely popular and it was "state-of-the-art" to be his fan. So I got infected by the Jacksonmania as well but there was something that separated me from the fans I knew at that time: Apart from his wonderful music, his incredible dance abilities and his marvellous looking, I got interested in the person Michael Jackson as well. I wanted to know how he became the superstar he was, what he liked and disliked. I started to read books about him, listened carefully to the lyrics of his songs to understand the message behind them (being a girl from Germany not always easy at that time, but it improved my English knowledge tremendously) and tried to look for the human being behind the superstar. Soon the person and the star were intrinsically tied to each other and this knowledge created a bond between him and myself which made clear to me that I would love and support him forever. I felt his pain when the tabloids were making up stories about him and I stood up for him whenever I had the feeling his reputation needed to be protected. As you may imagine, this has not always been easy in the course of the years because unfortunately there was a time when it was not as popular to be a Michael Jackson Fan as it was in the Eighties and Nineties. However, I have never had any doubts in his integrity and to me Michael was innocent from any accusations right from the beginning.
In the early nineties I was eagerly waiting for the release of Michael's next album and when the first single "Black or White" of his "Dangerous" album was released in 1991 – after four years of waiting and steadily learning about his past and the Jackson Five/Jacksons - I was happy to witness the release of a new Michael Jackson album and the hype which came along with it for the first time. When his Dangerous World Tour was announced, I begged

my mom for permission to go to at least one concert and fortunately she allowed me to go to the opening concert in Munich on June 27th, 1992 which was a three hours drive away from my hometown. My first live concert was a bit disappointing because I only got a ticket very far from the stage and Michael was about 1 inch tall. But what I do remember very well and what amazed me was that he set the total audience of 72,000 people on fire from the second he stepped on stage. During the hours I was in the stadium, waiting for the show to start, I was so far away from the stage that I was convinced that I would not be a part of the show, that I would watch it like a movie – but I was taking part! I was going wild and wondered how it must be to see Michael perform close-by and promised myself to make this experience – when I would not need my mother's permission anymore.

I continuously admired Michael over the years, became the president of a little formerly Austrian (unofficial) Michael Jackson Fan Club for some time, wrote letter after letter to him and none of Michael's birthdays passed without a present from Heidi in Germany sent to Neverland. By the way: My innumerable letters have all remained unanswered. However, another World Tour was on its way in 1997: HIStory. I watched both of his shows in Munich (Germany) as well as his shows in Cologne (Germany), Basel (Switzerland) and Copenhagen (Denmark) which happened to take place on August 29th, Michael's 39th birthday. For the first time I experienced the real thrill of going to a Michael Jackson concert. It is not only about the show itself or the Man himself, everything was so exciting! Standing in front of the stadium already in the early morning hours waiting for the gates to open. Running into the stadium at about midday/early afternoon, getting a spot in the first section in front of the stage and waiting several hours more for Michael to start the show. All the waiting was worthwhile once Michael took control over the audience. We were completely putty in his hands, helpless victims of rhythm, voice and performance who could not help but be grateful to witness this amazingly talented human being live on stage and watch how he touched the hearts of thousands of people at one time.

by Heidi Laurito

It was in 1997 when I first had the chance to not only see Michael onstage. After the concert I went to Michael's hotel in Munich. When I arrived there, everything was completely going wild. People were crowding the street, chanting his name, completely adrenalized by the show they had just witnessed. Michael was standing at the open window, waving to his fans and suddenly I felt so near to him. His suite was on the fourth floor of the hotel which was not built tremendously high. I could really see him! It was amazing and it seemed as if Michael had fun sharing these moments with his fans. I remember one situation: Michael was throwing autographs out of the window and at one time he wrote it on some kind of piece of cloth (maybe a little towel or table napkin?). To make it fly better he wrapped an apple in it, threw it out of the window – and accurately hit the police car which was standing in front of the hotel. Watching this scene made me laugh and I held my head up to watch Michael's reaction: He was clenching his fist, was laughing like crazy and I assumed to read the word "Strike!" on his lips.

I was lucky enough to see Michael personally during these days in Munich in June 1997 a few more times: When he went shopping (at a toyshop and a US American shop) and not to forget the many times when he showed himself at the hotel window. It was on one of these occasions when my friend got an autograph from him, by the way. His van had to wait at a red traffic light. As my friend was not prepared very well, Michael had to sign his calling card – Michael was nice enough to do so.

"Michael Jackson hotel actions" were something very special to me. It was as if a big family reunion was taking place. Therefore, a popular rap to entice Michael to come to the window was "Hey, Michael, meet the family!" I always had a thunderer whistle with me, so we would do raps conducted by the whistle. It was a circus, a magic circus of love. All races, ages and people from different societies were suddenly united heading to one single aim: showing Michael our love and support. By the end of the day, which would last until late night hours, we were completely exhausted, sometimes chilled to the bone and dog-tired but perfectly happy – and yet too excited to fall asleep. After some hours of light sleep

by Heidi Laurito

we found ourselves back in front of the hotel again to start anew. I remember one situation which was planned to be the ultimate banner presentation to Michael, but turned out to become a hopeless misfortune. It was in 1999, when Michael was giving his "What more can I give" concert (Michael Jackson & Friends) in Munich. My dear friend and Michael-fan-action companion and myself wanted to prepare a banner. A banner which the world had never been seen before! A banner which Michael would like so much that he would call us to his hotel room in a second! An "open the door to Michael's suite" banner. This was the plan, now we needed a good idea. So, we took a linen as big as four metres wide and two metres high and of dark-blue color. We went to a copyshop and enlarged the image of the Dancing the Dream book with Michael being in the clouds and tenderly watching down on some playing kids (what a different meaning this image has now). We chose a phrase from "Heal the world" and wrote it in big silver glimmering letters on the linen. But the clou was still to come: We all know that Michael loved glimmering and sparkling, so I found it to be a good idea to put "real" stars on the banner - in the form of electric light chains. Now the banner was finished, we had to find a way to supply it with current for the light chains – quite difficult on the open road where the banner was to be presented. I talked to a working colleague of mine and he had a wonderful idea: Why not use a power set? Perfect, where could I get one from? No problem, he said, I'll lend you mine. It was a Russian model, operated with fuel. I made a test at home (I was a bit surprised by the loud noise), grabbed the longest extension cord I could find in our garage and drove to Munich.
As we were so sure we would meet Michael this time, I had written a poem for him which we wanted to recite – so I repeated it on my way to Munich again and again, imagining how wonderful it would be to meet the Man himself and to finally be able to thank him personally for all he had given to me and to so many people around the globe.

After having arrived in Munich and having joined the "magic circus" in front of the hotel for a while, finally the time had come

by Heidi Laurito

and we went to my car to get all the stuff: The huge banner, the extension cord and the power set. I went to the parking space where I had left my car and… the car wasn't there anymore!

I turned around and looked whether I had confounded the parking spot, but my car wasn't anywhere to be seen. After a while and after having talked to the hotel staff and to the police, it was clear that my car had been towed as it was claimed to have been parked in front of the fire service exit! What to do next?

We jumped into a cab and drove to the place where my car had been delivered to. This place was quite far outside Munich which cost a whole lot of money. Having arrived there, I had to pay 300 D-Mark in cash, otherwise my car would not have been released plus a parking ticket of another 100 D-Mark. If that had not been enough, we now found ourselves in the situation of finding the way back to the hotel. We were all strangers in Munich and it took quite a while until we got back. To be exact, the whole procedure took at least 3-4 hours! Hours that were so precious to us!

When we finally arrived at the hotel again, the situation had changed heavily: There were so many people there now and the best spots for presenting the banner were occupied in the meanwhile. Nevertheless, we grabbed our stuff and went on. It took quite a while to get from the parking spot to the hotel, because a) I did not want to make such a terrible mistake again and parked my car further away and b) because the Russian power set was extremely heavy and had to be carried by my male friend who had to pause every now and then. As it had slightly started to rain and as I learned that water and current are not the best friends, I decided to take another blanket - on top of all the stuff we already had to carry - with which I wanted to protect the power set from the rain.

We must have looked real funny when we showed up. We luckily found quite a nice spot, put all our stuff out and I started to make the power set run. The loud noise it made (like an old lawnmower) was familiar to me in an instant as, you remember, I had tested the set before I left home. The power set had not even been running properly, when someone tipped my shoulder. First I did not react because my nerves had really been stressed after

by Heidi Laurito

all that had happened lately and I just wanted our big show to happen now. So I went on to make the set going. My shoulder was tipped again. I slowly turned around and looked into the face of a policeman. "Excuse me, lady, but what's this?" I decided to find this question very ridiculous because what we were doing was so obvious – at least to me. While continuously occupying myself with the power set, I muttered "That's a power set." But obviously this was not the answer the policeman wanted to hear. "Aha. And what do you need it for?" Now the policeman got my full attention all of a sudden. I turned around, stared into his eyes and said very slowly and clearly: "We need current. For our banner. Or how else could we make these light chains burn?!" Just as this would be the most normal thing in the world. My friend was watching the scene and turned from one to another. Then we heard something we did not want to understand at all: "You are not allowed to use this power set here. It's against our regulations." Against our what??!! A fevered discussion began between the three of us. Suddenly my friend shouted something into my direction and left. I saw him walking towards the hotel entrance where he went in. After a while he came back with the Public Relations manager of the hotel who continued the discussion with the policeman on our behalf now. The PR manager asked the policeman if he was aware that this could be a chance for us to be invited to Michael's room and whether it was possible to make an exception. The policeman shrugged his shoulders: "No. No exceptions. No permission."

To make a long story short: This is how the story ended. Michael was never meant to see our lovely banner, we were never meant to meet Michael and the policeman will never understand how little exceptions can mean the world for someone.

The tabloids used to describe Michael as a shy person who does not want to be touched due to hygienic reasons. Michael might have been shy but he was neither a wacko nor weird. On the contrary, in many ways (his vision of healing the world and seeing the children as our only future) he was much more realistic and down-to-earth than most people are. To me it is absolutely clear: If you dibble a seed of love, wellbeing and comfort in a child's

303

by Heidi Laurito

heart it will grow to a wonderful tree over the years. Adults who had a good childhood are very unlikely to harm other people, for instance in a criminal way. Adults who had a good childhood are very unlikely to start wars. And adults who had no childhood at all will try to compensate once they get older. Nothing to blame anybody for.

There is a time and place for everything and when you were lucky enough to hit them both, Michael was very willing to talk to his fans, hug and kiss them. Of course he did not like it to be pushed or feel his hair being torn out, but who would not want to escape from such kind of situation? I remember, it must have been during Michael's two weeks stay in Munich in 1998, one situation I will never forget: Again we were gathering in front of Michael's hotel and surprisingly at this specific time there had not been so many fans there. Across the street I saw Michael's bodyguards and some fans were running towards them. I thought, why not join them, maybe they distribute some autographs. When I got there I felt the tension immediately and I could not believe what I saw through the crowd: It was Michael himself who was standing there! He had obviously decided to visit us and say hello. I could not believe it. Michael was dressed all in black (long coat, his black fedora and face mask). After a little confusion and pushing within the crowd surrounding Michael, I found myself standing right left to him, about one metre away. Michael had a charisma which could be FELT and I was standing there, enjoying this feeling and had the strong desire to hug him. Suddenly the crowd began to push and grab for Michael, thereby the bodyguards decided to lead him through a door into the hotel which I could not pass.

I hurried to the main entrance of the hotel where a bellboy was trying to get in my way. But I was so strong-willed that I just ignored him, walked right through the hotel lobby, went through another door – and there he was. Michael was standing on the staircase, patiently signing autographs and having the fans take photos with him. It was so amazing, I was deeply thankful for having had the chance to witness this encounter. Many people have asked me why I had not tried to take a photo with him or

by Heidi Laurito

get his autograph. Honestly, I do not know a concrete answer, but somehow I always had the feeling that there were already so many people around who all wanted the same from one single person – somehow I did not want to be another one, maybe stressing him. I was waiting and hoping for an intimate moment. I did not want to touch him by quickly passing by. I wanted to shake his hands, look him in the eyes and address a warm and heartfelt Thank You to him and assure him that he will always have my love and support. If he then had wanted to hug me, I would have of course allowed him to do so, but I did not want to urge him. After all, he was just a normal human being with feelings like you and me – would we want to be hugged and kissed by any strangers crossing our way? I doubt so.

However, when I recall this situation, another story comes into my mind: There was this little 12 year old German boy who somehow managed to contact Michael during his Munich stay in 1998. It did not take long, this little boy was by Michael's side most of the time. He spent time with him on his hotel room, joined him visiting the circus and met Michael on various further occasions. I remember one afternoon, we were singing and shouting in front of Michael's hotel trying to make him come to the window. Suddenly something was going on at the curtains, the window was opened – and this little boy was looking down on us. He gave us signs to be quiet because he wanted to tell us something. It took quite a while until all the "shushs" had been noticed by everyone and I personally was so excited because I expected a special message, directly coming from Michael who wanted to let us know something important or meaningful. What the little boy had to say, was: "Could you please be a bit more quiet? We are having dinner up here right now." No more comments on this, but I really had a great laugh.

There were so many occasions when I saw Michael close over the years, be it live in concert, during a shopping tour or just a short glimpse at the hotel window. But not all of our undertakings were successful. I remember driving to Italy to see PavarottI & Friends with Michael announced to join him onstage – but Michael never turned up. The same for a press conference which was to be held

by Heidi Laurito

in Warsaw/Poland. A Fan Club had organized a bus tour which would bring the fans from Munich to Warsaw and me and four other fans wanted to be part of it as well. We were all driving in my humble little car to Munich. Just when we had arrived and were looking for the bus terminal, we got a phone call that the press conference had been cancelled. There were rumours now that Michael wanted to go to Gstaad/Switzerland instead. My companions and me did not have to think about it twice: Let's turn around and drive to Switzerland! For all who do not know: Gstaad is a ski resort which means it was COLD there. Have I mentioned that we did not have a hotel room? Have I mentioned that I only had a little car and that there were five adults on the road? Have I mentioned that we spent three days and four nights just sitting in my car in front of Liz Taylor's chalet, waiting for Michael? The days were dead boring. Outside it was freezing, inside the car it was warm but crowded. We were playing games from our kindergarten and school times and on one day we thought having seen something going on inside the chalet. This was our go! We grabbed all the Michael stuff we had with us for the cancelled press conference, grabbed some candles and climbed on Liz Taylor's garage roof. Up there we lit the candles, held our banners and posters in our hands and started to sing "Heal the World". In the beginning rather quiet, but then we became louder – but neither Michael nor Liz turned up. The neighbors around us felt so sorry for us that they were supplying us with hot tea, bread and Swiss cheese during the day. But we felt to have an insider information this is why we would stay and in the beginning there were also other fans turning up (I suppose we all had the same source).

The nights were freezing and uncomfortable. We all had to sleep sitting and I turned the heating on and off as I could not have the engine run all the time. Suddenly we saw a car slowly driving down the road. In the nights before, security came once in a while which made us believe that Michael would arrive soon. But this time it was not security, but a normal car. A man and a lady were getting out – it was in the middle of the night – and stepped towards us. It turned out that they were fans themselves and they could not believe that we had been waiting there for days. They

306

by Heidi Laurito

were very nice and the man told us that he had a Michael Jackson pub and asked us if we wanted to see it. We admitted to ourselves that probably nothing would happen at Liz Taylor's chalet anymore, so we decided to come with him. He drove ahead and we followed him. We visited his wonderful MJ pub with so many wonderful collectors and things to see and us being the only guests. After having spent some time there, the man asked us whether we wanted to come to his home. In the beginning we were a bit retentive, but then decided to accept his offer. We went to his beautiful home and his Thai wife was preparing wonderful food for us – in the middle of the night, somewhere between 4 and 5 am! Afterwards he offered us to spend the night at his home. He had such a big house that every one of us had his own bed (not a matter of course, from my point of view) and we were sleeping like stones after all these cold and uncomfortable nights until afternoon. Though our aim to meet Michael did not work out, we experienced the generosity of a couple who really lived Michael's message. Thanks again, you were our knights in shining armors that night. By the way, rumours say that the couple met Michael at Liz Taylor's Swiss chalet a few weeks later and I know this meant the world to them. The man had tears in his eyes when he was only talking about Michael.

Though I had been close to Michael for several times over the years, I never really had the chance to have a word with him. When he was around, I did of course yell how much he meant to me, but there has never been a one-on-one moment. This was a situation I dearly was longing for. Besides of it I felt the strong desire within me to give him something back. I wanted to please him with presents and let him know how much he meant to me and how much I cherished him, his art and his efforts to heal the world and support needy people. The ability of making people happy is probably the most precious gift one can share with the world and Michael was a lucky star for so many of us. And I was well aware of how much of himself he put into it.
When I watched the press conference in London this year, I went completely nuts! The last time I saw Michael live in person was

by Heidi Laurito

at both of his 30th anniversary concerts taking place in New York in September 2001. At the second concert I was sitting not so far from Michael during the first half of the show while he watched it from the audience, too. After so many years not having had the chance to see him, oh boy, I could not wait to get on the plane and experience the magic again!

After having had purchased tickets for the first and second show, I was spending the time of anticipation with preparing some presents for him: A three dimensional book and some bracelets. Unfortunately, none of the presents have been finished properly. I am sure that everyone – fan or not - remembers how he or she got the shocking and devastating news of Michael's tragic and sudden passing. I cannot even describe what I was feeling at that moment. I have always been convinced of being a fan until the end of my life – but would have never thought of Michael being called home by God so suddenly and soon. My thoughts and prayers went out to his children and family. I felt this incredible pain and needed some time until I could really understand what had happened and I still have this painful feeling inside my heart of having lost a dear friend and the world of having lost its most precious, warm-hearted, generous, charming, talented and above all loving creature. God moves in mysterious ways – yet it hurts that he is not around on this world anymore. The world is different since Michael passed away and will never be the same for those who loved him.

But I know that Michael is in a better place now. A place where he is not hunted, accused and slandered. A place where he can heal his soul for having tried to heal and unite our world. A place that is all about love. L.O.V.E. And music.

Thank you, dear Michael – Rest in Peace. We will never forget you and you will be missed forever.

by Heidi Laurito

March 17th 1996 – Paris, FRANCE...

by Kader, France

It was a Sunday, the last day of spring break. It was cloudy and windy, not the kind of weather that makes you wanna go out for a walk, so when my father asked me whether I wanted to come with him and my sister, I just smirked and declined. I simply sat back on my bed doing what I had been doing since the morning and would still probably be doing later in the evening... nothing!

However, the thought of it was so depressing, that five minutes later I desperately rushed out the door to see if I could catch them up... as I got out in the street I looked around, but I was too late and saw my father's car driving off, duh!!
I contemplated going back and resuming the whole bunch of nothing I had been doing when I remembered that the single for "They Don't Care About Us" had just been released. I thought it might be nice to go to the record store and check out the remixes - not that I usually like them - but then again, sitting back on my bed wasn't really the most exciting thing you'd wanna do!

Back then, when you wanted to go buy a CD, most people went to the Virgin Megastore on Les Champs Elysées (for those familiar with Paris) and I decided I would just walk even though I lived pretty far from there. An hour later I was almost there, and for whatever reason the only thing I remember about this uneventful walk is singing "Man In The Mirror" as I was a few minutes away from getting into the Virgin Megastore.

Les Champs Elysées is this huge avenue that we have in Paris that most tourists visit whenever they come. It's pretty busy and crowded cause there are plenty of stores, restaurants, sightseeing spots... and I kinda knew that I'd have to get in the line, before I could get to the headphones they put up in the store to let people listen to snippets of the CDs they wanna buy.

Just as I was walking into the store, these two girls passed me by in the other direction and one of them goes: "What now? She thinks she's all that cause she touched Michael??? Hell, no..." Being a fan and stuff, if you hear Michael, you think MICHAEL and I started wondering "Michael? Which Michael? Where?? Like 'the Michael'??", but then again I was like "Yeah right, whoever she was talking about, it wasn't him"...
You could ask any fan, hell, you could ask anyone: "Would you like to meet Michael Jackson?" I don't know a lot of people who'd decline the offer, and I'm just like anyone else, but reality is a bitch and it hits you in the face pretty hard.

Just a year before, I was reading an article about a fan who seemed to be a huge collector. He was explaining how he had spent more than $3.000 on Michael Jackson CDs, paraphernalia, merchandising and whatnot and as enthusiastic as he was, he said this terrible sentence that still sticks with me to this very day, he said: "As much as I admire him and love him, I know I'll never ever get a chance to meet him!" When I read that, any dream I'd ever had to one day meet Michael was just shattered, every time I would have hoped about one day meeting Michael, this article totally ruined it for me and this time, too, I thought about it: "I'll never get a chance to meet him".

Damn, was it crowded that day, it was kinda chilly outside, so I guess people were all keen on staying inside where it was a little warmer. I looked around to see where the listening spot for the single was and it was right to my right, it was only when I got closer that I realized that no less than 10 people were standing in the line!!! Seriously?? To listen to a song??? I was upset, but I thought "So what, I'll go to the library downstairs... hopefully when I get back they'll all be gone!"

So here I was in the library, checking out all kinds of books and some magazines too. After 15 minutes I decided to go and check out if it was any less crowded, so I could finally listen to the single.

You wish... It had gotten even more crowded in there!!! But that was not all. There was something else, some kinda tension in the air, I could feel it... something was going on, but I couldn't figure it out. And it just seemed like everyone in the store was looking up in the same direction to the balcony!

At first I thought there was a show case, which happens from time to time, so I looked where they usually put up a small stage, but there was nothing and clearly people were looking up! I wasn't thinking about anything else in particular, I'm just a VERY curious person, and something was going on and I was going to find out, one way or another!

Being kinda a recluse and pretty quiet person, I didn't like to talk to random people, but there was this group of girls looking up and talking about whatever was up there, so I kinda got closer and tried to overhear their conversation, but it was so noisy in there I couldn't make out what they were saying. This whole 'not being able to know what was going on' was really irritating me and this tension inside the store, the whole place was buzzing! God knows I would never have asked in other circumstances, like if I get lost, and I've been walking in circles for hours and I have no idea where I am, I'd rather keep walking in circles for a few more hours than ask someone for my way! Yet, this time, I felt compelled to ask and before I knew, I gave one of the girls a tap on the shoulder and asked: "Excuse me, what's going on???"

She turned around smiled and said: "Oh, there's Michael Jacks...." - that's when the time stopped and I almost fainted – "...son inside the store!" In a heartbeat, a violent adrenaline flush made my heart speed up, I felt my knees getting weak, and I was hyperventilating and I literally had to hold onto a shelf not to fall.

by Kader

I was telling to myself "NO, it can't be, it's not possible, it wasn't supposed to happen, I had wrapped myself around the fact that I would never see or meet him... This was never meant to happen, this can NOT be happening!"
In a few seconds I understood why everyone was looking up in the same direction! He was upstairs and judging by the huge flow of people walking down the stairs he had left. While I was downstairs in the library, Michael was upstairs and I had no idea, and I had just blown my only chance to ever meet him! How could I have come so close and still miss my chance??? Life was playing a cruel, cruel joke on me! I had come to terms with the fact that one of my biggest dreams in life would never come true! So why torture me like that??

It couldn't be. I still decided to go upstairs making my way through the flow of customers to get to the balcony until I saw two fans, one of whom was wearing a fedora talking to a security guarding a door. When I got there the security was telling those two fans how "you guys are crazy. You almost killed him!!! I have NEVER seen anything like that in my whole life!! This is insane!!!"

Apparently Michael had just left through that door, who knew, maybe he was still behind it, I still couldn't believe I'd missed him like that! I ventured a question to the security: "Is he gone?", he answered a stern "Yeah"... I was totally lost in disbelief; this was just too good -for lack of a better word- to be true!

This moment I had been waiting for several years!!

Hell, when the Dangerous tour came to Paris, I was 13 and my parents wouldn't let me go, actually I think they couldn't even afford a concert ticket. But we lived on the 9th floor and from this tiny window two meters above the floor, in our toilet, I had a perfect view of the stadium where the concert was and I thought if the closest I ever get to Michael Jackson is being able to see the concert lights... so be it! And I spent the entire evening looking through that window... but I couldn't see anything.

by Kader

I was devastated, but the fan with the fedora told me that dude was lying, Michael's car was still parked outside which meant he was still around. I thought, if I still had one last chance to see him it's when he gets in his car, so I rushed out, but when I got there it was pandemonium! All the people that were inside the store had gone through the same logic as I had and where right there!!!

What else could I do? There was no chance that I would even be able to see anything with so many people, and Michael still being inside, they could shut the store down to give him some privacy as had been reported before... the next best thing to do was to go back inside and see what happens! At that time I was thinking - thinking fast, I had to make a decision, I was getting a potential second chance, and I couldn't blow it!!!

I walked back towards the entrance when I heard people scream "Move aside, get back now, move", then I saw about 20 security people walking in my direction. I thought they were actually shutting down the store and I didn't wanna get locked out, so I rushed in. I was standing in the middle of the way when it hit me!!
They were actually escorting Michael out and he was coming my way! The adrenaline flushing in my system made it seem like everything was happening in slow motion, yet everything was going really fast!!!

This was too much, totally unbelievable... a couple of hours before I was bored to death sitting on my bed and here I was, about to see my biggest dream come true! I could have sworn it was a dream or a joke: Michael Jackson didn't exist anyway, he was just a picture on my wall, a video on my TV, a voice on the radio! He wasn't real... he couldn't just be there in person!! I honestly believed someone was gonna bring a TV screen and Michael would be in there and that'd be it!! I really believed that was the only thing that would happen.
But I could see the bunch of security walking in my direction and if this wasn't a dream at all I would soon see him.

by Kader

I was trying to figure out where Michael was, but I couldn't see much.... it was only when they got closer that I glimpsed the fedora. There was no turning back, my life was gonna change completely, starting now. They were moving closer and with each step they took the fedora was getting closer. I was dumbfounded, I was the only one who hadn't moved aside and it's only when the first security gently pushed me that I moved. And all of a sudden, he appeared.

I can't explain what one goes through at that moment, it's probably the best moment of your life and the most excruciating from all the emotions that flow through your body. I imagine that is what happens during an out-of-body experience even though I've never had one!

Michael was wearing the hat, the mask and this dark green/bluish jacket with yellow neon stripes going from the collar down to the wrists, black pants with the usual red stripes.

And I saw his face... Michael passed me by, and this was it, I lost it!!! I was living THE moment! I lost control and started calling his name, I grabbed one of the security guys by the arm and held onto him, I couldn't let go, I wanted Michael to see me!

I wanted him to know I existed and that he meant so much to me! I just wanted him to know that during all these years there was someone who never thought something like this could ever happen to him, someone who was just a fan, and even though he couldn't go to any concert, still loved him and I wanted him to know that this person existed and it was me!!! I wanted to shut up all those who had told me "Why do you bother defending him, he doesn't even know you exist!" At that time, I had so many things I wanted to tell him, it would have needed a whole life.

I reached out and shook his shoulder, but Michael was looking the other way, the security was yelling at me! I grabbed Michael's arm and that's when he turned his head and looked at me. He gave

by Kader

me one stare, looked me deep in the eyes! It lasted for a second or two, but I could have sworn the world stopped spinning at that moment. It was one moment, and he probably just meant "Dude, let go of my arm now", but for the young fan that one look meant the world!

You know how people say "I saw my life flash right before my eyes" - well I felt like I saw Michael's videography flash right before my eyes! The look... any fan who has looked Michael in the eyes knows what I'm talking about, the aura, the persona... it's so overwhelming! To this day I could describe those eyes in every detail. And Michael looked down and that was it, but that was a lot, too much, and I just let him go.

I stood there for a few seconds, but I thought if this is the only chance I ever get of seeing him up close, I should enjoy the moment till the very last moment. I caught them up before Michael got to his car, but I couldn't see much because of all the fans that were gathered around the van!

I took a glimpse through the tainted windows, but they were so dark I couldn't see through. I kept trying, I just wanted one last glimpse, yet a few seconds after the van drove off and he was gone!

And... I stood there! And what can be said to describe a moment like this?
I kept looking at people and I think I had to kneel down for a while. I couldn't think straight! Why? How? I had given up on the whole idea...

In an instant, he totally turned my conception of life upside down: I had always thought these kinda things never happen to people like me. For once in my life I had gotten a glimpse of what it's like to be extremely fortunate, to have something really good happen to you without asking for it, for no other reason than that you had gotten lucky! For once in my life... It was my moment, my dream

315

by Kader

come true, it was all for me!!! It made me feel special, he made me feel beyond special... I was looking at the people around me and I wanted to scream: "I SAW HIM, I SAW HIM!!!!" I wanted them to understand what it meant to me!!! Had they the slightest idea???

I had to share... this was too much to keep it to myself!!! I ran to the nearest payphone. After several attempts at dialling the correct number - my whole body shaking wasn't really helping - my mother picked up the phone. She had hardly said "Hello?", when I burst out screaming "Mum, oh my God, oh my God, I saw him, I saw him," she went "Who???". "Mum, I saw Michael Jackson, I saw him up close!!! I swear..... I saw him!" Needless to say she was kinda surprised, probably thought it was a look-a-like, cause she seemed kinda doubtful. I hung up, so what now? Was it over? What was I supposed to do?

Back then I was totally clueless as to which hotel he might be staying at. All I knew was that a couple of days before, I was having a totally random discussion with my father about the time when he was working as a repair man and how he once went to the "George V" hotel for an assignment and how fancy it was and it just so happens that the next subway station from the Virgin store is GEORGE V. I figured there was a street with that name nearby and hopefully said hotel would be right there. And if that day was to be my lucky day, then I should definitely give it a shot!

As I was making a left on George V Avenue, I was hoping I'd see fans outside the hotel, yet my sight was obstructed by the traffic and the trees. Once I was getting closer, I thought I was seeing fans and a few steps further I couldn't see anyone... It was only when I got really close, I realized that barricades had been put up and a crowd of 3000 fans were standing behind them chanting and cheering!!!
A few minutes later Michael made an appearance and waved to the fans and did so every 3 or 4 hours, every day of his stay in Paris. That's how random my first time seeing the King Of Pop was!

by Kader

This is my story as a Michael fan, a story that I will forever cherish, but a story that will forever leave a bottomless depth in my soul. Right now, I feel so empty and I realize now that part of it is, because I'll never get a chance to tell him that story, my story... I've always wanted to ask him if he had the slightest idea of what it means to a fan when something like this happens to him or her! Does he even understand, can he even fathom for one second what an instant like this means to someone like me? And to know this will never happen, is so depressing...

Sometimes I think back of that day when I was in school and how I wish that kid had never brought that tape of the freshly released "Black Or White" single and never played it to me... How I wish my little brother never called me over to the living room, one Saturday morning while I was in the kitchen doing the washing up, to show me the video for "Remember The Time" for the first time ever... I wish my friend never recorded the Dangerous tour live from Bucharest, Romania and never played me the video.... or do I? Do I?

I love you Michael, always.

by Kader

I love you

by Dagmar Herrmann, Germany

You're not only an illusion
Only a shadow of my thoughts
You're more than an imagination
You overcome every bound.

Neither oceans nor land
Nor heaven are able to banish you
Through that strong ribbon of love
The whole world you want united, too.

Even moves, the glaring limelight
You're apart from me, so far
Your dear face appears, bright
In reflection of the stars.

Once the mercy GOD has weighed
For you of gifts a brimful measure
In thousand colours now glistens fame
This lot of fate is hardly drawn.

You're often very close to me
Much closer than you can discover
Yet in your eyes it is to read
You call yourself my brother.

Seeing him live

by Gabriela Bejan, Romania

I have many memories about Michael. I became his fan by the age of 14 and I learned all his songs, listened to all his music and by the moment I saw my first MJ video, I went totally crazy, probably just like all his fans.

As he first came to Romania, I couldn't believe it. I was reading all newspapers and cut out all articles about him so now I have a real big collection of articles. I tried to buy all his albums which actually was very difficult at that time here in Romania, remember it was the beginning of the 90's.

When he came back a few years later, in 1996, I made an effort to buy a ticket for his concert. He was my life at that time and I wished so much to get a ticket so I could see him live, see him on stage, hear his voice, his wonderful voice and see his moves and his magical dance. I loved him so much. In the end I paid 38 $ for one ticket (which was a lot of money back then) but it was all worth it! He was so amazing and I was the happiest girl for I finally have had the chance to see my idol and favourite artist live!

Now, that he is gone, I will do all in my power that his music survives.

I will always love and cherish you Michael! God Bless You!

by Gabriela Bejan

HIStory Tour Bremen 1997 – Michael's arrival

by Kerstin Reinke, Germany

Early in the morning of May 28th 1997, I travelled to Bremen by train. There I met up with a few friends and we immediately made our way to Bremen airport, where Michael was said to arrive in the afternoon. Although it would only be possible to see Michael from far away on the small landing field, I was unbelievably nervous for it would be a unique experience nevertheless, I thought.In the meantime different "trusted" sources had told us that our chances to see Michael arrive would be much better at the Parkhotel, where he would be staying. I knew that driving there just now, shortly before his arrival, would near our prospect of getting a good place there down to zero.

But regardless of all that doubts, we last-minutely decided to opt for the "hotel arrival" and leave our good place at the airport. During the whole bus- and taxi-drive I asked myself if this was the right decision, but there was no way back now anyway. The airport had been overcrowded with fans but now at the hotel the same picture awaited us.
Fans were literally standing everywhere, close-packed and only somewhere way back in the tenth row there might have been a little place for us to stand. So the view was zero.
At first I was so mad at myself that I would not even get to see the tip of his hat when he gets out of the car. At the airport I might have been able to see him, if only from very far away and as a tiny figure, but I would have SEEN him at least.

By now we had walked a bit closer where the last barriers stood, right on the street. But there was no opportunity to even get a glimpse of Michael neither. Yet we didn't have much choice left. But then I saw a small gap of about 20 centimetres between a lamp post and the last barrier still left open. I managed to acquire exactly that little space just in time just as Michael's car, under thunderous screaming of the fans, was parked in front of the hotel.
Despite all, the feeling now was awesome, simply thrilling. But where was Michael?
I only wanted to see him for a short moment, yet it seemed impossible. So, I squeezed myself through that little gap and suddenly stood right on the street in front of the hotel. Immediately a policeman was on the spot and told me to go back behind the barriers. However he swiftly turned away from me to push back some hysterical fans that were just about to climb over the barricades. My plus was that I stayed completely calm. But as hard as I tried to tiptoe to get to see Michael, I just couldn't. Therefore I slowly walked on, step by step. From time to time a bodyguard came closer and beckoned me to move back. But as right next to me other fans again tried to get over the barrier the bodyguards were busy getting them under control and left me alone.

I had a small self-made silky pillowslip in my hand on which I had painted Michael with his baby son Prince in his arms surrounded by Mickey and Minnie Mouse on both sides. Based on the volume of the fan screaming, I assumed that Michael must be very close. And then the wall of photographers appeared directly in front of me. Again I tiptoed to get a better overview. Right at that moment the mass of press people, blocking my sight, split and right ahead of me Michael appeared.

"Oh my God" I thought, this can't be true. There he was! So close like never before in my life. I held the pillowslip up in the air and as Michael saw it he smiled and pointed towards me. Then he waved to me and gestured me to come over to him. It was such an unbelievable amazing moment for me. Should I really go over to

by Kerstin Reinke

him? I looked at Wayne, his bodyguard, and he also signalled me that I could walk towards Michael. It felt like a dream, yet it was real. Michael simply looked dazzling. He was wearing a beautiful silk-jacket, black jeans, black hat and sunglasses. All I could stammer was "It's for you, Michael!" and with a shaky hand I held my painted pillowslip in his direction.

A little boy shortly interrupted and got Michael's autograph. Then Michael looked at me again and said "Oh – lovely!" took the small pillow out of my hands and held it in front of his face. It looked like he was kissing the painted picture because his son was on it. He was all smiles and behind the pillow I could hear him laugh out loud one time. Then he said "Thank you" and signed me the book I was holding, too.
I could see that he wasn't really shaven that day and his perfume smelled gorgeous. How could I ever get out a word when he was looking so gorgeous, standing right in front of me. However after he gave the signed book back to me, I managed to thank him and told him "Michael, I love you so much". He just smiled back at me with his amazing and lovely smile and blew me a kiss. As far as I remember, I only stared back at him grinning blissfully.

Then he turned and walked back towards the hotel entrance, writing a few more autographs and holding my pillowslip right in front of his face again, hiding it behind this small piece of cloth. The press later wrote: "A girl gave him a handkerchief. Michael smilingly blew his nose with it."

But I know that he must have really liked it which made me simply happy.
A few moments later he disappeared into the hotel, still with the pillowslip in front of his face.
Paralyzed, I kept on standing at the exact spot a few moments longer and tried to realize what just happened. Tears of joy began to run down my face, my friends came, hugged me and shared this moment of happiness with me.
I will never ever forget that day. Thank you so much, Michael!

by Kerstin Reinke

The soundtrack of my life

by Glenda Furia, Italy

Michael,

How can I describe what impact you had on my life?
Well, maybe this way:
I remember a young lady, ten maybe twelve years old, her parents divorced and her travelling by train to her dad and grandparents house every weekend or summer holidays.

In her headphones you could hear the songs "The lady in my life", "Billie Jean", "Human Nature" playing all the time. Travelling through the landscape, the song's unknown lyrics got mixed with the other train traveller's voices yet they were only a noisy background to the main theme, Michael's wonderful voice and melodies.

I remember a young lady sitting in her bedroom, doing her homework while listening to "Liberian Girl" and "Dirty Diana" or being absolutely charmed by watching the videos to "Man in the Mirror" or the "Bad Tour" performances on TV.
And then "I'll be there" - just so much sweetness in that track.

I remember a young lady who saw this wonderful person as her friend, her first companion, who spent all the time with her. She never noticed his skin colour - he could have been rather black or white - it didn't matter.

Now I see a grown up woman. All English she now knows she has learned through Michael's songs, but she learned so much more than that. All the things he taught her about loving and caring for people who are in need and he taught her to respect each other.

School's homework now turned to work.
Train trips to her dad or her grand parents turned to work trips.
Her grandparents are now gone.
But one thing has not changed ever since: the music.

Now when she walks her dog through the country alongside cornfields and sunflowers the same music the same lyrics play in her head...

".. we're the party people night and day,
Livin' crazy that's the only way,
So tonight gotta leave that nine to five upon the shelf,
And just enjoy yourself,
Groove, let the madness in the music get to you,
Life ain't so bad at all
If you live it off the wall"

Thank you Michael for writing the soundtrack of my life.
I will never forget you.

324

by Glenda Furia

The Dangerous "balcony" Show in Tel Aviv (1993)

*by Julia Orendi, Birgit Hoffmann,
Dagmar Wendel & Monika Reimann, Germany*

After a whole lot of pondering, reasoning and quite some travel cancellations caused by the critical situation in Israel - so after some very stressful weeks, in the end, we nevertheless went to Tel Aviv where Michael was supposed to be playing two shows. Tel Aviv welcomed us with blistering heat. We took our luggage and went directly to the hotel where Michael who had arrived the day before was staying. When we got there, a lot of fans were already waiting in front of the entrance, over which a huge banner was fixed, telling us „The Hotel DAN Tel Aviv welcomes Michael Jackson and his Dangerous Tour 1993".
That evening we saw Michael in his bus after a one year break of his „Dangerous"-Tour and we were hardly able to believe that we would see him on stage in two days time. At around midnight we luckily finally found a hostel room where the four of us fell asleep totally exhausted.
The following day we experienced Michael's departure to Jerusalem, where he visited the old town and archaeological excavations. At that same time we went to Hayarkon Park, where the concerts would be taking place, to check out the best entrances. In the evening the whole stress regarding the tickets for the concert started, which we were still not holding in our hands due to two consecutive holidays in Israel. After some long telephone conversations with the lady of the local organizer of the concerts Haim Slutzky and with Marcel Avram from Mama Concerts, who

The Dan Tel Aviv Hotel

Michael performing during his Tel Aviv concert

stayed at Michael's hotel, we got our tickets on the following day without any further problems and so found ourselves at 7 o'clock in the morning in front of the park's entrance waiting for the gates to be opened. That happened at half past 3 in the afternoon after long hours of patient enduring in almost unbearable heat. We managed to get spots in the first row. After the opening act „Culture Beat", Michael, like always, did an incomparable performance, leaving out „Working day and night" and instead doing „Dangerous", which made us and the other 60 000 people go completely bananas. The mammoth show was ended with amazingly beautiful fireworks and was highly acclaimed by the press.

In that night, we were still sitting at the beach with some English fans, Michael suddenly appeared on his balcony to watch us. We took the opportunity to thank him for the unique, spectacular concert and when we told him that "Billie Jean" was brilliant, he waved at us enthusiastically. This was definitely the cherry of the icing of a special day.

On Monday we bought some newspapers, and while three of us spent the day shopping and swimming, Monika stayed at Michael's hotel. When Michael left the hotel, his van was surrounded by several enthusiastic fans. Monika, who gave a self-made picture book of children to his doctor several days before, wanted to know if Michael had received the book. On a banner she asked him if he got the book with its specific title. Michael nodded vehemently, which of course made her very happy. Monika followed then Michael who went to a Children's Hospital in order to make a donation. In the evening we were again sitting at the prom when Michael, absolutely unexpected, stepped out on his balcony to watch the beautiful sunset.

There were hundreds of fans at the beach that went completely nuts when Michael started his rather unusual performance. First of all he climbed over the balustrade of his balcony, sat down on the edge and let his feet dangle. Then he lay down on his tummy and leant his head in his hands, smiling and grinning all the time. People could hardly believe their eyes and went completely mad, yet when Michael began balancing fearlessly on the edge, his bodyguards appeared out of the blue and tried to end his dan-

by Julia Orendi, Birgit Hoffmann, Dagmar Wendel & Monika Reimann

gerous stunts. After a short discussion they disappeared again, and he continued his actions. When the sky was completely dark, he kept on showing and explaining the stars to the children that were allowed to spend the evening with him.
That evening reached its top when his bodyguards returned to hand him over something: a megaphone. With it Michael began to talk to the fans saying things like „Heal the world", „I love you" and „Can I come down?", what created hysteria among the fans. After twenty exciting minutes another bodyguard appeared, took the megaphone and told us, that Michael would now need to go to bed. Stunned by Michael's actions, we spent the rest of the evening at the beach.
The following day the second concert took place and over 100,000 fans were present to first see „Culture Beat" and to then become eyewitnesses of a perfect gigantic show by Michael that left everyone speechless. The heat was so unbearable that water needed to be sprinkled on the fans to prevent them from fainting. After an amazing show Michael said good bye: „I love you Israel!" „Heal the world" was the very last song and Michael left the stage, celebrated by his fans and accompanied by a seemingly never-ending applause. Unfortunately we had to leave in that very night, so we took our luggage and went to Mike's hotel for the last time. Sadly, we weren't lucky enough to see him. Later we were told that he had already left Tel Aviv and was on his way to Istanbul.
After those five crazy days we also left Israel and got back home, already looking forward to our next concert at Tenerife, where we again experienced many more unbelievable moments and a very special show: the stage, that was located at the harbor and surrounded by huge cruise ships, was much lower and so made it possible to see Michael from head to toe, usually a rather rare sight from the front row. From the beginning he was making eye contact with his fans in the first rows, what made us happy, because he continued to point at us every once in a while throughout the whole concert.
Monika got lucky as she got hold of Michael's Billie Jean hat, which is until today one of her treasures in her memorabilia.
The concerts in Tel Aviv and Tenerife were our first concerts

by Julia Orendi, Birgit Hoffmann, Dagmar Wendel & Monika Reimann

farther from home. We have visited many concerts worldwide since and got to meet Michael several times.

Michael, thank you very much for your wonderful music, your influence in our lives and your mission to „Heal the world". We will never ever forget you!

by Julia Orendi, Birgit Hoffmann, Dagmar Wendel & Monika Reimann

Julia & Birgit with Darryl Phinnessee, Michael's background singer in Tenerife

Monika with the "Billie Jean" hat from the Tenerife concert

Basic needs simply didn't matter

by Laura Czerska, Poland

I can't believe it's been almost 4 years since I went to London to see my dearest idol, Michael Jackson. It was October, the beginning of the academic year. I was a little panicked to hear there was so much for me to do to succeed in all my exams.

Then one evening I got a message via the official Michael Jackson website that said he was where? In London! It was his first official journey outside the US since his acquittal. My first thought was: 'What difference does it make? It's still far away from where I live'. But a few seconds later, I realized my brother was living in London. I thought that perhaps I could take the chance, go there and make my dream come true. I was desperate to see my idol as I had never seen him in person before! I knew the idea of going to London all by myself on the spur of the moment was crazy. I couldn't be sure I would see Michael as London is huge while Michael's behaviour unpredictable. I didn't even know how long his stay in London was going to be, not to mention the purpose of his visit. Anyway, I was ready to go, hoping to catch at least a glimpse of Michael.

I spent hours on the Internet, browsing through some MJ forums to get more information about Michael's London visit. I found out which hotel he had chosen to stay in, how he was spending time there and how great he was with his fans. I was getting more and more information. I also found out some stuff about how to get to the Dorchester Hotel, at which station I should get off, even where the nearest toilet was. The more I found out about fans who were lucky enough to get hold of Michael in Harrod's or at Madame Tussaud's, the more I wanted to go there myself. After a few days, it turned out I could go!!! Within the time of one morning I was all ready. I took my backpack, which I still have, I put into it a few indispensable things: a toothbrush, some underwear, some documents and a map of London. Then I took a mascot and a letter as presents for Michael, as well as a photo of him which he could sign. In fact, first, the thought of going to London scared me, but soon this feeling was oveshadowed by another one – the desire to finally see my idol!

When I arrived in London, I was overwhelmed with its huge airport, then with the Underground. It didn't matter, though, as I had one ultimate goal. As I found myself at Marble Arch Station, I asked a lady to help me find the way. Upon approaching my destination, I asked a motorcyclist if I was on the right way. He was very nice; "You have to go there!", he told me. I thought to myself: 'Oh, really?' I got really excited and started to run! Finally I saw a group of people looking like MJ fans. I knew I was there, in the right place. I could sigh with relief. But, as I was in front of the hotel where Michael was staying, I was constantly carried away. The first person I got to know was a girl who saw Michael right in front of her the previous day. She told me he walked past the fans and when he approached her, he said: "Hello". She quickly took a photo of him, but I guess her hand was trembling, so she only managed to take a picture of the lower part of his face. 'My God, how lucky she was! I would have been satisfied if I was in her shoes,' I thought. I also imagined how wonderful it must have been. There was another thrill of emotion when a male fan ran after a black car with tinted windows and shouted: "Michael!" Everybody followed him. I remember when the car pulled up; I was quite close, but unable to get any closer, as the fans were going really mad! They even touched the windows. It wasn't Michael who was inside, but the mere thought that it might be him made us crazy! The "chasing the wrong car" - situation repeated itself several times within the few days that I spent there. Each time the majority, including me, was running towards it. I didn't see Michael the first day of my stay, but I wasn't disappointed. I was

by Laura Czerska

excited to be close to him, happy to get to know some other fans, even from Poland and relieved to join my brother around 10 or 11 pm.

The next day around 1 pm I was again at the Dorchester Hotel together with other fans. I made friends with some of them, especially with one girl. Just like me, she was there to see Michael for the first time. Every moment we spent there together was so precious because we shared the same feelings. We also talked to other fans. From one I bought some pictures of Michael that she had taken. The atmosphere was nice. From time to time, some hotel staff told us that he might come down. Each time this happened, our excitement rose! It also rose when Michael's bodyguard approached us. I tried to give him a letter I'd written for Michael. Yet he was adamant saying Michael had so many letters and presents that there was no place for any more. That moment I was really disappointed. I came all the way from Poland and I thought nobody cared. Fortunately the disappointment was compensated with the sight of Michael on the window that evening. I remember exactly the moment when we were tired of waiting. We were so desperate to see Michael that we stopped thinking he might have problems because of our shouting in front of the hotel. We ran to the side on which his window was situated, and we started to call Michael. His window was on the top floor. It seemed as if the light was turned off or at least the curtains gave such an impression. I remember this moment very well when, all of a sudden, he emerged from behind the curtains. Step by step there was more and more light and then we could see our dearest idol waving to us! From time to time he hid and again he appeared and was waving. This moment lasted between 10 and 15 minutes and it seemed as if the time had stopped. There were passers-by who didn't know what was happening, some of them stopped to see, some of them did not. Some cars stopped to see what was going on, others were blowing their horns. The traffic got slower. This moment was really dear to me. I came home filled with bliss and I couldn't think or talk about anything else. It was so wonderful that it's even hard to describe. But I can tell it seemed like a revelation to me.

by Laura Czerska

Next day, another dose of emotions. Someone, somehow found out that Michael had left the hotel. It wasn't difficult to miss the moment when he left the hotel, as there were three entrances. He must have left via the parking lot. Then the fuss started! 'Where could he go? Probably to a place where he hasn't been to yet.' Such were our thoughts. Some fans thought he went to Hamleys, the biggest toy store in London. Therefore, I took a cab with a few people from Poland and we went to this shop. There were other fans, as well. We went on each floor, looking around. But there was no Michael. We thought that he probably wouldn't do the shopping during the opening hours so we waited until they closed the shop. Desperately we kept running from the front to the back entrance not knowing which one he would chose if he came. Then we were leaning against the shop windows, trying to see him shopping inside in case he had already sneaked in. I guess the staff had a great laugh! Eventually, we understood Michael was not going to visit Hamleys. Somehow, we found out that he went to the cinema which was close to the hotel. As we arrived there, he was already gone. I was a little bit disappointed at that moment. Nevertheless, I decided to head for the Dorchester Hotel. Soon the feeling of disappointment disappeared when I saw a group of fans in front of Michael's window. He was there! I could see the light in two of his windows and he was running from one to another and was playing with the curtains. He also waved to us out of the open window! It was incredible! I stretched my arm as far as I could and got the impression that our hands touched in the air. What he also did was show his face, as we shouted out: "Show your face". We also sang 'D.S.' That was probably what caught his attention. After some time, he closed the curtains. Then there was one of his bodyguards outside the hotel. We could ask him some questions, but he couldn't say when Michael was going to leave. I went back home.

Another day we gathered at the same time with the same goal. Whenever a black car was approaching the hotel or leaving its premises, emotions rose. What is worth mentioning is a situation in which I really held my breath. A black car stopped by the main

by Laura Czerska

entrance, naturally we assumed it was Michael. However, instead, we saw ... Jean Réno. I don't know how to describe the emotions at the sight of this actor. Surprise? Shock? Disappointment? Or all of them at the same time? It was nice to see someone famous, but he wasn't the one we were looking for! There was only one person among us that shouted: "Mr Réno!" He could enter the hotel without any fuss, which would be impossible in Michael's case! Anyway, we were still waiting for our idol. As usual, he appeared at his window in the evening. He was wonderful, he was sending kisses, he showed something (a pillow, I guess) where he'd written: 'I love you'. Actually, I didn't see this clearly because I'm short-sighted, but other fans told me so I tried to make this out. Anyway, it was great to see him again. The atmosphere was wonderful. Within these days, we made up some simple songs while calling Michael – songs like: 'We love you Michael, we do, we love you Michael...'. We also sang his songs (eg. 'You are not alone' or 'D.S.').

Next day, in the morning I was walking through the city centre to an internet café to read some news about Michael. I read about his visit in the cinema and about his jokes with the kids in the hotel. What I also read was that he had left London early in the morning. Somehow, some fans had known about that and followed him to the airport where they could wave him goodbye. I got sad at that moment. I wished I had been among those fans. How did they know? Again, I was a little disappointed because I wanted more! Michael has that quality that you can never have enough of him. I was glad I experienced what I experienced then, even though I wanted more. I hoped to shake his hand or make an eye-contact with him. But those who experienced that, wanted more anyway. And so it goes.

Now that Michael is gone, I'm really happy I could at least see him at the window. He was a wonderful idol because he was not indifferent towards us – I was a witness to that. His visit in London was more of a private visit. As he came to London just a few months after his acquittal, undoubtedly, he was tired of being in

by Laura Czerska

the public's eye; he wanted to relax and have fun with his kids. But he showed that he cared for his fans by appearing at the window and sending his bodyguards down. At the beginning of his stay, he was more open to his fans, but it was probably because he went out more often. I also found out that one day he had ordered pizza for his fans. That was before I got there, but frankly speaking when I was so close to Michael, I didn't need to eat or drink. He provided me with so much excitement that basic needs simply didn't matter.

by Laura Czerska

A fan's life

by Eva Lassmann, Germany

For me, all began sometime before 1992. I was 9 years old and Michael's "Dangerous" album had just come out. It's still a riddle for me and my family, why I absolutely wanted to spend my first saved pocket money for this album, how and when I even got to know Michael. All I know is, that I felt blessed when I finally held my first music tape in my hands (for which I already got put down from my sister as wacko). Ever since I had the feeling that this pure voice sang only for me. For example the words „Gone to soon", I misinterpreted as „Go to school". I thought it was very touching that Michael went through all this trouble, just to remind me to go to school. Well, with Michael's help I slowly learned the English language. Of course, as time went by, I began to understand more and more of his songs correctly. He took great influence in my life and the feeling of closeness to him stayed and grew quickly to love. To me, he never has been „Michael Jackson", even though we fans admire him as something transcendental we love him as „our" close friend „Michael".

1997, 5 years later, I saw him in concert for the first time. An experience I can't describe and will never forget. One year later Michael visited Munich, my hometown. He stayed for over two weeks for private reasons. In these two weeks, my family and friends didn't see very much of me (except in school). I spent every free minute in front of his hotel for two weeks, whether there was rain, snow or sun. Under his eyes I made my homework, sang for him, made banners, worked on my tan on the hotel's lawn and I made new friends.

This was a memorable time, in which my "fandom" reached a new level. I was not alone anymore with Michael and the magazines, which kept me posted on the news about him. I had to share

Michael. But that wasn't hard at all, because I could share dreams and hopes, frustrations and excitement as well. Now together, we informed each other about MJ-news, made plans, banners and travels, where we got more and more friends, literally all over the world.

I got intoxicated with felicity and bliss, a wave swashed over me, pulled me into swirls that spun me around and spit me out, back onto the top of the wave, where I surfed in happiness, as if there was no tomorrow. Blissful, exciting years went by like that, feeling high. Nothing was more important than Michael and his music. His ups and downs I lived through with him and every possibility to be near him was grabbed, regardless of the consequences. The rare meetings with Michael, for which we worked so hard, glittered in our hearts and were too big to understand on our own. Even though he was miles away, we felt so close to Michael, just because we had found other fans, with whom we could share our passion.

In retrospect I wouldn't want to miss this time, not for the world. It was an intensive phase. It will hardly be possible to ever live such an unapologetic life. The energy and enthusiasm carried me over all cliffs, such as foreign countries where we travelled without a penny left, nights in the streets, hours and days in the rain, snow or torrid sun, absence from school or work, fights with parents, sleeplessness, huskiness, emotional heights and depths in unhealthy alternation, missed flights home and a lack of understanding from the „outsiders". It was a life that took a lot, but the more we gave, the more we got back. It made me who I am.

In my case, it couldn't go on like that for ever. At some point this lifestyle had become "too much" and I asked myself, what for I was going through all that. Something stagnated. Slowly I got other goals in life, illusions vanished, and another future came in sight with my first serious boyfriend. He once told me: "That's not you", after I had told him something about Michael. That made me think and I asked myself who I really was and where I wan-

by Eva Lassmann

ted to go. And I recognized that I had lost sight of who I really was due to Michael. And I also said goodbye to believing that Michael needed me. Although I knew, that he honestly loved and appreciated us a lot, I felt that he was better served without the screaming fans, that wouldn't let him alone for just one second.
Again, a new period of my life started, this time Michael took the back seat. Getting independent from Michael wasn't an easy procedure at all. It hurt letting this love go. One or two "fan-friends" went through the same change with me but the other "fan-friends" I didn't see anymore. Frankly, it has become too boring and plain for me that they seemed to have only one topic: Michael – naturally! And that's exactly what I didn't want anymore.

This all happened around seven years ago. During all the years I hardly ever met other fans anymore and Michael was more or less just a musician to me. I started and completed my degrees in literature and found a good job, travelled and finally got to go sightseeing (not only Michael-seeing). And I got engaged with that very boyfriend and will soon get married. I went through my personal heights and depths and damn, I'm proud of that! Also this made me who I am.

It could have gone on like that.
But then that morning came, when the guys in the radio told me something unbelievable.
Michael Jackson was dead. Michael! How is this possible? I left my breakfast at once and the first thing I did was calling my old friends. How were they doing? I was sure they already knew, way before me. It was no question that I immediately went to see them.

After all these years I sat again in the well known kitchen of my good old friend, together with a bunch of other girls that used to be part of the old clique which actually hadn't existed like that for years now. Still it was the most natural thing in the world. After all these years I knew, that they would feel the same disbelief about Michael's death and the same emptiness inside. I also knew

by Eva Lassmann

that my grief was different to theirs. Not as broad and deep and more rational because I had filled my life with something other than Michael almost entirely – did I?
However I just wanted to be there if they needed me and I needed them to understand what was going on. Now a few months later everyone has found a way to cope with Michael's death somehow. Maybe we will never fully comprehend that he is really gone. But life, life goes on. And friendship goes on. That's the best heritage Michael could have left us: the friends that he gave us, the memories that we live through together again and again, the enthusiasm that inflames us when we hear his music.

When I see pictures of Michael, I feel deep gratefulness, love and security which you usually can only feel when looking into your parent's or brother's face. There is this familiarity that you can only feel with yourself. And there are the memories of thousands of intensive moments that I connect with thousands of different faces. My life was one like thousand lives together and still – life has just begun.

by Eva Lassmann

Escape!

by Dagmar Herrmann, Germany

Pursued through the shadows of the past
tormented by the shreds of memory
tortured by doubts of inadequacy
pressed through thoughts of hopelessness -
you don't find comfort
you are your worst enemy.
Is there no ESCAPE?

Walked on the stony way to success
controlled with iron will the wishes
denied the insistent desire
hidden the most affectionate feelings -
you're weeping the life afterwards
you see yourself in the mirror -
and search for the way out.

Showered with gold and gifts
changed the life in a constant party
climbed to the peak of immortal fame
unstoppable catapulted in dizzy heights -
you ask for safe ground
search for a hand which holds you.
Do you attempt to ESCAPE?

Do you try to escape from the morning
get away with gasping breath the persecutions
wounded by hate, envy and slander
crushed by force of the wrong emotions.
You search for warmth and for love
and trust your tears.
Do you find the way out?

Look deep into the bottom of your heart
explore the corridors of the time and experience
renew the oath of your youth.
Fulfill your childlike yearning
for love and pureness
other ways still stand open.
Escape! The gate into freedom!

BUT – too late!

by Dagmar Herrmann

My inspiration

by Mark Makowski, Poland

Everything started over 15 years ago, when my older brother introduced me to Michael Jackson on a pirate CD that he had bought for himself. In the beginning he wasn't anything special to me but after a few months I began to recognize and like MJ on the radio and on TV.

Finally, in the year 1996 I found out Michael was coming to our country Poland. He was going to give us his first concert in our history and his career.

Unfortunately I was only seven then, so I couldn't go and see MJ live because no one wanted to look after me at the show. They explained: „Do you realize how many people there will be? You can easily die in that crowd." So knowing that Michael was only five minutes from my home and all I could see of him was his cars leaving for the airport after the show made me very sad and angry and cried a lot.

After that time I told myself that I'm gonna be the second-best dancer, after MJ of course. So I started to practice his dance and still do to this day. My dream was to show Michael how I can dance for him. When I heard about his concerts in London, I knew that I had to be there and finally see him live, see him performing and just feel his genius of creation.

I was totally welling up when I got my ticket and knew that I was finally able to see him live.

However this time fate was very cruel to me and to all the MJ fans. From the day Michael passed away, I was crying for a whole week through. My tears didn't want to stop. Our genius of music, of dance, of songs and my moral father and biggest authority is gone.

by Mark Makowski

But he left me with his love and inspiration that I will follow for the rest of my life. I started so many things because of him and I'm not going stop. One of those things is teaching young people to dance like MJ because I believe they need to know who he was, the genius of creation and the most wonderful person and performer that the world has ever seen.

Thank you Michael, you're still alive in my heart and in everything you've done.

by Mark Makowski

Prague 1996 - MYStory

by Olaf Haensch, Germany

The many people who had gathered in the lobby of the hotel, waiting for HIM, started to forget their surroundings. Stoically, they focused the front doors, their nervousness increased with every minute. Now everyone was on their own, all others became competitors. If you didn't know what they were all waiting for, you would have guessed they would be getting something to eat after three weeks of starving. The scene had something animalistic in it, something threatening, instinctive. Through the glass doors we could see the people outside in the rain, who were overjoyed right now, screamed, waved and fought for their place. The reason was not to be seen, but we knew it. HE had just returned and in a few seconds this turmoil would break out right here where we were, in the protected lobby.

The day before, my friend and I had arrived in the Czech capital. We had both never been to a concert. And now we had specifically chosen the greatest show of all: the world premiere of Michael Jackson's „HIStory" tour. Associated with that were pictures that we knew from television reports about his past tours. So with these on-screen-memories of screaming, panicky and to unconsciousness exhausted fans in mind, we went to Prague full of expectation and nervousness. Fortunately, an accommodation was quickly found. Long before we reached the city, oversized posters greeted us and got us into the right mood. So it was really true, he is here, we have tickets, we will see him! Until then, it was just unreal and unimaginable. We only knew him from television, where he was always portrayed as supernatural, unapproachable and almost alien-like. How could it be that he was suddenly here in the same city? We only needed to go and that's it?

Quickly we left our luggage in our hotel and drove back downtown. Since we did not know exactly where the Letna Park, where the stage was, was located, we first headed to the hotel Inter-Continental, where already hundreds of fans had gathered. We caught our breath, this was something we had never seen before! So we quickly gathered ourselves and then joined the turmoil. We didn't have to wait very long. Only a few moments later, Michael Jackson himself came out of the hotel. He stopped briefly, waved - and came straight towards us! Only one meter away from the fence right in front of us he stood with his red jacket and gave a few autographs. Unbelievable! You sit in your car in the morning driving for several hours, then torture yourself through the Czech capital to find your accommodation and two hours later, the most famous man on earth is facing you. I still love to remember this moment, his incredible presence and the fact that he seemed very small to me.

What could now still go wrong? We had just arrived and had already gotten everything. To see him in real life only once, to be convinced that this is all real, put the lid on our shared passion. Michael had left his hotel in order to rehearse. We could now calmly search the stage after we had eaten something at the restaurant on the corner. Finding the stage was simple, it was loud enough. The typical bass sounds were banging through the town. On our way we guessed the songs: Scream, Off The Wall, Billie Jean... After all, we knew nothing about what should happen on the next day save one. Nothing, absolutely nothing was known about the show. There was no internet, which whispered every detail already days or weeks before. Like children, we barely couldn't stand the tension anymore and it was fine that way. As pleasant as the internet is today, sometimes I curse it. It robs the people of the unknown, the charms of novelty, the excitement.

So, together with other fans we stood behind big black blinds listening to the rehearsals, which went on well into the night. The next morning we were back on the spot, and here we got to know Ulrike from the Rhineland. She was there alone, was staying in

by Olaf Haensch

the same hotel as Michael and invited us to join her there. We couldn't believe our luck to suddenly be on the other side of the barricades. Outside, the fans stood in the rain, and we were sitting comfortably in the lobby with an orange juice and waited for him. Familiar faces from Michael's team walked past us. Bob Jones chatted at the bar, some musicians were sitting a few feet away.

Michael was somewhere in the city and we were waiting for him. We had seen him up close, had been at the rehearsals and of course finally I got the idea that I could try to get an autograph. I had precautiously gotten myself a postcard with Michael's portrait, had found a thick film writer in our hotel, and now I stood in the middle of this turmoil in the foyer at a, in my opinion, strategically good place. I had chosen a corner that Michael had to circle inevitably on the way to the elevator and so I hoped to get close enough. Now, everything went fast, much faster than I liked. The doors opened and a group of bodyguards came in. Michael had to be somewhere in between. At last I could see him as he wanted to give autographs. He didn't have a pen yet, but I had one! And indeed, yes, he had seen it and came directly towards me. I already thought I had made it, but what was that? A hand grabbed my card and the pen! But it did not belong to Michael! One of the bodyguards had realized his request and gave him the pen. Michael, however, did not at all what I had expected, but went a few meters back and signed albums, books and maps, then got back closer to me and - past me - straight into the elevator. What an impertinence, I thought, having already the total loss of the card and the borrowed pen before my eyes. So here I was now jostling with the masses behind the 6 or 8 guards and begged for my card. The elevator opened and I already saw Michael disappear with my borrowed property. But ultimately, the unexpected happened. I saw a hand reach over to me with my card, signed! Whose hand it was, I'll never know. But Michael had not forgotten me and I had now actually received something from him personally, an illegible scribbler on my card, which could with a little imagination be identified as „Michael Jackson". The card immediately disappeared into my jacket, because the

347

by Olaf Haensch

fans around me were out of control and I had to be prepared for anything. He had kept the pen, of course ...

Those were my first real and the most intense experiences during my time as a fan. They should never be topped. But I have never aspired to more. He has given me everything he could give. Thus I was and am satisfied. I'll never be able to understand the reckless manner in which some fans have harassed the human being Michael Jackson, just to be closer or grab something from him. Together with friends I got to experience 7 concerts. The beautiful experiences in Prague and at the other concerts I will never forget.
In 2002, Michael came to Germany again. I enjoyed his stay mostly behind the scenes, and I was deeply shocked by the selfishness of men. I experienced a cursing, discontented and whimsical filmmaker who did not get the „material" he wanted. He had even organized a fanparty to film the superstar along with his fans. I saw selfish fans who begged for Michael's visit to the party, although the chosen disco had no proper safety precautions and the organizers themselves seemed to be quite disorganized and overstrained. At first, there was no one there to sell tickets and lottery tickets were sold although there were no prizes. A show program did not exist. The party was a fiasco, and no one had taken care of Michael's safety. Our team then phoned Michael's former manager, who was almost on the way to the nightclub with Michael already, to warn him and to cancel the visit. This decision was not easy for us, but the person was more important than the personality. After all these experiences, I decided to retire almost entirely from the fan scene, although I had been one of the most active fans behind the scenes for years. I could no longer endure fans and business people who hazarded all consequences in order to get their very own piece of the pie.

Today I still enjoy hearing the unique music and sharing it with friends. His death hit me harder than I had expected. We had previously thought about it occasionally, how it would be - afterwards. Of course it's different. Even now it remains hard

by Olaf Haensch

to understand many reactions and opinions. Michael Jackson's death became a worldwide media event. People who have previously ridiculed him are now suddenly his followers. People follow a trend, in our paradoxical world it is „in" right now to buy and listen to MJ music. Everyone quickly wants to go with it, publish a biography, organize a memorial concert, be on TV - before the source of money finally runs dry. I take the „Dangerous" album off the shelf, dive into the memories, into the wonderful music. The news fade while the music fills the room and myself. The images in my mind are the last moving pictures of Michael when he was rehearsing for „This is it". He is high-spirited, full of joy and expectations, laughing. I feel good.

by Olaf Haensch

In the eyes of those who love him

by Sandra Mojas, USA

Sandra Mojas is a photographer who has done extensive work in capturing images of fans during the Michael Jackson tria

„Beat me, hate me, you can never break me
will me, thrill me, you can never kill me
...kick me, hike me, don't you black or white me."
--Lyrics to They Don't Care About Us

„....and I just hope that one day that they will be fair and portray me the way I really am, just a loving and peaceful guy ...I want to be a joy to the world. "
--Michael Jackson

Who MJ really is, is who we all really are. And that, in essence, has to do with how bright or how dim the light is that we emit (and inspire). Who MJ is can be seen in the eyes of those who love him and defiantly stood for him. Love opens people's hearts and dilates the soul. These people were loving Michael, and as a result were open to a channelling of God's light (both reflected and inspired) that can be seen in the photographs. Through the portraits we get glimpses; and without knowing it, these individuals serve to create a composite portrait of Michael's true identity.

Of varied ages, races, nations....backgrounds, sensibilities, and forms of expression...his supporters represent different elements of Michael Jackson. They are diverse and multi-faceted, but at the same time, one, in the light that testifies on his behalf.

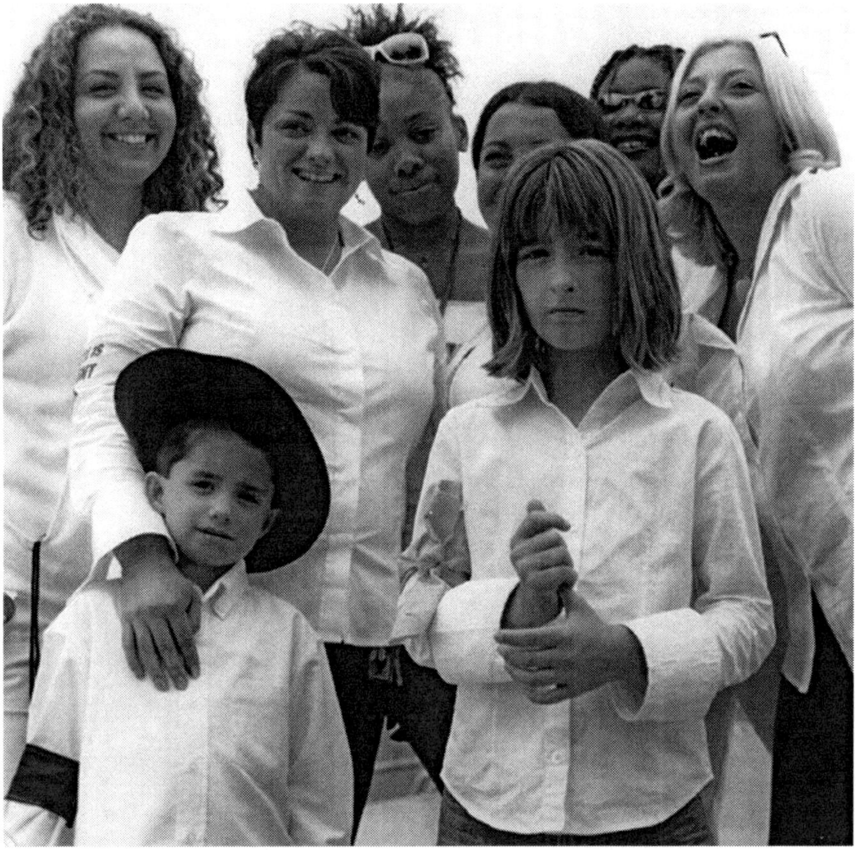

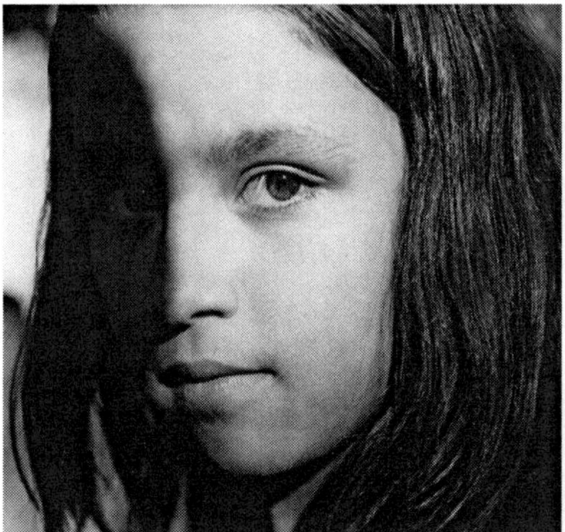

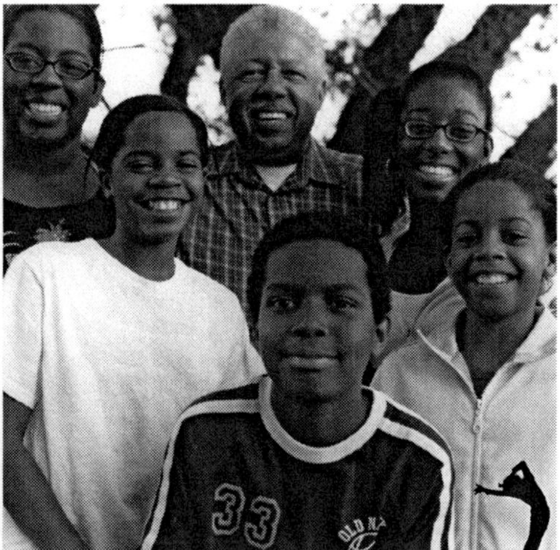
33

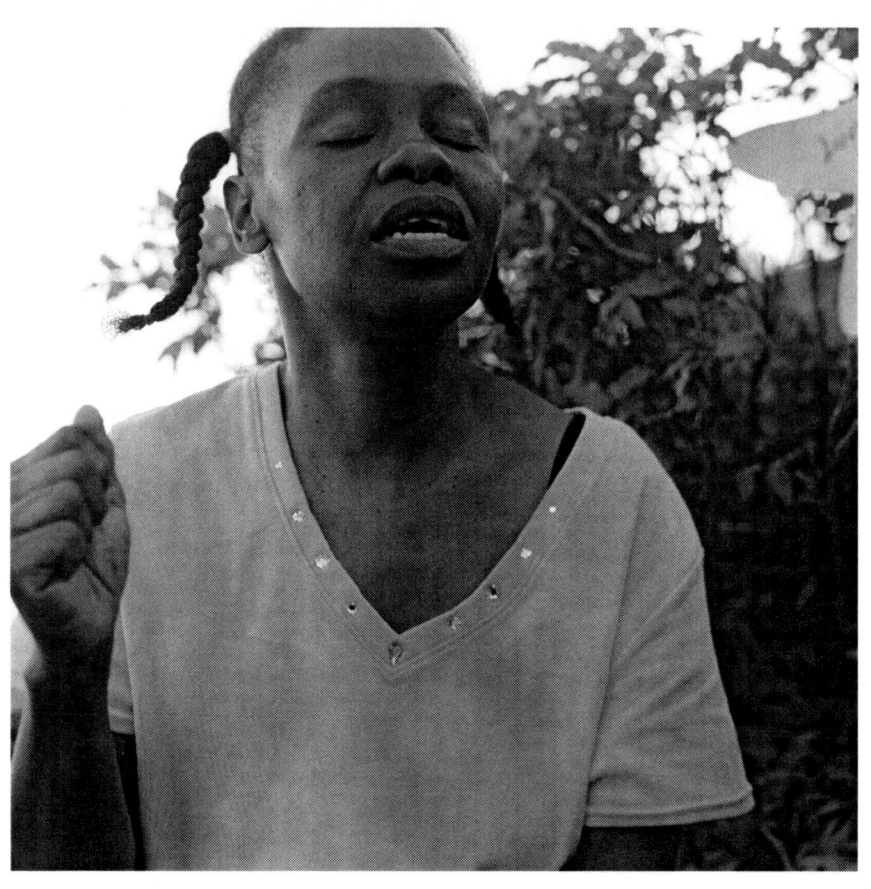

for more Sandra Mojas pictures of Michael Jackson fans please visit her website: www.reframingmichaeljackson.com

"I give you more than a hug"

by Sybille Wittmann, Germany

My name is Sybille and I'm a huge Michael Jackson fan since 1989. Ever since watching his movie „Moonwalker", I couldn't wait to see him live in concert...thankfully, a few years later he started his „Dangerous" Tour. I desperately wanted to see him - and I did. So then, the greatest moments in my life were seeing Michael at his concerts in Bayreuth and Munich for the first time ever. I always tried to be in the front row and managed to get there most of the time. During every show I envied the girls who got the chance to hug him on stage during „She's out of my life" or „You are not alone". I wanted to meet him so badly, only get the chance to hug him once in my life. This was my biggest dream which I never thought would come true...until the announcement was made that MJ would come to Berlin to receive the Bambi Award in 2002. Berlin should change my life forever.

I have to say in advance that I had already prepared a big poster for MJ a few months before. Since I knew he loved children, I put a lot of effort in it and collected a lot of additional baby pictures. I already had the banner with me on a few MJ events before, like London for example. Michael saw it once in London and he waved to me, but I didn't get the chance to give it to him because the car drove by too fast to follow. I was quite disappointed that I didn't get the chance to hand it to him during his stay in Britain back then. Little did I know that this would be the best thing that could have happened to me. That is when I learned that everything in life happens for a reason.
Then the big day came, MJ arrived in Germany. I urgently had to prepare everything to make it possible to get there: take off some

days from work and talk to my best friend Nicole about how and when we should get to Berlin. Luckily she has relatives in Berlin where we could stay.

So, on Tuesday, November 19th 2002, I entered my train to Berlin. In the afternoon, my friend Nicole called me and was all excited, she could barely speak. She told me that she had met Michael on his way into the hotel, at the entrance. There even was a picture of her in the newspapers the day after. Now she was amongst the group of lucky girls who met him. I didn't expect to get that lucky myself though. I felt very happy for her, because I think she really deserved it, but I have to admit that I was a bit jealous, too. Nevertheless, as soon as I arrived at the Adlon hotel, Nicole called me to get into a taxi. She would join me so that we could drive to the restaurant where Michael had dinner at that time. Once there, I found a good spot which was pretty much in the front part of the fan crowd. Shortly after, the moment arrived, Michael came out of the restaurant and hurried into the van that was waiting for him in front of the building. Everything was very hectic at that time, but I was just happy to see him again. It crossed my mind that it would be best to run in front of the van, so MJ has the chance to see my poster, which I did. I positioned myself in front of the car, held up my poster, as all of a sudden one of the bodyguards came up to me and asked me to hand him over my banner because Michael wanted to have it. I never ever believed something like that would happen to me. I told him that I wanted to give it to Michael personally and he replied he would go and ask Michael. I couldn't believe my ears: HE WANTS TO ASK MICHAEL! Right! My heart was jumping when he came back and told me that Michael had said yes! Soon after that, I found myself standing at the door of Michael's van, talking to him. I just couldn't believe what was happening there. Is this really happening? Is this really me? I was lost, like in a dream. Michael, however, was so kind to even help me by telling the securities that they should let me in. Well, first thing I asked Michael, a moment I longed for my whole life, was, if I could get a hug to which he replied, "yes, of course, I give you more than a hug!". He talked

by Sybille Wittmann

to me while we hugged and I looked him in the eyes. God, that was the happiest moment in my whole life and I even have it on DVD.

Since then I know that dreams do come true! You just have to believe in yourself and work hard for your goals. Michael was such an incredible person, such an inspiration and so full of love. I do miss him dearly, but I am very grateful for all the happy moments Michael brought into my life and all the unforgettable experiences I made together with the other fans during his concerts and the time spent in front of the hotels. He will be in my heart forever! Michael, I will always love you!

by Sybille Wittmann

The purest smile I have ever seen

by Goncerenco Sherin, Romania

When Michael visited Romania for the first time in 1992 I was only three years old so I didn't comprehend a lot. But as he came back in 1996, I finally saw him. Not in concert since I was still too small for that but I was there when he arrived at the airport in Bucharest.
Now I realize that that day was the happiest of my life so far.

There were a lot of fans but I was in the front together with my grandmother and my aunt. I screamed to him as loud as I could: "Michael!" And indeed he turned around, looked and then he smiled at me. He wanted to come over and give me an autograph but his bodyguards didn't let him. However his smile remained with me through all the years and each time I listen to his songs I remember it - the purest smile and look I have ever seen.

Dear Michael

by Brigitte Bloemen, Germany

You made us laugh,
you made us cry,
you taught us love,
why did you have to die?

You showed us the way,
opened the doors for others to follow,
lived your dreams day by day,
why does every day now seem so hollow?

The walls of the world you tried to break,
To give is the way, not just take.
But who listened to your word,
Who saw how much you hurt?

You always saw the best in others,
Wished for all people to live as sisters and brothers.
You dreamed of a better place,
While the world only watched your face.

The media said you are mad,
Now they praise you as a dad.
For Prince, Paris and Blanket we pray,
May your love in their hearts always stay.

All for fame and glory,
No-one ever dared to say sorry.
All the pain you had to feel,
Still the world didn´t wanna heal.

by Brigitte Bloemen

Now everybody is a fan,
Using your name whenever they can.
Where were all those people when you needed them most?
Probably reading the Mirror or the Daily Post.

Now everybody loves you.
They buy your music, too.
But still they don´t understand,
Years before you reached out your hand.

Through your trials and tribulations,
Your real fans from all nations
Stood by your side
Knowing there was nothing to hide.

You walked through the court door,
Showing love is worth fighting for.
And those who knew it before,
Now feel it even more.

Your presence still lingers here,
And to those who loved you it´s clear.
You will live forever in our hearts,
Long after you left the charts.

THANK YOU, MICHAEL!
For the inspiration, your soul and your art,
For your open, caring and golden heart.
I know now why God took you away…
Nothing gold can stay!

…still everyday I sigh,
Why did you have to die?

by Brigitte Bloemen

A cold winter's day in Berlin

by Agnes Spett, Hungary

In November 2002, Michael travelled to Berlin to receive the Bambi Award. Me and my friend went to his hotel, and despite of the freezing cold there were hundreds of fans from all over Europe and overseas waiting for him. Each time he looked out of his window, everyone was screaming and waving to him, showing their banners, just being happy, it was an incredible feeling. Only Michael could create this atmosphere that we have experienced in front of this beautiful hotel Adlon near the Brandenburger gate.

We went to his hotel early in the morning on the 21st of November and just waited and waited in the cold winter. Around noon, after he woke up, Michael immediately came to the window to greet and play with the fans, still wearing his pyjama pants. We kept showing him our banners and he pointed at us. We saw him explaining something to his bodyguard who appeared at the entrance of the hotel a few minutes later and asked us to go inside. I was both, really excited and nervous at the same time, because I knew that something big was going to happen! Actually I never ever expected to meet Michael because I thought it was impossible. Fortunately I did not have much time to think about this as only a few minutes later we were already standing in front of Michael in his hotel room.

He welcomed us, and from the very first moment we realized how nice, straightforward, funny and sweet he was. He may have realized that this was our first time meeting him and so I think he made sure that we feel comfortable. We absolutely did not feel

Agnes (left) and her friends at the window with Michael
Pictures by Heike Arbter

the fan-superstar distance. He joked, smiled a lot, and was very down to earth. Michael even invited us to sit down on his sofa, he asked us to say some words about our banners we had made for him, he kindly gave us autographs - actually his bodyguard told us that if we wanted to get something signed we could ask.

Michael did not mind that I had brought several things to get them signed for my friends. He hugged us and he even was so open and trusting to show us his son Prince. When a friend, who was still standing down on the street as she did not come up with us, called me on the phone, I gave Michael my phone to pick it up to surprise her. And he did and talked to her. He was simply amazing.

The "window door" to a French balcony was open in his living room while we were there and we could sometimes hear the fans chanting "Sony sucks" (which Michael joined in the room and repeated) or simply calling him to look out of the window. At one time he decided to do so and we went with him. That was real fun!
Because we were used to chanting with the other fans down on the street when Michael used to look out a lot during the previous day, we couldn´t help but join their excitement, although we now were right beside Michael looking out. Michael thought this was really funny and started to laugh really loud - he must have experienced what was going on down in the street by being right in the middle of us.

Me and my friend will never forget those 20 minutes we got to spend with Michael and are very thankful for the love and experience he gave to us.
Thank you, Michael! We love you...most!

by Agnes Spett

My life as MJ "fan"

by Harald Hehmann, Germany

Michael Jackson had to die to become human again.
A sad conclusion for many, but at the same time we, his fans, had the privilege to often experience him not only as an artist and entertainer, but also personally as a human being!

Michael gave so much to us and I am utterly convinced that we also meant a lot to him. He for sure thought highly of his most devoted fans. The press often wrote that Michael Jackson needs to hide from his fans and that he has to conceal his face and later on his children, only because of the fans. Fact, however, was that he just wanted to protect himself and his children from all bad things. Bad, for sure, was the press which only dumped malice and ridicule over him during the last 10 years, but his fans loved and admired him and vice versa. Us, he did not fear…

In 1996, when I was 16 years young, Michael Jackson was just about to inaugurate the "Colorado MJ Thrill Ride" rollercoaster in the "Phantasialand" near Cologne. About 3000 fans were in the park and I was amongst a few hundred fans who had gotten free tickets. It was said it had been Michael's wish that the fans standing in front of his hotel will get those free tickets. I don't know whether PR was behind this or if it really was Michael's wish, but what happened on the same evening after all the tumult was over, showed the true Michael and was simply unbelievable. About 150 fans including myself were waiting in front of the hotel in Cologne, dawn was already falling, as finally a van arrived. Teddy Lakis (Michael's then-appointee to care about his fans) got out of the car and told us that Michael wants to say Thank you. So it came about that the van drove into the hotel garage at the back entrance. After a few minutes the gate opened up again, a chain of hotel employees built a barrier and on the other side Michael

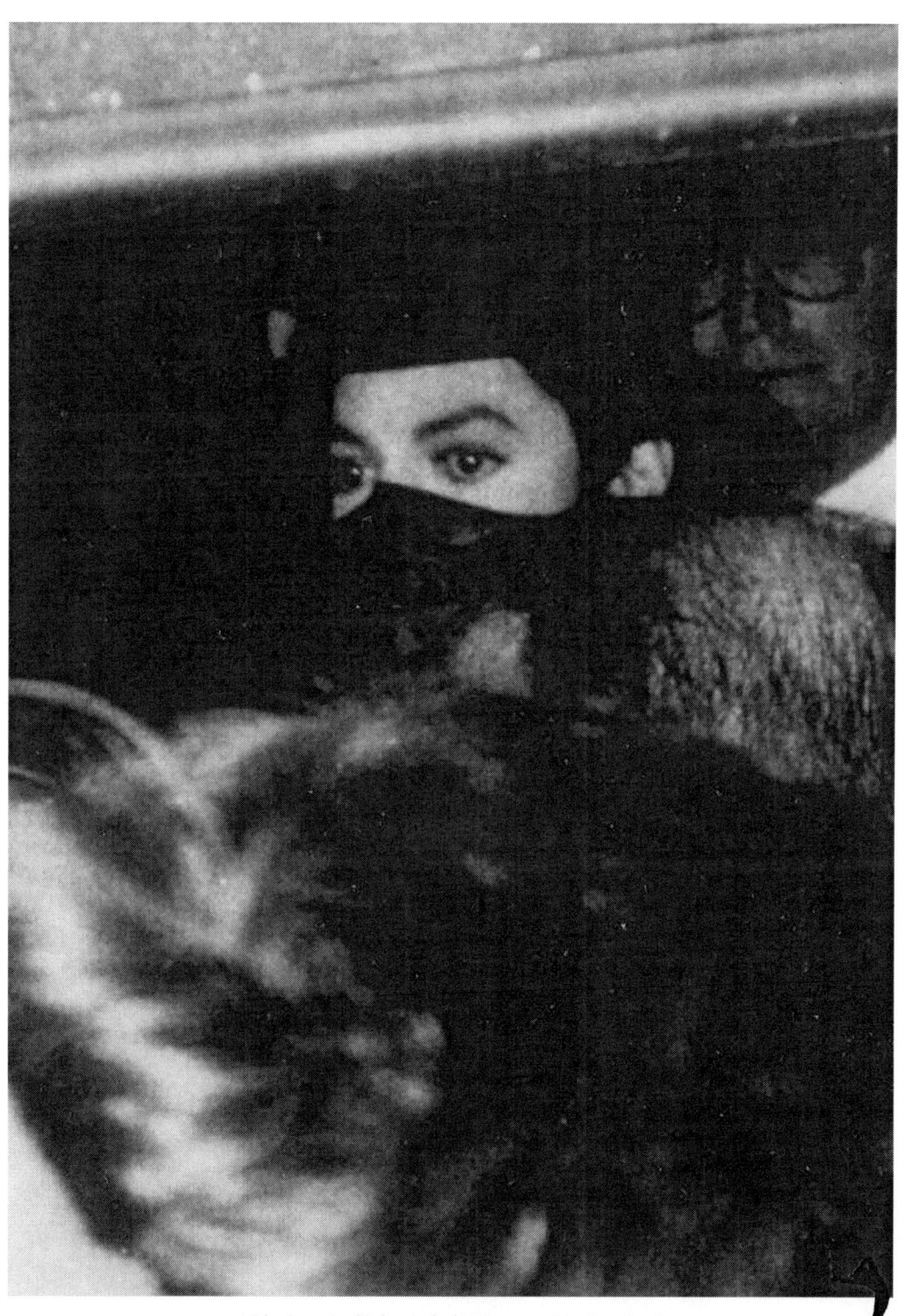

Michael meeting his fans in the hotel garage of the Hyatt hotel

stood and waved to his fans. No big turmoil, no cameras, just us fans and Michael. I was all excited! The whole thing only lasted a few minutes, but it was magical. In the same year I travelled to the HIStory concert in Amsterdam. The night after the second show, about 50 fans were standing in front of the hotel windows. 3 other fans and I made our way to a fast food restaurant at about 2 am ... well, the drama was perfect! When returning to the hotel, about half an hour later, the remaining 30 fans were totally freaking out. Michael Jackson had just successfully completed an extensive "window-action". Michael had thrown two pillows with autographs and messages for his fans out of the window. One boy and a girl managed to catch one each. I don't remember the messages completely, but it was something like "Tell all my fans I love them and thank you for your support, Michael Jackson".

Even though we had missed all that by mere minutes, everybody was happy and joyful. I need to add that those concerts took place at the end of September. The night temperatures were around the freezing point and fans camped in sleeping bags in front of the hotel at the canals of Amsterdam...

In the summer of 1997 the HIStory Tour stopped over in Germany. I went to the first concert in Bremen, to Cologne, to both Munich concerts and to round it up, to the show in Hockenheim. A summer I will never forget...

Munich was phenomenal. Michael stayed at the hotel Bayerischer Hof, together with his then-wife Debbie Rowe and his son Prince. Between the two concerts there was a day off. On this rainy summer day (it really didn't stop raining!) Michael kept the whole city on the go. Michael crossed all through the town to an Army Shop. Me and two other fans started our pursuit. Thanks to the city traffic, the three of us found ourselves standing at a red light along with Michael's car. Suddenly the car window opened and his bodyguard asked who wanted to have an autograph. And so it happened that first the two girls got one and then, just when it would have been my turn, the red light switched to green and it

by Harald Hehmann

Michael in Munich

was over. The car sped off! Admittedly I didn't even have anything with me he could have signed in the first place. My backpack and everything inside, even my clothes, were completely soaked from all that rain… anyway, I further ran behind the slowly moving car with other fans closely behind me. When we arrived at the Army Shop, we saw Michael was in a shopping mood. After half an hour he left the shop and walked right past us, waving happily. The few fans who were there, however, were too shy to say something, me included. No hysteria, just silence! Michael went on shopping in a toy store as somewhere along the road I lost my breath… In the evening everybody gathered at the hotel again, had a little party and just had fun. Eventually Michael joined us. He was high-spirited. Around 11 pm MJ jumped from window to window and played with the curtains. The fans were screaming. Chantings of "Michael Jackson", or simply "Michael, Michael!" started. A pillow flew down, again a message to the fans: "Burn All Tabloids" was written on it. Bed sheets with more messages from Michael were thrown out of the window. The fans heavily fought for each of them. It was a jolly and happy atmosphere. Michael showed his little son at the window and Debbie waved every once in a while. Obviously, Michael wanted to show us his family. We were overjoyed. That evening totally compensated for the bad weather. Of course, none of that was reported in the media…

All the concerts were spectacular. The shows in Munich were recorded for television, despite the rain. The Hockenheim show, to the contrary, hit the hottest day of the year and so many of the 90.000 people in the audience collapsed. For most of the concerts Michael was directly flown in from Paris, where he and his family stayed at the Disneyland Hotel. So there was no "hotel action" in Hockenheim, but the show itself was terrific enough.

In 1999 my first trip took me to Saarbrücken where Michael was the special guest at the "Wetten, dass..?" show. Sadly, I didn't make it into the studio, although some free tickets had been given to fans again. So I doughty waited outside. After his appearance in

by Harald Hehmann

Michael in Hockenheim

the studio was over, Michael entered his van, drove a few meters and then, exactly in front of me, the side door of the van opened. Michael Jackson was sitting there - I still see that picture in my head! He smiled like a little boy and pointed towards me with his finger, just like he wanted to say "Hey, don't you have something better to do?" During this short time so many fans gathered around the van that people's upper parts of their bodies moved along with the slowly driving car while their feet stayed at the same place on the ground. Eventually we all fell in a slanting position and finally all tilted over. Michael laughed out loud and sped off - it must have looked very funny indeed. Weeks later, I still had bruises on my head and knee. Such contusions and smaller injuries needed to be accepted when following Michael around.
That same summer the "Michael Jackson & Friends" concert took place in Munich. Again, Michael prepared some "hotel action". His arrival was celebrated by more than 5000 fans in front of his hotel. He walked past the screaming crowd - it was gigantic - I still have that yelling recorded on my old walkman. Total goosebumps-feeling! Michael seemed laid-back and relaxed, even though he had just returned from Korea where he performed the first "MJ & Friends" concert a day earlier.

The night after the show, Michael had to stay in a Munich hospital, because a bridge on the stage disengaged and fell down. Michael hurt his back during this accident. The next day, however, he seemed to be quite fit again and enjoyed standing at the hotel window once more. He collected gifts from his fans via balloons, self-painted posters were brought into his room and those fans who put a lot of effort into their presents and pictures were even allowed to meet Michael in person. This had already been common practice during the HIStory Tour. A bodyguard collected gifts, banners and letters and brought them to Michael. Later he came down again with certain pictures or gifts, asked who made them and the lucky one was allowed to meet Michael. I never was a big tinkerer or painter, therefore I sadly never had that privilege.

by Harald Hehmann

Unfortunately my flight back to Cologne was on that afternoon, so I missed a few things. But later, I saw pictures other fans took on that day. Michael really had a lot of fun...

In the year 2000 I went to Monaco. Michael received the "Artist of the Millennium" Award at the World Music Awards. The former German Michael Jackson Fan Club "Angel" had organized a cheap bus ride, so I hopped on. Unfortunately a ticket for the Award Show was not included, but that was not necessary either. We had a blast doing our singing and celebrating in front of the hotel where everything centred on MJ. The other "stars" became minor matters. The show was broadcasted on huge screens at Monaco's beach. The atmosphere was relaxed and I met a lot of nice new people there as well as some old friends from the days of the HIStory Tour. With some of them I am still in touch today - Michael unites! Luck wasn't on my side in Monaco though, somehow I always managed to be in a place where I could not see Michael at all. Others were lucky enough to see him all the time. Michael was good-humored, signed a lot of autographs, shook some hands, took some gifts and waved into many cameras, just not into mine. He was always friendly and just adorable. By all means that is what was reported to me.

Again I found myself aboard an "Angel Fan Bus" driving to Oxford/UK in March 2001. We gathered at the university where Michael was supposed to deliver a speech on that evening. It was raining! Michael walked on crutches, but he still insisted to thank his fans. He crawled out of his van, hobbled towards us, waved and took a bow before finally walking into the building. Only a short moment, but so worthy.

In summer 2002 I was on my way to England again. This time Michael Jackson visited London to attend the "Killer Thriller Party" organized by a British Fan Club. Earlier that day a demonstration took place in front of the Sony Centre near Oxford Street. Over 5000 fans had gathered there. Around noon Michael himself joined the demonstration and passed the crowd on a typical London double-decker bus. The sun was shining and the bus was open at the top.

by Harald Hehmann

Michael grabs banners from the top of a double-decker bus

Fans demonstrating in the streets of London

Michael ran around on that bus, waved to his fans and shouted via megaphone "Sony sucks", "Burn all tabloids" and "I love you". He smiled and was virtually euphoric. Once he even dangled himself over the bus rail to grab some fan banners. That scenery: Michael hanging down from a London sightseeing bus, surrounded by 5000 fans - simply unbelievable! And I was in the middle of it all. At the end, when the bus had to turn around the corner, you could hear the crunching of a pub's window, because those masses of fans were pressed against it. It was total frenzy. Finally the bus was gone. The whole spectacle had lasted for over half an hour...The same day Michael went to his own fan party and celebrated with around 3000 fans there. At the end of the evening Michael held a 15-minute speech in which he thanked his fans, talked about his differences with Sony and told us about his upcoming projects. Naturally the fans went nuts, but as soon as Michael talked we were all ears. At that party, there had also been a lottery. There had been several prizes like signed MJ items, collectables and the first prize of course was a meeting with the man himself. I only missed that by one lousy lottery number! If I had bought one more raffle ticket, I would have met Michael, damn! Anyway... after the show was over, Michael left the stage and, as usual, collected all the fan gifts he could carry and even climbed over and hung down the balustrade to grab some last pictures and banners. He always was kind of reckless regarding presents for him - one of his many childlike, wonderful and loving qualities.

The last time I saw Michael was in 2006 when he appeared at the World Music Awards in London. I was standing in the first row. At the end, during "We are the world", Michael took a little walk-around on stage and gave some fans a high five. At the last "high five" he looked me directly in the eyes while deciding to shake the hand of a hysterically screaming girl who was standing right next to me. The heck with it, I thought. Afterwards he threw his jacket into the audience. A hand full of fans was still fighting for a piece of that jacket long after the show had ended.

I can't tell whether Michael Jackson behaved differently towards his fans in the 80s, for I became a MJ fan in 1987 when I was 8

by Harald Hehmann

Michael on stage during the "Killer Thriller"-Party

Harald mourning Michael's death with other fans in Cologne

years old. In the 90s I started travelling around to see him, until the year 2006. I had also booked tickets for his London shows in January 2010. During my "fan time" I always got to know him as an open, friendly and loving person, as much as a "fan" can get to know his "star"...

Michael Jackson, to me, was more than just a "star", he was a part of my life, more like a family member...

RIP Michael!

by Harald Hehmann

Argentina 1993

by Anonymous, Argentina

Back in 1993 I was a member of a fan club and we all waited for Michael to finally arrive in Argentina. He passed by us in his van, looking through the window and watched our banner saying "Welcome in Argentina, Michael Jackson, We love you".
One day we saw Michael through the windows of a shop as he was about to shop for some clothes and even tried some on. We were so excited.

We waited all night in front of the Hyatt hotel, singing his songs and waited for Michael to wave down to us. One day Michael came out on his hotel balcony and stayed there for about 10 minutes, just waving back at us and looking at the enormous banner we had made for him, which said: "Your heart is as enormous as your talent" It was so amazing!

I am very glad that I have recorded a video of those incredible days which honestly were the best days of my life! Even though I was only 18 years old back then, I still feel the same way about Michael today. Michael's heart was at least as big as his talent. I am very grateful that I was lucky to have been able to visit three of Michael's concerts here in Argentina.

I will never forget those days.

My meeting with Michael Jackson

by Gina Banic, Germany

Before I begin to tell my story, I have to say how much Michael Jackson influenced me and how much richer he made my life overall. If I imagine to have lived in an era without him, I must say that I probably would have missed out on countless magical moments.
It is 1997, Michael Jackson is in the process of touring through Europe with the History World Tour, which kicked off in Prague in 1996. The King of Pop is all over the news, hysteria is everywhere – he is simply on top of the world.
I had just graduated from college and decided to treat myself to a trip leading me through numerous parts of Europe in order to see Michael Jackson perform live. That has always been a dream of mine and it certainly was the most exciting experience of all time!!! And let me tell you, I feel so sorry for all the people out there, who have never gotten the chance to witness the man live on stage. It was out of this world.

It was July when I jumped on a train all by myself – I was completely determined and I didn't care about being alone, I wasn't afraid, all I felt was mere excitement and joy about my journey. On my way through the different cities I met some really cool people, who were all fans from all over the world following Michael. It was just like a big family travelling together. And than I met one girl, who became my best friend on the road – Lisa Marie (Fio). She was so nice, cool and not as crazy as some other people. Needless to say that Fio and I spend the rest of the tour together, which in the end made it 10000 times better.
My god, I had so many things with me, things I wanted to give

to Michael, like a coat I had made, a very large collage which is an assortment of photographs and drawings from children from all over the world. I had given some of those kind of collages to Michael before and he absolutely loved them, so I continued to make more, because I wanted to give him something to show my appreciation.

So one day, we are about to go to the show in Oslo (Norway) and Fio and me are sitting in front of the lockers at the train station, where we had stored our luggage. For some reason I felt the need to bring the collage to the concert that day, which I had never done before, because I was always afraid that somebody might break it, since it was very large and tough to transport. Well, that day I did it anyways.

So we arrive at the Stadium, we manage to make it to the front row – yet again, and that in itself was always a blessing. I cannot begin to tell you how great Michael and his people were to us. He made sure to let the fans who went to all theses shows in before everybody else. How wonderful is that??!!! I don't know any other person who does that, but that's Michael for you. It was just amazing.

So usually what happens before the show is, that the crowd inside the stadium is being filmed and shown on the jumbotrons, which are the large screens next to the stage, and that was always a lot of fun. This would happen to the funky tunes of Motown classics ranging from Diana Ross to the Temptations and many more. So today Fio and I are being taped, which normally happens with the people in the front rows. I have put my banner out and was waving it from side to side, so that everybody could see it and all of a sudden a man appeared in front of me, asking me if this was a gift for Michael. I answered yes and he wanted to take it with him right away. Before I let it go I asked the man if it was possible for me to get an autograph from MJ, because I had already been a fan for 10 years and I didn't posess one and that that would be the coolest thing ever. He said no problem and told me that he'd be back. "How cool is this" I thought to myself, all excited that I'd finally receive a personal autograph from MJ. We couldn't

by Gina Banic

believe it. The next thing I know is that Michael's stage manager (Anthony) stood in front of me, looked me in the eyes and asked me: "Do you want to meet Michael?"

First, I thought I heard wrong and just stared at him and all I could do was nod my head. Within 5 seconds I was pulled out of the front row and I was on my way backstage to meet Michael Jackson. And remember, there wasn't a lot of time before the show was about to begin, so I am totally freaking out inside and I am desperately trying to think of things I've always wanted to tell him and not to have a nervous breakdown.

When we entered Michael's wardrobe, I saw him dressed in his golden stage outfit. He walked over, gave me a firm handshake and said: "Hi Gina, how are you?"
I could not believe that he actually knew my name!!! Well, maybe somebody told him, but he knew and with him being so calm, friendly and down to earth I felt very much at ease in his presence. I finally answered to MJ: "Well Michael, I am very well – this must be one of the greatest moments of my life, so thank you very much. You are such a big inspiration to me and everyone out there and I am following you around Europe. I really enjoy all your performances."
It seemed as if Michael was very much used to hearing things like that, but he was very kind and thanked me for being there for him and supporting him and showing so much love.

Then I gave him the present I made for him, he opened it up and kept staring at it as if it was the artwork of Michelangelo. His ability of being excited like a child about a present amazed me. It was so nice to see that the biggest entertainer of all times is so normal and sweet. It was exactly what I had always imagined it would be. Michael kept thanking me over and over again: "Thank you so much for this beautiful artwork, I love it, I love it, I love it. You know, I keep all your presents (from the fans) at Neverland. I have a special place where I keep them. It means the world to me. Please promise me to make more of these – it's absolutely

by Gina Banic

beautiful." I answered "Off course I will Michael". He then took the present and handed it over to Michael Bush, his personal stylist. He told him to make sure to put it on his seat in the plane! He said it in a very demanding tone. I loved it.
At that time, Michael just became a father and Prince was too little to travel on a plane, so MJ kept flying back and forth to Paris to be with his child.

I asked Michael: "So how did you know that I had this present for you?" He put his arm around my shoulder, turned me into another direction and pointed at a TV screen that showed all the fans inside the stadium. MJ: "You know, you guys always think you're watching me, but in reality I'm watching you" and he starts laughing really loud. I couldn't believe what he just said and I felt kind of embarrassed, because we as fans always did so many silly things. So now both of us were laughing. While I tell Michael how unbelievable and great that is, he is now looking in the mirror and putting on the final make-up touches. The funny thing was that I kept thinking: Why isn't he telling me to leave? It's been minutes already and he is so comfortable with me being there (and nobody else around by the way), that he simply doesn't care. "I just don't know how you do it?" MJ said "All the traveling and standing in the sun all day long for the shows and waiting and all that. It always amazes me. You have so much love – it's a beautiful thing and it warms my heart." "Well Michael, when it's worth it – it's just worth it" I answered confidently.

At some point Michael Bush walks back in the door again, looks at Michael and says: "Michael, we have to get ready. It's getting late!" So Michael walks over to his stylist, who starts putting on the silver shining knee protectors. "I'm so sorry, but I'm going to have to go on stage now. The show is about to start. Thank you so much for coming" he says to me, walks over and gives me a biiig hug. All I remember is holding Michael very tightly and him doing the same. We were cheek by cheek for quite a while, as if we had been friends forever and said our good-byes. He smelled very good – a mixture of perfume and make-up – extremely pleasant.

by Gina Banic

As I thanked him for this wonderful experience I just remember him smiling at me and I have to say to everyone out there, who never stood in front of Michael Jackson that his smile was phenomenal, his aura was one of a kind and he was the sweetest and kindest person you could ever meet. And I have met and worked with many celebrities in my life, but he was one of a kind!!!

So I turned around to walk out and told him my last "I love you Michael", while he responded "I love you more and watch out!" I didn't know what he meant and within a split second I have hit my head so hard on some type of metal, which made us both laugh. Well, me due to embarrassment, him out of amusement I guess, but that was ok with me. I waved at him and he disappeared. The stage manager, Anthony, was holding my hand and walked me back out into the stadium. The interesting thing is, that I was calm the entire time I was with Michael and that it really hit me what just happened, once we walked back into the stadium and I saw this sea of screaming people, just waiting to see Michael Jackson. Anthony lifted me back into the front row, where my friend Fio was waiting for me. We looked at each other and started crying and so did all the other fans around us, because they were aware of what just happened!!! Only a few brief moments later the music for the show trailer started and of course the hysteria began. That night it felt as if Michael came over to our side of the stage and waved a lot, while we threw kisses and waves back at him.

It was a magical experience and a day I will never forget. It has taught me that anything is possible, you only have to believe in it and put some effort into it and it will happen, so never give up on your dreams!
I was lucky enough to have met Michael Jackson several times throughout my life, I have been to Neverland twice and I have met the most amazing people and made numerous friends worldwide through being a fan of his. I am eternally grateful that I have lived in the era of the greatest entertainer of all times.
Thank you Michael.
All my love to all Michael Jackson Fans, Friends & Family. He will always be a part of us. Let's continue to heal the world.

by Gina Banic

Gina today

Gina with some friends mourning at the memorial in Munich

The Elephant Man's left hand

by Sandra Mojas, USA

    Feet trailing phosphorescence in the sand;
    You are firefly jelly, the golden hour and
    The Elephant Man's left hand.

    Slide down a dune, throw a balloon,
    Rejoice with a farmer's reserve;
    Not for the rain, but for the pain
    That God inverts to flower
    As earning converts to deserve.

    Now,
    Press your wrists inside the door jamb,
    Children inventing flight;
    Bright slate sky dumps change
    And reverie,
    Arms floating up to catch the light.

by Sandra Mojas

"Wetten, dass..?"

by Petra Fischer, Germany

Wednesday, November 1st, 1995
None of the other fans knew whether Michael would arrive on Friday or whether he possibly has been staying in Cologne since Monday already. I arrived yesterday evening, but there were no other fans in front of Michael's hotel. Today, I am stading in the rain again, alone, and I wonder whether Michael has decided to choose another hotel, not the Hyatt?
I decide to go and get some newspapers, but unfortunately they aren't writing anything new about Michael's stay in Cologne. Worried, I try to call some of my fan friends. Maybe they have heard something. But I am unable to reach them, so they are probably on their way already. No, mobiles are not commonly used yet – remember it is 1995! About two years from now, the most well-to-do fans will be able to afford their first mobile.
All I can do now is hope that I will meet my fan friends somehow. Cologne is not a small town and if Michael has decided to stay at another hotel, I will have a problem for I won't know about it until it's too late.

Two hours later, on my way from the main station back to he Hyatt, I finally run into some of my fan friends and now we are standing in front of the hotel together. That's better! It's still raining, but at least I know I'm waiting in the right place. According to the latest rumours, Michael is due to arrive on Friday. A Michael lookalike turns up, but we're not interested in him. We want to see Michael, the real Michael.

Thursday, November 2nd, 1995
In the morning, we are meeting in front of the Hyatt again, standing in the rain. At the moment, there are only about 30 to 40 fans from all over Europe. Some of them have travelled as far as

Mexico and Japan to see Michael perform during his „Dangerous" tour. They are the so-called hardcore fans. My friends and I aren't in the best mood because waiting in front of a hotel is no fun at all without Michael being there. However, I decide to stay at least until noon as I don't want to miss anything. Teddy, one of the people in Michael's entourage, said that he would be back to inform us at what time Michael will arrive tomorrow and whether there will be buses from the Hyatt to the airport for us.

Friday, November 3rd, 1995
Finally things are getting exciting! Sony has indeed provided five buses for the transfer to the airport, where we will be able to welcome Michael. That's service! Not only will we be permitted to enter an area of the airport which is usually closed to the public, but we won't even have to spend money to get there on our own. How cool is that!?

However, distributing the fans among the different buses is not as easy as one may think. First, Teddy names five fans as „leaders" for each of the buses. Then, he chooses the fans who will go on the bus. As he picks them from the first two rows, there is a big jostle among us. And as if this wasn't stressful enough already, there are TV crews shooting the chaos. We certainly don't feel like going on TV now, but there isn't much we can do about it. We need to get on the bus, so we can't just leave.

Again and again we are being counted. Each time we get more scared that there won't be enough seats for all of us. But in the end, they decide to let some fans ride on the „press bus" and we all fit in. I am so relieved that this stressful situation is finally over.
We are told to get off the buses next to an airfield access road, which is behind a closed gate and can only be reached by special permission. There, beneath an underbridge, we are allowed to stand behind the pedestrian railing and wait for Michael. The railing is quite dusty, and the whole place smells of exhaust gases. But who cares? We'll see Michael!

by Petra Fischer

It takes only half an hour or so, then a convoy of cars is approaching slowly. As the convoy is getting closer, someone is standing up inside, waving through the open sunroof. It's Michael! Michael! He ducks, gets out a bouquet of flowers, which he throws to the waiting fans, then he ducks again. He does this four or five times, throwing more flowers to the fans. Then he's gone. That was all. It all couldn't have lasted longer than a minute, but we are happy. We have seen Michael.

Back at the Hyatt, we are wondering whether we should go to Duisburg now, where the „Wetten dass" show will take place. There are rumours that Michael will rehearse this afternoon. However, we decide against trying to see him in Duisburg, which is about 100 kilometers north of Cologne, because we don't know our way around here. Keep in mind, it's 1995 and navigation systems weren't widely used either.
Only a few fans went to Duisburg, as they later tell us. Michael waved briefly, then disappeared into the Rhein-Ruhr-Halle to rehearse his show. So we had made the right decision staying in Cologne.

In the evening Michael is back at the hotel. He appears at the window and we are all very happy and excited to see him. But unfortunately, his suite is too high up and besides, the windows can't be opened. Michael tries to open them several times, but to no success.

Saturday, November 4th, 1995
The big day has finally come! Tonight, the "Wetten dass" show will take place. Unfortunately, I have had no success in getting a ticket yet. In front of the hotel, some of the fans are arguing about how to distribute the few tickets of the fan clubs among the many fans hoping to see Michael tonight. I am not in the mood to listen to them, knowing I will not be among the lucky ticket holders anyway. So I decide to buy some newspapers instead, as a souvenir of what happened yesterday.
It's two o'clock in the afternoon. Two of my fan friends were

by Petra Fischer

lucky in winning tickets for the show, which they have to pick up before four o'clock. So we are leaving for Duisburg, where we drop them off at an office somewhere to collect their tickets. They'll then take a bus. The rest of us are now looking for the broadcasting hall, called "Rhein-Ruhr-Halle", which we soon find in the industrial area of Duisburg. Our first impression is that it is rather ugly. It lookes like a carpet warehouse.
Many fans are already waiting there for Michael to arrive. There are barriers all around the hall, and the police are closing the remaining gaps with their cars. Even the access road is blocked by a police car. Behind the hall, big screens have been set up for the fans to watch Michael. But I don't want to see him on one of these screens! No way. I need to get inside.

Two hours later, someone announces that Michael has already entered the hall. At about the same time, an ambulance drives past us and disappears through the gate. That's strange. Maybe Michael is in that ambulance, going inside? I've heard that he does that sometimes. Anyway, it doesn't look as if we are going to see him enter the hall, so now it's time to start looking for tickets.
I wonder whether I will be able to afford a ticket at all. There are rumours that the price of a ticket may be as much as DM 2,000, which is about EUR 1,000 and certainly more than I can afford. After all, I'm only a student.

I can't see anyone selling, so I write a sign that I am looking for tickets. Some unfriendly, greedy people approach me and say things like: „How much will you pay? No, that's not enough." „You'll have to come up with more than that." „Mine are DM 450." Time is running out. The show is due to start at a quarter past eight, and I am certain that they won't let anyone in once it has started. After all, this is a live TV show. Yet, eventually, I am lucky. Someone offers me a set of two tickets, and at the same time, a girl appears next to me. She's crying desparately, because she also wants to get in, but people only want to sell two tickets, not one ticket. We ask how much the tickets are, and I ask the

386

by Petra Fischer

girl how much she has. In the end, we are able to buy the tickets for DM 200 each.

Overjoyed we enter the hall, refresh ourselves and quickly go to find our seats. They are a bit high up but we don't mind. We are inside, that's all that matters. The show will start in about five minutes, so we only just made it!

Shortly before the show, Thomas Gottschalk, the host of the show, comes in and welcomes us all. He seems to be very relaxed. Five minutes later, the show begins and the widely known opening theme sounds through the hall. Now Mr. Gottschalk appears again, but this time as the professional host of Europe's biggest TV show. We are on air now.

Although I have watched this show at home many times and liked it a lot, I don't like it today. It's kind of boring. But never mind. We have something to do anyway, and that is to find better seats so that we can be closer to Michael. Luckily, we find two empty seats that are closer to the stage. The fans who got their tickets from the fanclub have special seats right in front of the stage. And there are some more fans in the audience, like us. We now stand up and move to the crowd barrier that separates the upper level and the lower level of the hall. Michael is coming!

We are standing behind the barrier, and a few moments later, Michael appears onstage. All the fans scream from the top of their lungs. We are so excited to see Michael perform the song "Dangerous". As usual he is simply amazing and perfect! All too soon it's over and the security guards are now sending us all back to our seats. The next few minutes of the show flash by me and then, Michael comes back onstage. Again, the fans rush closer to the stage. On the huge monitors to the right, the video to "Earth Song" is shown for the very first time! Yet at the same time Michael is onstage, so we don't know where to look first. It's truly outstanding! Michael's performance is beyond comparison. He is standing on a crane, not too high above the lucky fans down there. They later told me that they could see the hair on his chest! But I think they may have been exaggerating.

by Petra Fischer

Michael gives everything, his talent, his heart and soul. The entire hall is filled with his presence and everyone in the audience is touched by his performance. Again, way too soon the song is over. Now, Thomas Gottschalk tries to talk to Michael to keep him on the show a little longer. But Michael is not so much into talking. He kindly thanks everyone and shakes Mr. Gottschalk's hand, then he is gone.

Many people ask me whether it was worth paying so much for this performance. After all, these were just two songs, not a whole concert. My answer always is, „yes, it was definitely worth it!". Michael usually performs in a big stadium with thousands of people watching, and he moves them all. Now, we experienced this same power, this presence in a little hall. Yes, it was worth it!

Sunday, November 5th, 1995
Was that all? Many fans seem to think so. They are leaving the Hyatt and go back home. But then, there are rumours that Michael wants to so something today, so I decide to wait. One or two hours later, we realise that Michael is about to leave. Two of my friends, my sister and I wait in our car. Some other fans wait in their cars or in cabs. Finally, after about half an hour, Michael's van leaves the garage and we follow it.

First, the whole convoy crosses three red lights, and then they take the motorway. One of us is reading the map and tries to find out where they might be going. Will it be the "Phantasialand" amusement park? We're headed in that direction. Ok, we are not even sure whether Michael really is in the van we are following. It might be a diversion. And to make matters worse, we even lose sight of the convoy shortly before reaching Brühl, which is the exit for Phantasialand. We decide to go there anyway, as Michael might be there.

Soon we see that it was a good decision. A lot of press and curious onlookers have gathered in front of the entrance. We quickly park our car and join the crowd. Just moments later we catch sight of

by Petra Fischer

Michael holding a blue umbrella while walking towards the entrance with his guards around him. The press tries to take pictures, but he skilfully blocks them with his umbrella. Then he disappears behind the gate and we wonder if we will see him again. Phantasialand is closed to the public at the moment, because their winter break began last week.

But suddenly, my sister recognises one of the other fans inside the park! Quickly, we decide to give it a try and indeed we are allowed to enter, just as many other fans. That can't be! They just let us in, they let us all in to be with Michael. As we approach the gate called "Berliner Tor", we are told to stop there and wait. Teddy tells the fans to stay calm and behave, as Michael will come here now. We don't believe a word of it. This has never happened before, at least to my knowledge. And yet, Michael really comes to see us! We try hard to keep as calm as we can. And, as unbelievable as it may sound, it really works. No one is running towards Michael, everybody behaves respectfully.

It's hard to describe the atmosphere. We fans are now standing face to face with Michael, who is only a few metres away from us, with no barrier in between. And we aren't just some kids that happened to be at the amusement park that day. We are young adults from all over Europe that have come to see Michael perform at the "Wetten dass" show. For most of us this isn't the first "Michael trip" nor will it be the last. This is why we are doing this, to meet Michael, to be close to him. It would now be so easy to just rush towards Michael, to touch him. Yet we don't, because to us, Michael is not just one of the most gifted entertainers the world has ever known, but above all, we see him as a human being. Michael doesn't want to be jumped at, just as we wouldn't like it if someone did that to us.

This encounter with Michael lasts a few minutes. Then, someone throws a stuffed toy in Michael's direction and some others follow their example and throw their scarves. Finally, one of the fans throws a flag with Michael's own picture towards him. He

by Petra Fischer

doesn't seem to have a stuffed toy with him. When Michael sees the flag, he starts to giggle, then he laughs, turning aside as if he didn't want to hurt our feelings by laughing about us. I guess he needn't have worried.

Then, Michael rides the carousel with some kids and their parents. I recognize Brett Barnes and his sister among them. We cheer for Michael whenever we see him because he's on our side of the carousel. Afterwards, Michael disappears in the direction of the wild-water channel, but we are not allowed to follow. Due to all the excitement, some of the local fans are getting loud again, and the Phantasialand crew tell us to calm down or they will kick us out. Just because of a few inexperienced fans? Luckily, they calm down again and we can stay.

We are then permitted to wait for Michael near the wild-water channel. We start to sing „You are not alone" there, and a few moments later, we see Michael again. He smiles at the fans and pretends to conduct our singing. It is great fun for us. Then, someone of Michael's crew informs us that Michael invites us all to ride the roller coaster, followed by a ride called "Space Center" which is a spaceship simulator. Rumours go that he is watching us during the ride. He could have, using the security cameras of the park. Afterwards, Michael himself rides this attraction. We wait for him to come out and a few minutes later he indeed walks past us and is shaking the hands of some fans. Unfortunately, I can't get close enough.

Michael talks to one of the children that are with him, and to his crew. All too soon, we understand that he is about to leave, so we all call out „Thank you, Michael". He smiles and waves to us one last time before he and his entourage enter the bus again. Then Michael leaves. We are left behind with blissful memories that will remain with us forever.

by Petra Fischer

A poet's notion

by Carina Lanes, Germany

1st:
It was June
and the night was quiet
I will always remember
I smelled the rain
when the news
almost made me surrender
I looked up
for the sign of a lie
praying for a wonder
I'm caught alive
in a blaze
craving for a blunder

Hook:
It's a poet's notion
to fall away too soon
I fall away with you
I'll make it a better place
like you told me to
even if I fall away too

2nd:
Is it too late?
am I overcome
by a rational fate?
How can I turn back time
or buy eternity?
'cos you're the one we need

Hook:
It's a poet's notion
to fall away too soon
We fall away with you
We'll make it a better place
like you told us to
even if we fall away too

Download this song for free:

www.mjjbook.com
Password: Poet

by Carina Lanes

Like a big brother…

by Michael La Perruque, USA

Mike La Perruque was Michael's personal bodyguards for many years.

The first time I ever worked for Michael Jackson went pretty quick. We exchanged no words. He gave me a glance and a nod—and that was it. Michael was filming „You Rock My World" on the lower lot of Universal Studios in Hollywood.

I was a Deputy Sheriff with the Los Angeles County Sheriff's Office, assigned to the substation at Universal Studios. Through that, I came to know the Director of Security for the Universal Hilton Hotel, where Mr. Jackson was staying. Like everybody else, I really paid the bills with off-duty work—security for celebrities, community events and so on. When the director pulled together a team of security people to work the filming, I got the call. It was all about being at the right place at the right time.

It was a busy set. And for me, a kid who came from Korea, [Mike didn't know this detail] — the biggest celebrity around was Marlon Brando. Later, I met his son Miko, a very close friend of Mr. Jackson. And someone I would now call one of the "good guys." Of course, like everybody else, I'd also grown up with Michael Jackson; but I certainly would never have called myself a fan. I never had any of his records or tapes. I didn't know pop music and I hadn't followed his career. Once I saw him on MTV and remember thinking, "that guy can really dance." But that's all I knew about him. And I certainly never had any ambition to learn the moonwalk.

What I saw on that first assignment was a nice guy who was extremely professional. Always polite to the people on the set, and yet a real perfectionist; he'd keep doing take after take after take — over and over again until he was completely satisfied. And everybody else wanted to get it right, too. He seemed to inspire that in the people around him. When it was time for him to take a break or consult with some of the creative people on the project, my first duty was to simply escort him off set and into his private trailer. In those early days we didn't say anything to one another. He just knew I was there. Whenever I escorted him anywhere he would smile, say thank you, and that was it. It was completely natural and matter of fact for him — like someone else brushes his teeth or walks to the mailbox. But what I came to see was something very different. A life of isolation surrounded by staff, fans and the media — that does something to a person. Then you have the entourage — the good guys and the bad guys.

This time, as in years to come, Michael always brought his children with him. When I first met them, Prince was about 5, and his sister Paris, about 4. While Michael was on set, he would want a security person to stand by at the Universal Hilton to be on call should the Nanny see a suspicious person in the hallway near the suite or need assistance at anytime. And if fans knew that Michael was in a particular hotel, they would walk the floors, try to find his room, try to slip notes under his door, and so on. We were always called when somebody was being persistent like that, trying to get a glimpse of the children. Michael was incredibly protective of them. As he had to be.

The Kick into High Gear

I worked for him like this two or three times — nothing special. Just security at the trailer or back at the hotel with the children. And I thought that when the video was finished — I'd move on to something else.

Then I got word that Michael was going to have a 30th anniversary show at Madison Square Garden in New York. Michael's Chief of Security called and asked me to meet them in New York and help with security at the two shows. The first show was set

by Michael La Perruque

for September 8, 2001 and the second was scheduled for September 10. So I asked for a leave from the Sheriff's Department and thought I was off for an adventure. I had no idea how close I would come to the Twin Towers on that historic moment.

Going to New York City was a big deal for me. In fact, it was only the second time I'd ever been east of the Rockies. I got picked up at the airport by a chauffeur and limousine — the real star-treatment! It was pretty exciting, I thought, "Wow!" Here I am going to work and somebody's picking me up at the airport. You know how you always go into an airport and you walk by those drivers standing there holding signs with somebody else's name — somebody important you think — and you're never one of those important people. All of a sudden, I was one of those special people being picked up. It felt great. I remember thinking that the man I was now working for had this feeling every day of his life, every moment, and everywhere he went.

I enjoyed that big limousine. I was totally relaxed, enjoying the view — the excitement of the city, people rushing everywhere when suddenly we came to the Palace Hotel in Upper Manhattan where the Jackson party was staying — and I had to hit the ground running. Michael was on his way to rehearsals at the Garden and I barely had a minute to drop off my bags and join the security. That's when I got my first real lesson about the die-hard Michael Jackson fans! They always seemed to know where he was and when he was moving. First of all, they must have a highly organized network. Like most of us, Michael had his favorite places to stay, and the fans had contacts, whether bellmen, or front desk people, or kitchen staff — who kept them posted. And I'm not talking about a few people — but hundreds of fans — everywhere Michael went. Every public place. In London, the crowds got up into the thousands. And in Germany, you couldn't believe it!

That morning I was assigned to the "chase car." Our job was to follow the limo and be ready to move should any vehicle come up along side of Michael's car. I was told to wait in the VIP parking

394

by Michael La Perruque

area until I got the radio signal that Michael was being brought down from his room. What struck me first was the noise from outside the garage. Literally hundreds of screaming, chanting fans were being held back by a huge roll down chain link gate. They called his name. They cried out to him. It was frantic. I'd worked crowd detail before in L.A., but never had I seen anything like this spectacle. The door opened and the crowd went berserk, I could hardly hear the voice in my ear phone telling me that Mr. Jackson was at the garage. He moved quickly to the car and in what seemed like an instant he was inside. The door slammed and it was all over. If I'd turned my head for a second I never would have seen him.

It was a closed set, and so my job during rehearsals was to walk through the audience area as workers were setting up equi pment and so on making sure that no one was taking photos or videos. If someone had a disposable camera, I'd confiscate it. I'd just make the guys with digitals erase the memory card.

The first night of the MSG show, Elizabeth Taylor was waiting for Michael in a limo in the parking garage. She was going with him to the Red Carpet festivities where Michael was scheduled to speak with several members of the media. I stood at the open car door waiting for him to come down the elevator, sprint to the limo, and leave for the Garden. The screaming crowds were there as usual; only this time, Michael dressed in a bright sequined jacket, stopped at the car door and turned to the fans. This time he wanted the audience. He waved and smiled, flashed the "peace" sign, and posed for pictures. I was standing right next to him and I thought, this guy really knows how to work the crowd — but most of all, I could see that he loved it — even needed it. It was as if their energy was charging him up.

Suddenly from inside the car, I heard the unmistakable voice of Elizabeth Taylor. "Michael! Michael! What the fuck are you doing? Get inside this car right now! We have to go!!" Michael of course heard it, but he just looked at me out of the corners of

395

by Michael La Perruque

those big eyes as if to say, "Did you hear that?" For a moment, he looked like he'd been caught doing something wrong. I think he was actually embarrassed.
So I said, "Well, I guess we'd better go, huh?"
"Yeah!" he said as he smiled and jumped into the car.
That was our first connection and from then on he always acknowledged me in little ways — like we were school kids who'd both been scolded by the principal for some kind of a prank. First we had to work out the name thing — that we were both named Michael. In public — whenever anyone else was around — I was always respectful. I called him Mr. Jackson. After all, he was the employer, and I had been hired to protect him. He was my client. That was my job. Once when we were alone he said, "Stop calling me Mr. Jackson. It can just be Michael." So he became "Michael" in person. "Mr. Jackson in public." And I was always "Mike."

I was only a year older than Michael Jackson, but in that one moment I felt very much like a big brother. Protecting him was my job — my profession. But he was somebody you instinctively wanted to protect — even from the well-intended scolding of his friends.

by Michael La Perruque

Home-to-him sickness

by Marina Dobler & Katharina Roggendorf, Germany

„Ladies and gentlemen, it's Tuesday, March 6th 2001 and we are about to arrive at London Stansted airport in approximately ten minutes. The sky is clear, 5° Celsius and rain is expected only for the evening..." The captain's announcement filled the room with collective relief - especially we, Eva, Gitti, Katha, Marina, Sonja and Ramona sighed deeply as if a heavy weight was lifted from our hearts.

„Yes, here it must be – it's Hyde Park corner, let´s get off the bus!" We approached the Lanesborough hotel with hesitating yet determined steps. Our eyes caught sight of hundreds of fans equipped with cameras, pen and paper, banners and presents, waiting imploringly behind crowd barriers, squeezed like sardines in a can. We quickly got our banners out too and with them our red envelopes containing invitations to Munich to his „Scary-evening", a surprise custom party we were preparing for Michael's next visit to Bavaria's capital. Suddenly, screams, yells, unbelievable noise and hooting filled the air. Camera flashes danced, all vacant hands waved, banners and pictures were held up high and people finally went completely bananas. The short and the long of it was, that he hobbled out of the back entrance, dressed in a red baseball jacket, his right leg in black plaster and supported by a crutch. Our knees were shaking like jelly and our hearts were beating so fast they seemed to be bursting through our chests. Neither for love nor money could we have averted our eyes. This very moment was like a monster that hungrily opened its mouth and greedily swallowed all our thoughts, feelings, sorrows, fears and doubts, which were weighing down our hearts. It swallowed

Marina, Katharina and friends waiting for Michael in front of the Lanesborough Hotel in London

our past, it stopped the world from turning and it covered us with a blanket of happiness, which was for the first time in our lives not too short and wrapped us up completely. Our minds were trying hard to capture every little second, but we felt like being a sponge trying to absorb a sea of impressions, we were condemned to fail. He was standing there between the two hoods of his vans and waved into all directions. The crowd took pictures and the fans waved with their presents, of which his bodyguards collected some for him.

On top of all, even all the employees of the office building located right opposite from the hotel's back entrance seemed to be attracted by this surreal scenery, because they pressed their noses against the office windows in order to catch a glimpse of him, too. He limped back to his van, managed to enter it, the drivers set the vans in motion and they slowly rolled towards the four lined driveway being followed and surrounded by screaming fans that pounced upon the vans and hit against the windows. „It must be like driving through a carwash with all those scary giant brushes around you. When I was little, my Mum had a tiny rusty Italian „box" of a car. I was terribly frightened, that the brushes would crush us, I even cried. But imagine those brushes screaming your name!"

We didn't make it to be in Oxford in time. Not having had a bite the whole day we irresistibly trotted towards the closest Pizza Hut. For a moment it really seemed as if we would lull into contentment while enjoying our meal and feeling our hands and feet become warm again. But all of a sudden we glared at the clock on the wall "Oh jeez, he just must have begun his speech there and we…we are sitting here as if it was a commonplace day!" Instantly all our appetite was gone and replaced by a much more unbearable hunger called longing.

While we eventually made our way back to the Lanesborough, rain began to make its way down from above, falling on the city's silhouette which mirrored in the puddles. „Come on, let us try the view from up the wall, it looks quite comfortable once one has made it up there!" The act of climbing the high gray stonewall right opposite the Lanesborough's back entrance and the first impression we got while taking a good look around reminded us involuntarily of „Dead Poets Society", that we had watched only a few weeks ago. Robin Williams teaches his students, that it is important to always look at things from different points of views for that might lead to decisive changes in one's way of thinking. Indeed, it cleared our mood that was momentarily clouded by the rain and a certain homesickness which came up as he left the city going to Oxford and we left his hotel. But as soon as we had found out how to manage to keep our balance on that wall, Tuesday night turned into a magic one. Watching the yellow blades of light of the black cabs and red double-decker busses cut through the wet darkness and alternately looking down the lighted road that he took hours ago and up the lighted hotel front let all-day life blink like a distant fog light in a stormy sea.

As the night wore on and rumours that he would spend the night in Oxford spread like wildfire, many of the other dedicated fans who had besieged the places right behind the crowd barriers so untiringly and defied the ruthless rain turned away, disappointed for they began to feel stood up by him, with which we all had reckoned already hours ago. No word was spoken but in the silence we would ask a wordless question and in the silence we would answer it wordlessly: Not ten elephants could have put us off waiting. „Imagine we would be in the first row when he gets back!" Indeed there was just enough time before fate took its course.

He arrived with two buses full of thunderer whistles equipped "Angel" fans inconspicuously following him. Once his two vans had parked, we imploringly yet smiling made eye-contact with Michael's attendant to hand him over our letters. With a tiny gesture he kept us optimistical and made us hang on while he piled through big, colourful, marvellous banners and collages made by other fans for nights on end with lots of love. Michael and his kind attendant suddenly turned and moved into our direction. Never ever before had we been so close to him and had enough time to sense things like his fragrance. But his immense aura made us feel like being in a vacuum, everything around became insignificant and even the screams and thunderer whistles seemed to be much softer then. Unlike most people who walk on the face of earth he had something mysterious about him that puts one under a spell and amazes one, for he himself was magic without being dependent on any conjuring tricks at all.

Before he hobbled back towards the hotel's back entrance, we began to sing "Simply the best". Yet there were still the red envelopes which we longed to pass on to him. Everything already seemed to be in vain but in the very last moment his attendant jerked around as if remembering his promise and quickly collected our letters before rushing back to Michael. Together they receded behind the door leaving us behind in the cold, dark night, although not leaving us forsaken but with a glowing heart – and wet as poodles.

It was Wednesday evening and the moon was already riding high in a cloudy heaven as we got on a red double-decker bus, heading all the way to the city's west to „Hammersmith Apollo" theatre to attend the „Tenth Annual MJ Day". After the security had checked our bags, we piled our way through to the theatre's stall in order to equip ourselves with popcorn, coke and „m&m's". Shortly after everybody had taken a seat the hall auspiciously darkened what transformed the expectantly exciting chattering of the fans into deafening cheers and screams that came rushing out as we all allowed our emotional gates to open up. To top it all, a huge screen was slowly led down to smash his fucking brilliant performance at the „1995 MTV Music Awards" merciless into the cracked up audience. The moment he slowly loosens his tie and opens his shirt with his eyes closed had caused us butterflies and planes regularly inside our stomachs when watching it at home and that evening it certainly wasn't any different.
Looking around we saw kids, teenagers and adults of all ages

by Marina Dobler & Katharina Roggendorf

in the audience, people of all races, some obviously seemed to prefer Rock music, others loved Pop and still others seemed to give their distinction to Classical music. Though their ways of living probably couldn't be more different at the first sight they still had one great thing in common which is that they allowed him to get through to the deepest feelings that sleep inside every human being's heart and which, as soon as he has woken them, change everything.

„Finally! That girl will need good nerves for each time the phone rings on her birthday her heart will surely be in her boots!" The birthday call by Michael himself was the last item to be sold by auction in favour of "Heal the Kids" before one outstanding brilliant performance began to chase the other. Rabbi Shmuley eventually set foot on the stage and presented his passionate speech in a way as if he wanted to brand every single word on our minds. He screwed up our passion just like someone shaking a bottle of champagne to a point where ecstasy began to meet insanity. But what finally made the „cork pop" and us „bubble over" was the moment he hobbled on stage! The hall reverberated, its walls rattled and the floor vibrated for the adrenaline that had scratched on our nerves made the pent-up tension burst at once and filled the room with an incredible energy, sensible for everyone inside.

"Excuse me, would you please be so kind and take a picture of my husband and me in front of the "Tenth Annual MJ Day" placard?" asked an elderly lady that could have been our Grandma excitedly while handing us over her camera. It flashed twice. Afterwards we started a lively conversation with them about Michael. "He is such a wonderful man but to be honest I worry about him because he seems to be a little fragile and I missed his unique smile." The elderly ladies words dropped directly into our hearts and shattered them into thousands of pieces because they expressed the truth so simply and yet hit the nail squarely on the head. "Last time my wife and I saw him was in front of the Wembley Stadium during his BAD tour. He was passing by in a van and as he saw us waving to him he really seemed to be more surprised to see us than we were surprised to see him at first. But then he began to smile so much that corners of his mouth almost reached his earlobes while making the victory sign to us." Spellbound we listened imagining the scene. "Or did you see him smile the other day?" the lady still pondered solicitously. Unfortunately we had to negate and told her that she had taken the words right out of our mouths and that we worry about him too. "He really shouldn't forget about himself after all" gave the elderly lady a simple yet sometimes so hard to fulfil advice which we all wished he would take to his heart. With hanging heads and close to tears we agreed and waved them Goodbye as they linked arms and went away.

Even though we already sat in the right bus that would have taken us directly home to our hotel, where a warm and snug bed and a hot cup of tea was waiting, we simply didn't have the heart to pass by the stop at Hyde Park Corner without getting off the bus. We couldn't! No way!
„I think he urgently needs some kind of diversion" said Sonja to us while wistfully looking up the hotels illuminated „backfront". We were still in low spirits and on top of it, it had grown chilly at the turn of night so even cuddling close together didn't help. In the middle of all that downcast mood Katharina suddenly noticed some kind of motion in her visual angle, what induced her to turn her head a little and discover Andre, a Swiss fan, who sat „chillig" on the wall and waved inconspicuously towards one of the windows at the „backfront" from time to time. For a while Katharina kept on watching Andre without attaching too much importance to his action, but somehow she couldn't get rid of a certain feeling, that something bigger was at the bottom of it, what finally made her turn around and, following his lead, look upwards.

What she saw convinced her, that the first appearance hadn't deceived her, for a man she thought she had never seen before appeared at the window. She felt relieved but also confused

by Marina Dobler & Katharina Roggendorf

for Andre still kept on waving to that window every once in a while. „Why on earth is he waving to that man up there?" she finally spoke out aloud, hoping that Eva, Gitti, Marina, Sonja and Ramona would either share or dissuade her from her presentiment. But it was like talking to a brick wall for they still discussed Shmuley's speech and were completely absorbed in the question, whether he and Shmuley may have written it together or not.

So she bravely risked a second glance and now saw a man with long hair and a familiar contour. But the cold, the weariness and the musing atmosphere made it hard for her to accept the so unlikely truth though it irresistibly sneaked into her mind and forced her to look a third time. Her knees were a little weak by now and indeed, the very moment she looked, he looked and now there was not the slightest doubt left.

As if bitten by a Tarantula, Katharina jumped off the crowd barrier and uttered a shout, giving vent to her surprise, excitement and joy. Her scream set our teeth on edge and made our hearts beat at a hard canter. „Up there! It's him!" she gasped and excitedly waved about with her arm, pointing upwards to the mysterious window, while her face began to flush more and more.

Unlike an alarm clock, that rips you out of your dreams, Katharina's scream had first ripped us out of our lethargy and then pushed us into an incredible dream. But as our eyes followed the invisible extension of her forefinger and had reached the aforesaid window there was nothing to be seen. Sonja stammered „but his suite is said to be on the park-facing side of the building, right? So why should he look out of one of the „backfront"-windows?"

But as our dream already menaced to disintegrate, the curtain was suddenly slowly moved aside and with it the thoughts that had depressed our hearts were moved aside simultaneously. We felt like ship wreckers flung by the waves of our feelings as we recognized Shmuley appearing at the window, just like a lifebelt in stormy waters. But what's the use of a lifebelt for the moment

Michael came to the window waving at us aroused a tidal wave consisting of euphoria, relief and happiness that flooded us and penetrated into every little corner deep inside our souls.

Thursday we found out that Michael planned to stay another night to see his friend Macaulay act in "Madame Melville". Inspired by Michael′s idea to go to the theatre we decided to do the same and bought tickets for the evening. "It's really too good to be true that he changed his mind and also stays until tomorrow now, that really takes a stone off my heart, for it is always the same if he leaves the city earlier than one does. Even though one intends and would love to discover and experience the foreign city and it's sights, one never really manages to enjoy it, for as soon as he has left an inevitable „home-to-him" and „homesickness" starts spreading out inside."

Of course we couldn't really concentrate on the play for our heads kept turning and our eyes looking for Michael in the auditorium. As we later found out Michael didn't show up. So after the play we immediately jumped into the next available taxi and went back to the Lanesborough driven by a strong uneasiness. But as at lengths we turned around the last corner reality lashed right into our blankly faces just like an icy hurricane turning up out of the blue.

„No! Oh nooooo. „Please don't let this be true...it can't be true" we all implored almost simultaneously as we realized what our eyes had to see. The place that we had expected to be crowded with other fans was totally deserted and devastated and as far as our looks went, all the trash and trampled down newspapers covered dismally the cobble stones. On top of it all the crowd barriers were displaced and mixed up and looked as if they had gotten worsted in the fight of preventing all the desperate fans from running towards him or his vans in their despondency.
Not bearing the fact that we had missed our chance to say Goodbye to Michael and to not know when we would see him again, we decided to go on a walkabout through the inner city to dis-

by Marina Dobler & Katharina Roggendorf

tract ourselves. A sparkle of hope that he might still be around somewhere kept us from despairing so we visited some places we knew he had been during his stay. It was close to midnight when the longing to be close to the place he had stayed grew more unbearable minutely, comparable to a mosquito bite that itches so much that one can't help but scratch it. And so before long we were heading down Piccadilly Street towards the Lanesborough again.

"Pinch me, oh my God you got to pinch me!" There they stood again in rank and file on the spick and span cobble stones, parading like toy soldiers awaiting their commander in chief. If anyone had still been out in that street that late he probably would have taken these crowd barriers standing on a deserted place behind just another luxury hotel for only meaningless crowd barriers that had remained from a seemingly meaningful event. But to us they were the embodiment of pure happiness that took over and advanced into every tiny cell inside us for they indicated his non-departure.

Soaked with easiness and that very special kind of love one feels when he is near, we were suddenly struck by a flash of consciousness that now is here and here is now. "Bumbumbumbumbum, bumbumbumbum, bumbumbumbum...rescue me!" For someone who loves to sing though can not sing our heartily singing sounded proportionally, well actually – pretty good. Though much more important than perfection was our devotion to joy that expressed the unique variety of emotions we felt inside.
Even though it was in the middle of the night the hotel guests seemed to take it astonishingly easy to be ripped out of their dreams – or whatever else, for in one and the other window we discovered curious and amused faces looking down at us. One particular window caught our special attention for someone there kept waving shyly from behind a curtain every now and then. As eventually at 4 am the melody of "My destiny" was fading away we agreed to allow ourselves a little break after such a long and exciting day. We made a compromise to be back latest at 5.30 am.

by Marina Dobler & Katharina Roggendorf

„To the Lanesborough, please!" we panted nervously as if having the big white rabbit from „Alice in Wonderland" with his incorruptibly ticking pocket watch in the neck while heaving our bulky backpacks into the old fashioned taxicab. Luckily the taxi driver instantly caught the seriousness of our situation and brought his old car effactually yet respectfully to the limits, as turning left into Park Lane. While preparing the money for a quick handing over, we left the roundabout at Hyde Park Corner, entered the drive of his hotel and the taxi stopped in front of the Lanesborough's main entrance. Our skin instantly dressed up with goosebumps before our hearts turned somersaults for we had become trapped in a headlock of our imagination. „Are you checking in?" wondered the austere looking doorman aghast when he got sight of our bulky backpacks and our widened surprisingly staring eyes. Feeling taken red-handed we couldn't think of a cleverer way out than „no". „Drive us to the back!"

Luckily we made it in time to be present at his departure. The urge to reveal our true feelings one last time became stronger and stronger. We decided to sing again for him when he would come out to hopefully make him smile a little. "`Too good to be true` would be an appropriate song!" one of us suggested, trying to win over the rest of us. But before we were either able to agree or disagree, a grey-haired man who seemed to belong to his crew walked along the crowd-barriers with a searching look and said in a deep, respect filling voice: „He's not very well today because some fans ran him over as he was about to enter a fish and chips-restaurant. Therefore he had to cancel his plans to go to the theatre." Then he paused for a moment trying to attach more importance to his words before proceeding: „You will see him coming out in a wheel-chair and believe me today none of you guys will cross these barriers! But if all of you keep to that simple rule, he will drive along the crowd barriers to say good bye to you."
Shortly after, the door of the back entrance opened and there he was, indeed sitting in a wheel chair. Slowly rolling over the bumpy cobblestones he looked quite exhausted and weak, his countenance was grieved. We were condemned to watch him

by Marina Dobler & Katharina Roggendorf

warding off the camera flashes that merciless bombarded him. In that moment two ever present facts that are like cat and dog to each other collided inside of us. We wished so much to be able to surmount this wall that keeps us, being no celebrity in any term, and him, being the world's greatest entertainer of all time, apart. More than ever before our hearts were yearning for a way to express our unconditional love for him and the only possibility for us in that situation was to sing, for melody and words were all we had. And so we sang from the depths of our hearts. Once he had managed to enter his van he instantly took off his sunglasses and looked between the two front seats and through the open sliding door right into our direction. The moment our eyes met felt like coming home. Michael expressed his thanks to us fans by folding his hands.

Too soon his driver closed the van's sliding door and severed the invisible bond of our glances. We wished so much to be able to thank him too for though we never met each other, he yet woke feelings that we never knew and that we don't ever want to miss, either. Until an uncertain day in the future we would have to do without the incomparable feeling that spreads inside one when he is near.
As the van withdrew from our vision an overwhelming sadness rose inside us and tears came rushing out of our eyes like dammed up water through opened flood gates.

From now on society and all-day life would slip us over their straitjacket again…

by Marina Dobler & Katharina Roggendorf

Dream come true

by Marjorie De Faria, USA

The sun was slowly rising over the mountain, its bright yellow-orange rays shone through the large puffy clouds. It was going to be a beautiful warm summer day. A day I've been waiting to have pretty much all my life.

All night my mind was racing around, my heart pumping like crazy, I couldn't sleep; I was filled with anxiety. The one thing I've been wishing was coming to a reality. The chance to meet and dine with the one and only Michael Jackson, no one could be as happy as I am right at this moment.

It all began with a contest from Q-106 and radio personalities Jeff & Jerr had to plug one of Michael's new videos "In the Closet." The person who would win would have the opportunity to go onto the site where the video was being shot and have dinner with Michael and also meet Naomi Campbell. There will be 35 selected fans, fan club members, a buffet, and a Caribbean band as well. All you had to do was write why you wanted to dine with Michael. I never thought in a million years that I would be one of the 34 random fans chosen, and one special guest, but I was and I was extremely happy.

I quickly jumped out of bed and got ready. I had to be in L.A. at 8 am and had to take the train out of San Diego to Los Angeles to meet up with others that were going to the location where the video was being filmed.
When I finally arrived at the L.A. train depot, a huge air-conditioned bus was waiting for us to board. There were many fans from UK, Germany and Holland; these were the head club members who were doing reports of the event. The rest of the fans were from the California area.

I sat with a few young girls about 12 years old and asked why they liked Michael, they answered, "because of the way he dances!" It felt good to get on the bus with others that shared the same feelings as I did and we could speak about what we all love about Michael without fearing being criticized for it.

Our destination was the Mojave Desert, a perfect setting where Michael could be filmed without any problems with excessive fans bothering him. The ride was really long and it took us at least five and half hours to get there, but we stopped from time to time to stretch our legs. The noise of chattering, laughing and even crying was really ear –splitting.
Then came the lectures of what we should and shouldn't do while in the presence of Michael. "Do not ask Michael any questions about surgeries, or skin problems, or anything involving his personal life." "Make the questions pertain to his art, music and his dancing and tell him how you feel about him!" "One question per person only," Michael gets really nervous when flooded with too many questions.

Do not grab, touch or even try to kiss Michael. Do not give him any presents, please hand any gifts you may have for Michael to his security personal. Do not take pictures of Michael unless told to do so by Michael himself. Mike has his own photographer. So all cameras you have must be given up at the entrance of the tent we're going to enter. Give Michael room, don't crowd him and most of all have fun. You will be assigned seating arrangements at the table where Michael will be and the Special Guest will be at the right of Michael. If you all understand these rules then please sign the legal form we're handing out to you and return it back. [This was so you wouldn't go blabbing to the talk shows or rag magazines or shows.]
The rules seemed pretty common sense and well from what I could gather it sounded like if anyone did the opposite of this, it would mean Michael would run for cover and the whole dinner thing would be ruined and none of us wanted that. The winner was the lucky one, and funny she had a name just like the one,

by Marjorie De Faria

who he adored, which is Elizabeth Taylor. That's right, her name was Elizabeth Taylor and she had dark hair and was beautiful, just like Liz, only she had brown eyes and not lavender, was married, and was in her middle twenties. Her husband went with her too.

Finally, at 2 pm, we arrived at the location. There were make believe Spanish Villas, dancers, camera equi pment, animals, and loads of people buzzing around the vicinity. This made us even more nervous. Slowly we all got off the bus and followed another one of Michael's guards to a mobile home where we were to rest before we went to the special dinner.
The guard left us, leaving us with our thoughts running a wild. Hot and tired, most of us just wanted to sleep for a few hours, and most of us did just that. The younger kids were all poking their heads at the window in case Michael could be seen walking around.
You couldn't really see much, except for props and other camera equi pment, and the set where the actual video was being shot was like a 100 yards from where we were. Herb Ritts could be seen though, walking around towards a battered car, talking to another person and pointing at something. The clouds were getting darker overhead and it looked as if a thunderstorm would pass through before the day was over.

Finally it was 8 pm, it was time for all of us to have dinner with Michael. The same guard who brought us to the mobile home was now going to take us to Michael. My heart was beating so fast that I thought it would pop right out of my chest.
The guard reminded us that we all had to remain quiet as he led us to this huge white tent where tropical music was blaring. As we entered the tent the lights suddenly blinded us as they began taking photos and filming all of us.

We were brought to this beautiful tropical looking area with a huge long table that would fit all of us. The hibiscuses of yellow, red, orange and pink hung overhead and were also laid out in the middle of the table surrounding the food that sat in the center.

by Marjorie De Faria

Palm trees surrounded the entire dinning area. Each place had white gold trim plates with nametags with Michael's eyes and our names printed on them. The table linen and napkins were of soft peach and lei's of orchards laid across the backs of the chairs. Beautiful water fountains in the back of the room made the scenario seem so relaxed. This was very impressive for all of us.

The guard told us we could relax and dance, while waiting for Michael to come. Kids being kids got out on the dance floor and started dancing and so the rest of us followed suit. It felt like an eternity as the time was passing by and it was getting later and later.

Then things quieted down, and the guards said, "He's coming!"
The lights got brighter again, as we all stood there watching, waiting, hearts pounding, but too scared to make a peep. Michael got out of the blue van; he saw the crowd and ran back into the van again.
Elizabeth goes, "Oh no, that's it, he's not going to come out, so this is it, it's ruined!" The guard beside her told her to hush as Skipper, one of Michael's personal guards, coaxed Michael to come out of the van. Whatever he said, worked, because out comes this shy, very thin, tall person, wearing a black silk shirt with a red banner on one arm, and black silk pants. He walks past us waving and we all started waving back, this man is gorgeous, I mean GEORGEOUS. Not like what you see in magazines, or on television, even more beautiful. His pale color makes him appear so fragile; his hands so thin and bony look as if they'd break if one would grab him. But his skin looked so smooth, and he even had a little 5 o'clock shadow. His bone structure is deliciously strong and sexy looking and like Elizabeth and I said, Michael is just reeking with sex, and that's no lie.

Finally a spoken word, "Welcome," softly spoken with a slight quiver in his tone. Michael waved us to the dinner table. "Please join me!" He bobbed his head up and down and kept waving his hand towards the table, patting the little boys on the head and kis-

412

by Marjorie De Faria

sing babies, as mothers, who were trying to maintain, passed by to sit down. Elizabeth shook his hand and he kissed her. I thought she was going to faint, but didn't. She returned the kiss back. Michael giggled and then took her by the hand and sat down with her. [We all envied Elizabeth that moment!] We later found out from Elizabeth that his face is so soft and he smells so good, he was wearing some soft expensive cologne and that his hands felt like silk. She was still shaking from the entire experience. Her husband in the meantime was way at the back, somehow forgotten, but just looking on at what was going on.

Suddenly the food began to arrive. We all thought, "Oh this is going to be good, Michael's a vegetarian and we're all going to be eating rabbit food here." Much to our shock we saw pizzas, not one but about sixteen of them being brought to the table. French-fries, hamburgers, yes meat, chicken nuggets and other finger foods. They even brought soft drinks and other beverages for us. It was very evident Michael knew what kids loved to eat. One kid said, "Yea Michael went to McDonald and got all this stuff." This made me laugh.

We were afraid to eat with our fingers, as we were in the presence of a very important person, so we all waited and watched how he did things. Naturally Michael, being a kid himself, began picking up the pizza and pulling the cheese off with his fingers and started eating. The kids already had started eating and so we relaxed and started ourselves. Michael also ate a cheese taco, too and licked his fingers. He was very normal, not a fancy snobby person at all.

Satisfied with eating we all needed to move around. The music was getting really good with and well Elizabeth broke a few rules, she touched his hand and asked Michael to dance. The rest of us thought, uh-oh, we expected the guards to topple her but nothing happened. Michael surprisingly said yes, and he invited us all to follow him.

by Marjorie De Faria

We got on the dance floor, and two of the Caribbean dancers started doing the rumba, as we all held onto one another, Michael included, and began dancing all around the floor. The camera's flashed; cameramen were filming like crazy, and out of the blue came Naomi Campbell to join us. She is so tall that she had to wear flats, but is so beautiful, not to mention sexy.
All of us laughed and danced and had such a good time. Michael was giggling and turning the wrong way, we did too, and then he giggled again. The music changed and he and Naomi danced together. I noticed, too she would constantly be bending her head next to Michael's ear and Michael seemed very annoyed with her that after a while he left her and danced with the kids.

Finally the time for our fun was coming to an end and Michael had to go back to his mobile home to rest. But before he left, he told his photographer to take a group picture of us all with him in it. He thanked us all, and gave Elizabeth another kiss and showed his appreciation her for being his dinner date. He waved to us all, and we waved back at him. The tears were flowing down all of our faces, sad that Mike was leaving, as Skipper took him back to the van.
We were told we could stay at the tent and dance more, if we wanted to, until the bus would come to take us all home. But none of us felt like dancing anymore, without Michael it wasn't much fun, and we were all ready to leave now.

Finally the bus showed up and we all boarded it, not like the first time, where the noise was rather deafening, but more somber like. We all loved Michael and would have loved to spend the entire night with him. Michael did however give us all two hours of his time, more than what the guard had told us he would do. Excitement lead to exhaustion and well, we all slept with our dreams accomplished and embedded forever in our minds as we drifted off to sleep all the way back home again. It was a special day where our dreams had finally come true.

by Marjorie De Faria

Meeting Michael – How one single day has changed my life

by Silke Milpauer, Germany

It all began with a beautiful voice coming out of the radio. My heart immediately started to beat faster as I had never heard something similar before in my life. In awe, I listened to the wondrous melody. To me, it seemed as if an angel was singing. That's why I was even more surprised when the radio host announced that we had been listening to the brand new Michael Jackson song "Heal the World", taken from his new album Dangerous.

My brain started working immediately: Michael Jackson – wasn't that the manic guy who slept in an oxygen chamber and had a chimp as a pet? In the media, I read constantly about his bizarre way of life and learned that he seemed to live in an ivory-tower instead of the real word. But if this was indeed the case - why would this man sing with such emotion and intensity about healing our world? Wouldn't such a person be indifferent to our world and other people's suffering? But there he was, Michael Jackson, singing his heart out trying to get his message across. So could it be – a daring thought, really – could it be that the picture the media conveyed to the general public was actually a wrong one and didn't correspond with the truth?

Had I been manipulated? I couldn't get this thought and his voice out of my mind. The very next day, I went into a mall and bought „Dangerous". I still remember how nervous I was when I put the cassette into a tape recorder – imagine that I didn't even own a CD-player back then – and pushed the Start-button. I also remember the headache I got while listening to it. But I had to give it a chance! After all, I had never really been interested in music before and might have to get used to Michael's style.

Tell you what: I am so glad that I didn't just switch off the tape recorder after "Jam"! While some songs gave me a serious headache after first listening to them, others were a revelation. But after listening to „Dangerous" again and again while reading the lyrics at the same time, I found that I grew to like this album. A lot. The booklet informed me that Michael wrote all the lyrics himself and basically, I was quite impressed. Pretty soon, I acquired a taste for Michael and his music. Soon, I owned all his albums, read fan-magazines (such as the very popular „Black & White"), Michael's autobiography „Moonwalk" and, above all, „Dancing the Dream", which has enchanted me ever since then.

During a stay in the US in the summer of 1993, I discovered Taraborelli's biography "The Magic and the Madness" and devoured it completely in only three days. Among other information, it told me the location of Michael's Ranch, and after I had begged my parents to take me there, they finally did. I will always be thankful for that wonderful experience of being able to stand right at Neverland's gates and to be so very near to Michael. Well, when asked if Michael Jackson lived here (great question by the way, hm?), the friendly security guard just told us that he wasn't allowed to tell, but that we should take all the pictures we wanted and "be happy"! And we were!

So basically, within a couple of months and due to my intense research for "the man behind the mask", my previous, media-created, contorted and false image of Michael Jackson had changed a great deal. I started to think of him as Michael, or even Mike. Now I thought that he had to be a very sensitive and shy human being, who pretty selflessly – and even to the point of self-abandonment – dedicated himself to the concerns and needs of others – above all, of course, to the needs of children. I thought

by Silke Milpauer

of him as a gentle person who had suffered and who had been hurt and misunderstood to such an alarming extent that he found it necessary to erect immense walls around his soul. I thought of him as an outsider, a hermit who had often been laughed at and who had too often been called "Wacko Jacko" right to his face.

Let's turn away from Michael (for now) and let me tell you a little bit about myself. I was 14 years old when I "discovered" Michael for the first time in 1991 and a pretty introverted teenager who was picked on regularly for being so shy. I didn't like talking about boys – usually a favourite pastime for girls that age – and hanging around with other kids my age. Instead, I preferred the company of my books. I have always loved books and could disappear into the fantasy worlds they provided me with for hours. In this respect, Michael was someone I could identify with and I even imagined that I knew how he had to feel like. I could relate to him very well.
Anyway, his music and his messages meant a lot to me and always supported me during this difficult time in my life. And there were even more positive aspects, as my English started to improve. Well, that was hardly a surprise, considering the amount of time I spent translating his songs, lyrics and interviews, driven by the wish to understand what he had to say. Frequently, Michael spoke about the power of our dreams. The notion of "wishing on a star" had a very special meaning for him, and it would soon get a special meaning for me as well.

My wish to meet Michael and to speak to him became bigger and bigger with each passing day. By now, the autumn of 1993 had arrived - and it was no good time for Michael, euphemistically speaking. It was a hellish nightmare for his devoted fans as well. I just couldn't believe what was happening and was distressed all the time. Mind you, not because I considered for even a millisecond that these absurd accusations could be true, but because I was deeply worried about Michael and about the effects that this would have on his gentle soul. How could anyone use his good heart and his love for children as a weapon against him?

by Silke Milpauer

I failed to understand this, however, they could not have found a better weapon in order to hurt him deeply.

Back then I had discovered a particularly bright star in the night sky which I never failed to find. Just like Michael in „Moonwalker", I focused on this star every morning and prayed very intently: "Please God, let Michael come out of this unharmed and well." And then, a bit less selfless: "Let me meet Michael and talk to him!" This was my morning ritual for some weeks in a row. My best friend at that time had also fallen for a popular wrestler, and together we imagined what it would be like to meet our "darlings". "We just have to believe in it 100 %, then it will happen"; I told her again and again.

And in fact, it did: On 3 December 1993, a letter from „Bravo", a popular German youth magazine arrived. They had stood by Michael and supported him a great deal during his most difficult time and thus had good connections. I was told that I had won a meeting with Michael and could present him with the award that he had won in the category "Best singer in 1993". And guess what? Three weeks later, my best friend received a similar letter, telling her that she had won a meeting with her star. Out of 80.000 participants, they had drawn my name, and hers was also drawn out of several thousands. So both of us, best friends for years and years, coming from the same city and living just two streets apart from each other, had won! Can you believe that? How could that have been a coincidence? Ever since that fateful day, I believe undeviatingly in miracles.

A long, hard and exhausting time of waiting began. At times, it all seemed to me like a dream, a thing that I had made up in my mind. Had I indeed imagined everything? But no, a call from senior journalist Alex Gernandt put me out of my misery more than a year later: He told me that the meeting would take place. In several days. In Chicago – and did I have a passport? Luckily, I did. My joy was enormous, but on the other hand I was pretty scared: What if Michael would be totally different from how

by Silke Milpauer

I imagined him to be? What if I couldn't get a single word out? And, to make matters worse, I had to communicate in a foreign language! Don't get me wrong, I love English and have already had a good command of it back then, but nevertheless: In such extreme situations, you sometimes automatically slip into your mother tongue... and wouldn't it be embarrassing if that indeed happened to me?

But first things first. Before I could think of meeting Michael, I had to get the formalities out of the way. My parents had to inform my school and fill in a request for me to be excused from lessons for about a week. Not everyone was understanding. My French teacher, for example, reacted as if I had personally insulted her: "If meeting Michael Jackson is more important to her than her French class test – well, she must know herself...", she sighed dramatically in my absence. However, I didn't care one bit. All that mattered was that I would meet Michael, even though I admit it was a bit surreal, sitting next to Alex in business-class, sipping champagne and doing a test in a fanzine entitled "What would you do if you met Michael?" while the plane flew across the Atlantic. Even more surreal was the poor guy's face at the airport who asked me what the reason for my visit to the States was. At first, I simply told him: "For pleasure". But he wasn't quite content with that answer, insisting on details. So I replied: "To meet Michael Jackson." His face plainly told me that he thought me lunatic, but nevertheless, he let me pass.

The next couple of days were like a perfect dream. In fact, I felt like Cinderella in the expensive and luxurious hotel - the same hotel Michael lived in, by the way. Besides doing a bit of sightseeing, we met a lot of people from Michael's environment: Adrian Grant for example, who was great (even though it wasn't nice of him to bring up the movie "Speed" while we were in the elevator). A lot of time was spent with Bob Jones to whom I immediately took an absolute dislike and who observed my every move closely. I guess he tried to anticipate my reactions to Michael, whether I would faint or scream hysterically upon seeing him.

by Silke Milpauer

In fact, I had promised myself that I would do neither, as I found nothing more disturbing than fans who screamed their head off when laying eyes on Michael or forgot all dignity (their own and Michael's!) or even touched him uninvited.

Being a very empathic person, I always asked myself how Michael had to feel in these situations. Of course I understood the motifs for such actions and the emotions behind them well enough. But even though Michael seemed so familiar to us, we were still strangers to him. And who out there enjoyed being touched, stared or screamed at by strangers? That's why I vowed to myself not to lose it and to try to treat Michael just like I would any other human being. I could do all the screaming and crying afterwards when he wouldn't hear and see.

Sightseeing, shopping, diving head over toe into Michael's world, topped by an enormous amount of extraordinary experiences. One time, for instance, Mr. Jones took us to dinner in one of Michael's favourite restaurants. As we were getting ready to go, the chef rushed to our table, bearing a present for Michael: He had baked a giant chocolate-cheesecake for him and asked Mr. Jones to give it to him with compliments from the chef. Clearly, Michael was liked a lot here.

Time flies when you are having fun. Being in such close proximity to Michael was a surreal feeling. He "escaped" yesterday night and went shopping in the hotel mall, Mr. Jones told us filled with indignation at the breakfast table one morning. Michael dared to do that even though he himself had forbidden it, he added and sounded as if he owned the man. What gave him the right to treat Michael like a child, I pondered while eating my pancakes. And what I found even sadder was the fact that Michael obviously had no other choice but escaping under the cover of darkness. Granted, Jones` reaction could have been triggered by fear for Michael's wellbeing; after all, it was never safe for Michael to just do plain normal, ordinary things without being well-protected. However, I gained the impression that it was less Michael's well-

being that was predominantly on his mind, but his money.
Then everything happened very quickly: We were put in a minivan, and James-Bond-Style-like our journey to an unknown destination began. Not even the driver knew where he was taking us and got his instructions concerning the route while driving. And as if that alone wasn't exciting enough, not knowing if Michael would already wait for me was nerve-wracking. You cannot imagine how hard and fast my heart was beating when I stepped into the old warehouse where I was supposed to meet the man who meant the world to me. It was a huge place, with old machines being everywhere. Michael had chosen this place in order to take pictures for his „HIStory"-Booklet, Mr. Jones told us.

In the left-side-corner of the hall, a small photo-studio had already been built: A white screen served as the background, to its left and right, spotlights were placed in order to provide sufficient light. And of course there was the camera plus Jonathan Exley right behind it. I enjoyed talking to him, but nothing could take away my nervousness! And nobody could tell when Michael would arrive. So I did a bit of exploring, walked into a small adjacent room where I didn't believe my eyes: There were sweets everywhere. In fact, the biggest buffet I had ever seen – and it consisted solely of sweets. In between, some toys were placed. It was fascinating!

Now, the long wait began. To say that it wasn't very warm in the building would have been an understatement. Every now and then Mr. Jones` cell phone rang, and finally, he lost patience and went shopping, muttering under his breath how Michael could even dare to let him wait. He was gone for some time and when he returned, he had done some Christmas-shopping. Finally, everyone started to get bouncy. By now it was almost half past six pm and three hours had passed. "Michael will be here soon" – this whisper suddenly filled the air and then Wayne stepped through the door and made sure that everything was safe for Michael. Alex and I rose from our chairs in the right corner of the hall, starring mesmerized at the door. I was hot and cold at the same

421

by Silke Milpauer

time and I feared fainting from sheer nervousness. Was it possible to suffer a heart attack at 17?, I wondered because of my heart which beat as if I had just participated in a marathon.

Suddenly, joyful children's noise filled the warehouse: Some kids ran into the room and threw jellybeans at each other. As fascinating as this was, my gaze remained firmly locked on the door through which Michael stepped just a moment later. It seemed as if the whole atmosphere in the room changed immediately. It was as if I had a vision, so unreal seemed the man who passed by several meters away from me. That he was wearing black trousers, a red-checkered flannel shirt, a black scarf and his hat – all these details escaped me. My eyes were solely fixed on his features and his wonderful dark eyes. He must have felt my eyes on him, because now his glance conquered the distance between us and met mine, looking at me enquiringly. Embarrassed to have been caught openly starring, I quickly looked away. Out of the corner of my eye, I realized that the corners of his mouth twitched in amusement. In the meantime, he posed for some pictures. When I next looked at him, as I felt his eyes once again resting on me, it was him who looked away quickly. We repeated this game again and again.

„Now", Mr. Jones signaled to me and Alex and I crossed the room and moved towards Michael. For me, everything seemed to happen in slow motion now. Suddenly I stood next to the camera, directly in front of Michael who was now only about three meters away. Later, I wouldn't be able to tell what Michael wore. I saw the details which I have described above – that he wore a scarf and a hat, for example – on pictures a couple of days later. But at the moment, I was too mesmerized by his incredibly dark eyes which formed such a strong contrast to his fine, pale features. His complexion didn't seem to be that of a white person, but lighter than that. I have never seen anything comparable to this. His face was so symmetric and smooth like porcelain. His lips were a natural red, no lipstick. Just like Snow White, I couldn't help thinking. As I was looking at him, he was studying me as well.

by Silke Milpauer

After Jonathan had taken some more pictures, someone pushed me towards Michael and I tried hard to keep balanced and not to stumble across some wires. As if I were on autopilot, I crossed the five steps still separating us and put out my hand. Treat him normally, and don't stare at him, as hard as it is – this thought kept running through my head. Shocked, I realized that he had flinched slightly when I had reached out in order to shake his hand, and that his eyes had widened noticeably. He is scared, I thought. He is just as nervous as you are. The fact that he obviously thought that I, a shy and harmless 17 year old girl, could attack or harm him in any way shook me to the core. What this guy must have experienced in this regard… I have to move slowly, I thought, and speak quietly and calmly. In this moment, Michael didn't seem to be Snow White any longer, but a timid deer. Bambi.

Before the meeting, I had practiced a little speech. Now I pulled myself together, greeted Michael and shook his hand. He returned my handshake gently but firmly. At that moment, something astonishing happened: My whole nervousness and fear disappeared in the very instant that he touched me. After I had introduced myself, Michael replied quietly: "Hi. I am Michael." I remember that this almost distracted me, but that I found this gesture unbelievably cute. In order not to lose my thread, I explained to Michael who I was and why I was here: That I wanted to present him with the "Golden Otto Award", as the „Bravo"-readers clearly thought that he deserved it the most. I then offered my congratulations and put out my hand with the award in slow motion. Michael very carefully took the award (which has the form of a little Indian, by the way) and admired it at length. "Oh, he is so cute!", he called out and offered his heartfelt thank you. I got the impression that it really meant a lot to him. "I know", I replied and grinned. "I wanted to keep it for myself, you know", I teased and Michael giggled, then bit his lips. I didn't know what to do, but it seemed to me that honesty would be the best solution. So I admitted that I was pretty shy and very, very nervous because of all the people around and the cameras. I didn't want to tell him

by Silke Milpauer

that he was the primary cause for my nervousness, that would have been too embarrassing. Michael opened his mouth, clearly surprised, and abruptly, I was pulled into his arms. "You don't need to be nervous. We'll get through it together", he whispered and patted my shoulder. As it was time for some pictures, he put his arms around me. While we posed for Jonathan, he told me in a whisper that he still wasn't used to all of this and that he was so very nervous and shy himself. "They always think that somebody wants to kill me", he added quietly and rolled his eyes, his gaze now fixed on his bodyguards who babysat the children nearby.

Now, the ice was broken, so to speak, and in the next couple of minutes we talked to each other. I had promised myself that I wouldn't ask personal things and wouldn't treat him like some random yellow press – reporter. Therefore I was relieved that he seemed interested in my life and asked a couple of questions. I told him some things about me and my everyday life. When I mentioned that our meeting had originally been intended to take place on the day before, he seemed incredulous: "You cancelled your flights because of ME?", he asked as if he found it hard to believe that he was important enough to justify such an action. When I added that I had waited more than a year for this day, he looked even more shocked. "Because of me?", he repeated. His humility was amazing.
"I didn't even know there was supposed to be a meeting... I was only told some hours ago", he told me. After that, Michael was supposed to pose for some pictures alone and I returned to my place behind the camera, enjoying to watch Michael in action. Somehow all the people around us disappeared one by one into the adjacent room and all of a sudden, I found myself alone with Michael. I was surprised and Michael also seemed confused by this. But then, a grin appeared on his face and he waved me to him. In the run-up to the meeting, I had been told by Mr. Jones that I shouldn't stare at Michael's nose (as if!) nor ask Michael anything, and that I shouldn't request an autograph. But as we were on our own and I didn't think he would mind, I got over my qualms and did it. "Do you mind signing my Dangerous

by Silke Milpauer

booklet?", I asked him politely and Michael smiled brightly. "Of course!". I held out the booklet and a pen for him and he spontaneously decided that the knee-high and broad stone situated right next to the photostudio would serve us as chairs. He used the sleeve of his shirt to wipe dust from the stone, then, very gentleman-like, offered me a seat. I was so impressed – he was so very, very polite! Thanking him, I took a seat and observed him as he sat right next to me and flipped through the booklet to find a suitable page for his signature. Somehow, it felt as if there wasn't a distance – locally or emotionally – between us anymore, and so I admitted that I thought that Mr. Jones wasn't really likable and that I was quite afraid of him as he seemed to be so strict and domineering. Michael only laughed in a quite amused way and patted my shoulder. "You don't need to be scared of him. It's just the way he is. Even I call him Sir after all this time, can you imagine that?"

Once finished with writing a dedication into my booklet, he stood up and took my hand to help me get to my feet. I looked across the room where one of the playing children had caught my attention: "Oh, she is so cute!"; I exclaimed and pointed at the curly-haired beauty. "What's her name?" Michael followed my gaze, then broke into laughter. "That's a boy!"; he called and I felt heat rising into my cheeks. "Oh, I... I didn't know that", I stuttered and was quite embarrassed. "I'm sorry!", I apologized, and suddenly, Michael became more serious. "These are all boys", he said and his voice was... I don't quite know how to describe it. Heavy with meaning, perhaps? I was silent, as I didn't know how to reply to such a statement. Filled with absolute horror, I realized that Michael's eyes were now filled with tears. Then he whispered: "I really love children. Do YOU believe me?" The way he emphasized the „you", implying that a lot of people didn't believe him, ripped into my heart. The demons from his past seemed to haunt him and wouldn't leave him alone. Now I knew absolutely for certain what I could only have guessed before: They had hurt this man deeply, pushed a knife into his heart and twisted it around. They had done him such a great injustice...

by Silke Milpauer

Silke presents the "Golden Otto Award" to Michael
printed with permission from Alex Gernandt, BRAVO

I was only 17, and he was the man that meant the world to me, the man to whom I felt so close. I was at a loss at what to do. My first impulse was to embrace him tightly and comfort him, but I fought this impulse because I assumed that this would be unpleasant for him. I also didn't want to destroy the fragile band of trust between us. In retrospective, I regret deeply that I didn't follow my heart. What I did was to return his enquiring gaze and nod fiercely. "I know Michael. I know", I whispered. I was but a small moment away from breaking into tears myself, and he seemed to feel this, shook off his desperation and sadness and brightened up again. In order to distract us both, he introduced all the children around us to me. They were his nephews, he told me among other things.

"Michael, you have to go. The children are waiting!"; Bob Jones called indignantly, repeated it several times and pointed towards the door where indeed Michael's nephews had assembled . The feared moment was there: Even though I didn't want to be separated from Michael, it was me who reached out for his hand and shook it, whispering my good-bye, saying that it had been so nice to meet him and that I hoped that all his dreams would come true. I turned around and intended to walk away, but Michael grasped my hand, turned me around and pulled me in his arms, embracing me sincerely and kissing me on my left cheek. I was so baffled that I didn`t realize what was happening to me. So unfortunately, there really was no time to enjoy the moment. It all happened so quickly. I think I returned the kiss, but I don't know whether Michael said something to me or not. As if in trance, I returned to my place and watched Michael being ushered out of the room.

After the door had closed behind Michael, I let my feelings run free. All the emotional tension was released. Later on at dinner, Mr. Jones asked me if I was happy to have met "the King of Pop". How I hated it when people referred to Michael by using the third person, as if he was no human being! My eyes were still slightly reddened as I met his eyes: "I am glad that I have met Michael!", I replied and returned my attention to my food.

by Silke Milpauer

After that day, in the years to follow, I saw Michael several times, continued to follow his life and his career. But it was this day that has changed my life and that has given me so much. Looking back, I can say that without Michael, I would never have become the person I am today. That's why I agreed to write down my story: I wanted to share my experience, convey to others what a wonderful, generous and loving human being Michael was. He isn't – wasn't – how people imagined him to be, and I have much to thank him for: Without Michael, I would never have studied English and I would never have had the wish to work with children and young adults. Without him, the shy young girl from then would never have turned into a self-confident woman. Today, I work as a lecturer at a college in Germany, teaching English and German to young people aged 16-25. Among the youths, Michael is popular as never before. It is downright cool to be his fan. I only wished the reason would be a different one…

But I also know that he is well now, and even though it sounds cheesy, that he is in a better place. Thank you for everything, Michael! I will never forget you.

by Silke Milpauer

Silke today

„Thanks Michael, it means the world to me, I love you"

by Kader, France

When I last saw Michael in March 2009, he sat in his van for a while and decided he would sign a couple of autographs for some kids whose parents were working in the buildings around after leaving the doctor's office. I hadn't asked for an autograph for 10 years, but I had my Michael Jackson limited edition iPod and I thought this would make a nice souvenir. I ran to the car and grabbed my iPod, it is so precious to me that I still have the plastic covering the screen. Since the security was anxious to leave, I figured I'd just give it to Michael and get it back when he comes back to Carolwood and rushed back to our car to follow him to wherever he was headed next. My friend started the engine, but the security called me back and gave me my iPod. I thanked Michael, only to find out that he was so concerned about covering the markings on the back - which was exactly where I wanted the autograph - that he signed it on the plastic covering the screen!

God knows I would never have asked for more in other circumstances, but I just knew the autograph would probably fade away with time and I thought I should ask him if he'd do it on the back... „Michael, would you mind signing it on the back, please?" The security said: „No, sorry, we're late, we have to go!" I said: „Ok, no problem, thanks again Michael!" and ran back to our car. As I was opening the door, I heard someone calling me. The security guy was telling me to come back. I ran back to Michael's Escalade, the guy grabs my iPod again and gives it to Michael and asks me where I got it... then I hear a voice coming from inside the van asking: „Where did it come from?" And I've met Michael tens of times, however, no matter how hardcore a fan you are, when Michael talks to you, you're gonna stutter. And he kept asking about the iPod, so I proceeded to explain to him how I got it and where and other things that he wanted to know and a few seconds later, Michael handed it back to me and God, was I right to ask for a second autograph!!! It was perfect.... I thanked him so many times, I said: „Thank you, Michael, it means the world to me, I love you" and ran to the car. Michael wanted to go for some shopping, but the stores were closing down and Michael's Escalade started heading to Carolwood. Michael kept waving to us as we were right next to his car all the way back to his house. We could hear him say „I love you more" in reply to our telling him that we loved him...

He kept waving and we were happy, and I was so glad, cause after all that had happened to him in the last few years, I felt like for the first time in close to 10 years Michael had that spark in his eyes I once recognized the day that I first saw him.

„Thanks Michael, it means the world to me, I love you" - those were my last words, they came from the heart and I meant it!

by Kader

Kader's iPod with Michael's autograph

WE are Michael Jackson

by Franziska Neurieder, Germany

During the days, weeks and months after Michael left this world I continued to ask myself why this loss hurt so much. Why did the death of a man I never spoke to personally touch me so much that it put my whole world upside down? Why was I unable to sleep for so many nights? Why was I in total denial for several months? Why do I still start crying when someone mentions his name or when something reminds me of him (even if it is only the full moon that makes me recall the Moonwalker)?

Yes, I love his music and it does mean very much to me. His way of expressing his innermost soul be it musically, with the help of lyrics or through dancing always touched me and made me feel at home, made me feel secure. For me, Michael was always there at the same distance. No matter where I was, how far away from family and friends, he was always there as he had always been. No matter how lonely or abandoned I might have felt Michael was always there. His music, his voice always offered me a safe haven.
The mere knowledge that he was out there allowed me to feel close to him and gave me hope and strength to live in a world that for sure did not always feel like "Neverland". In his humanness and gentleness he was a good example for me. His vulnerability and weakness allowed me to accept the truth and importance of my own fragility.

Over the years I met many people who felt equally and it was always a pleasure to share those emotions and those experiences with them. And even more: I could share his message of love and friendship with them more than it was possible with others, those who did not understand him the way I felt that I understood him. I was truly "not alone".

And then there were those rare occasions when I had the honor to see him in person. Whether it was a concert or one of his other appearances, it was always (despite all the chaos) a magical experience. Being close to the man who influenced my life in such a lasting way made me feel as if I was taking a holiday from reality, as if for some hours or days that what was most important in my life also received my full attention. And yes, sometimes seeing Michael in the window of some hotel or on some stage or even just in a car made me feel stronger as if his mere presence approved my whole being. Close to him I felt good with being myself.

So how does it feel to live in a world without him? It feels as if the colors were taken away from this world, as if the only force that shielded me from the "cruel world" was taken from me. But what exactly have I lost? I lost a mentor. Someone who let me see the world as a good place to be in, someone who showed me what is possible with a little faith and trust. I lost a friend who showed me how much joy and happiness simple "being" can bring, how important it is to never stop dreaming. I lost a guide that was by my side for years, through good times and bad times. I feel like a tree that has lost a main branch and is now completely out of balance and deprived of an essential part. And now I am afraid that if I try to accept his death, if I try to live with it, that I would somehow betray his memory. Sometimes it seems as if the only way to remember and to love adequately is to suffer.

Mourning is like living in an upward spiral that starts at Michael's passing away. I will come across this date or a memory of him again and again and yet every time this happens more time has passed, more experiences were made and I have grown a bit "wiser". So how can I "sufficiently" store him in my heart and at the same time reduce the suffering? What do I do with the wound that is left from the branch?

by Franziska Neurieder

Maybe I will just try to do the same as the tree. Grow a new branch. No matter how tiny, how weak how seemingly unimportant and insufficient this branch might be at the beginning, it is there for sure. I do not believe that we were made to suffer, so there simply MUST be a little branch. Maybe I should allow myself to look at it. It is by no means there to replace Michael in any way but as time goes by there simply IS something that is growing from this wound.

What could that be for me? Maybe I could try to loose my fear of this big, scary world and try to see things more in the way he did. That is what he tried to teach us anyway. So why not simply take a risk and try it? Why not attempt to live, to be what I admired in him? Be more human, be more caring, more giving, less receiving, simply: more loving! Michael was always a great teacher and I truly believe that he would appreciate it if I, if we all, finally followed his path. We might not reach his mastery but that is not our goal anyway.

The goal is simply to try it, to never stop trying, never stop dancing Michael's dream. It is through us that he continues to live. Through our words, our deeds, our love. Now WE are truly the ones to make the world a better place. We have not lost Michael! He is there, maybe even closer to us than ever before. "Michael Jackson" is no longer a man; he is a concept, an idea. WE are Michael Jackson! There is no need to be sad; there is no need to despair! We have lost a messenger, not the message, a lover, not love! This world needs his message and we are the ones who will continue to live it. Because We Are The World!

by Franziska Neurieder

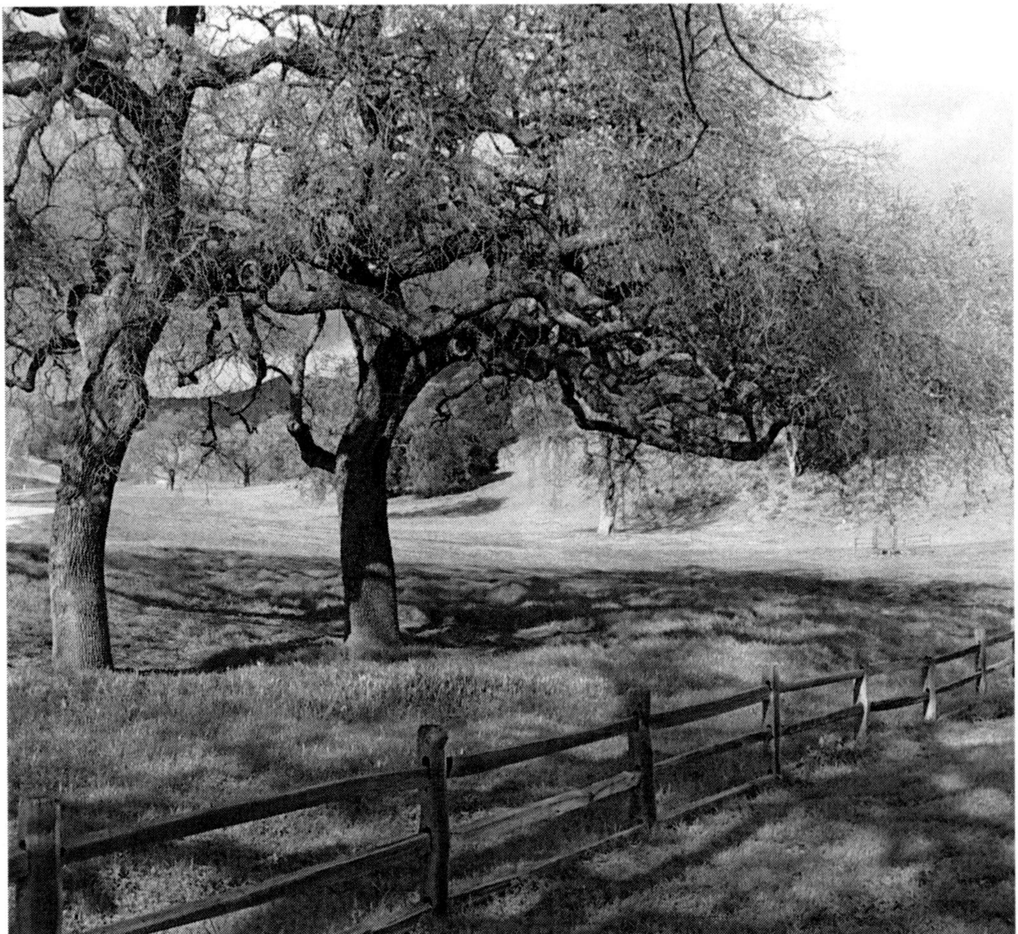

Quotes

by Michael Jackson

I'd like to thank the World Music Awards and especially the fans. You are the reason why I continue to do what I do. I've been performing since I was five years old, so I haven't had what you call an ordinary life, but I've been blessed with so many extraordinary opportunities and so many wonderful, wonderful friends all over the world that I wouldn't change a minute of it, really.

I love you more! I thank God, and I am so proud God gave me the gift of song. And the world gave me the opportunity to be heard through music. And it's because of moments like this I can say with all my heart that I'm very proud to be an entertainer. And... You ain't seen nothing yet!

World Music Awards Acceptance Speech (May 10th, 2000)

I just wanna say: fans in every corner of the earth, every nationality, every race, every language, I love you from the bottom of my heart. You know, thank you for your love and support and understanding during this trying time. I would love your prayers, and your goodwill. And please be patient and be with me and believe in me because I am completely, completely innocent.

Jesse Jackson Interview (March 29, 2005)

Geraldo: How do you feel, Michael, about the continuing support you've gotten from your fans despite all you've gone through.
Michael: Well, Geraldo, it's because of my fans that I am calling you today. I mean, I feel they are the best fans in the world and I decided rather than having anyone else speak for me that I would

do it myself, you know. And I want to thank my fans for their strong support over the years.

They could have been anywhere today, you know, and they chose to be in New York in Times Square. And I want to thank them from the bottom of my heart. They have written thousands and thousands of letters, and have made hundreds of calls regarding the Eminem video. And I love them so, so much.

MTV Rally Phone Interview (November 16, 2004)

Rick Dees: Where do they [the fans] get the craziest? I saw some shots in Japan where they're carrying people out and everything. Does it get craziest in Japan or where?

Michael Jackson: To tell you the honest truth, Rick: It's the same wherever we go. It really is. The love and appreciation is so wonderful. The fans are so happy and animated and it just touches my heart. It's love. I pray is what I do. I thank God.

Halloween Interview (October 30, 2003)

I would like to thank my wonderful fans so very much for this event. I cannot believe what enormous effort you have put into this. Thank you for putting together this fabulous party and for travelling from over 30 countries. I am deeply moved and touched by your love.
I want you to know that I appreciate my fans not just on occasions like this -- but every day of my life. It is your presence, your faith and your loyalty that has given me great strength during difficult times, and it was you who inspired me to work hard and deliver, I owe you. Over the years we became a family. You are all my family. My children are your children and all children of the world are our children and our responsibility.
45th Birthday Party Speech (September 3, 2003)

And to the fans around the world, I love you. I couldn't be me without you.

Billboard Music Awards Speech (December 2002)

Paris is imitating me now. When I call ‚I love you' to the fans she also calls ‚I love you,' ‚I love you, too from the bottom of my heart.'"

Bunte Interview (November 28, 2002)

Thank you to all of my fans for understanding how important it is to me to protect my family from the public eye. I have lived in a „fishbowl" all my life and I want my son to live a normal life. You've stood by me throughout my career and now you share my greatest joy. I love you.

OK Magazine Interview (April 1997)

I love our fans. Everyone who buys our records. From my heart and my work. I appreciate the fact that they enjoy it.

Beat It Interview (1982)

Ed Bradley: Michael, what would you say to your fans, who have supported you through all of this, and who today, some of them might have questions? What would you say to them?

Michael Jackson: Well, I would tell them I love them very much. And they've learned about me, and know about me from a distance. But if you really want to know about me, there's a song I wrote, which is the most honest song I've ever written. It's the most autobiographical song I've ever written. It's called, „Childhood." They should listen to it. That's the one they really should listen to. And thank you for your support, the fans around the world. I love you with all my heart. I don't take any of it for granted. Any of it. And I love them dearly, all over the world.

60 Minutes Interview (Dec. 28, 2003)

I would like you to put this in quotations: 'My main love for what I do is the admirers. I love the fans. Like when I'm doing a show and I see the fans out there dancing and screaming, excited, and we're bringing that joy to them, that's what I love most. And it's just the greatest feeling in the world. You're up there and you're giving them that energy and that love and they're just throwing it right back at you. And it's great. And that's my main love, the stage and making those admirers happy.'

Ebony Interview (December 1984)

You can feel the audience. It is love we are talking about. Ooh, you can definitely feel them! You hear them, they are swaying and screaming and fainting, the reactions are always lovely.

Interview in Morocco (July 1996)

Again, to my friends and fans, thank you very much for all of your support. Together, we will see this through to the very end. I love you very much and may God bless you all. I love you.

Michael Jackson's Message from Neverland Ranch (December, 1993)

Molly: Well how do you cope with all the hysteria? I mean wherever you go, whether it's London, whether it's Munich, whether it's New York, whether it's Bangkok, whether it's Japan and even

here in Australia, how do you cope with the hysteria?
MJ: I know it's all love, so it makes my heart very happy and I like to give it back, you know through however I can give and it puts a smile on my face to see all the children and all the teenagers and the adults, the demographics. It makes my heart very happy, I love them, I love all the fans very much.

Interview with Ian ‚Molly' Meldrum (19th November 1996)

Your unquestionable support has been my strength over the past year. I may be the captain of my faith, but you provide strength for my soul.

HIStory Booklet (1995)

It's the worst thing in the world for me to let my fans down

Press Release on cancellation of his concert in Wembley Arena (August 1st, 1992)

I realized that I have family all over the world, everywhere I go. Coz my fans show me the love and I love them just as much!

Private Home movies (2003)

Your love, support and loyalty made it all possible. You were there when I really needed you. I will never forget you. Your ever-present love held me, dried my tears, and carried me through. I will treasure your devotion and support forever. You are my inspiration.

Message on MJJSource after Michael's acquittal (June 2005)

Thank you's

The help of the following persons is highly appreciated.
A very special thank you to:

Lisa Hochmuth
Carina Zieroth
Katharina Roggendorf
Olaf Haensch
Sonja Boch
Glenda Furia

Cover
Olaf Haensch/Miriam Lohr

Layout
Jenny Yo Zimmermann

Writers
Special thank you to all the authors
Without you this book would not have been possible

Communities
Thanx to
the following MJ communities for supporting mjjbook
MJJCommunity (www.mjjcommunity.com)
Malibu (www.malibufanclub.de)
Jacksonvillage (www.jacksonvillage.org)
MJSN (www.mjsn.org)
Jam FC (www.mjfc-jam.com)
FttF (www.mjfriendship.de)

Xtra special thank you to Michael for your art,
your love, your strength, your courage...
for just being YOU and making US who we are

Pictures
All pictures taken by the authors of the respective stories unless otherwise noted.

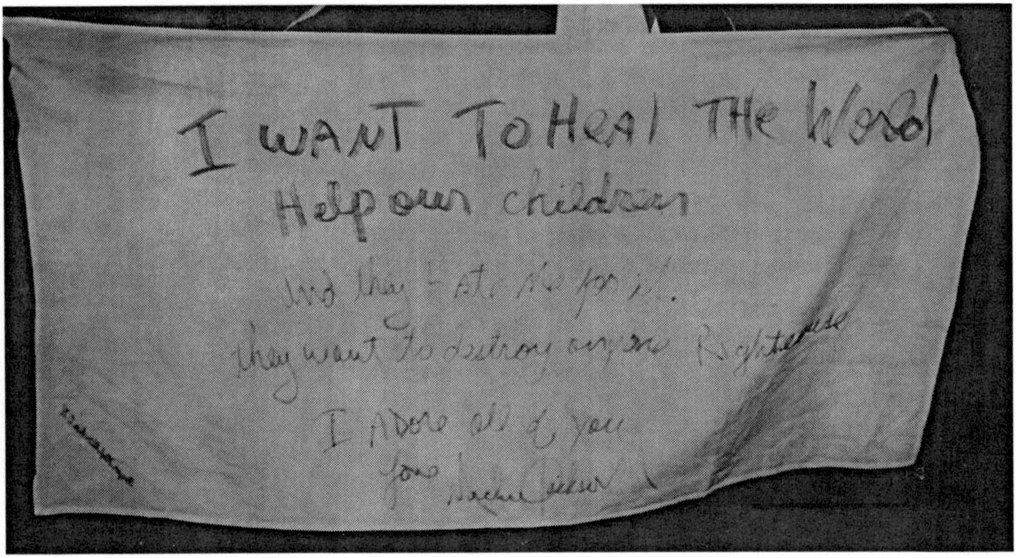
I WANT TO HEAL THE World
Help our children
I Adore all of you